T0355217

Through Iceboxes and Kennels

Through Iceboxes and Kennels

*How Immigration Detention Harms
Children and Families*

LUIS H. ZAYAS

OXFORD
UNIVERSITY PRESS

Oxford University Press is a department of the University of Oxford. It furthers
the University's objective of excellence in research, scholarship, and education
by publishing worldwide. Oxford is a registered trade mark of Oxford University
Press in the UK and certain other countries.

Published in the United States of America by Oxford University Press
198 Madison Avenue, New York, NY 10016, United States of America.

Library of Congress Cataloging-in-Publication Data
Names: Zayas, Luis H., author.
Title: Through iceboxes and kennels: how immigration detention
harms children and families / by Luis H. Zayas.
Description: New York: Oxford University Press, [2023] |
Includes bibliographical references and index.
Identifiers: LCCN 2022040690 (print) | LCCN 2022040691 (ebook) |
ISBN 9780197668160 (Hardback) | ISBN 9780197668184 (epub) | ISBN 9780197668191
Subjects: LCSH: United States—Emigration and immigration—Government policy. |
Immigrant families—Government policy—United States. |
Noncitizen children—Government policy—United States. |
Noncitizen detention centers—United States—History. |
Detention of persons—United States. | Unaccompanied refugee children—Care—United States. |
Psychic trauma in children—United States. | Post-traumatic stress disorder in children—United States.
Classification: LCC JV6483.Z394 2023 (print) | LCC JV6483 (ebook) |
DDC 325.73—dc23/eng/20221024
LC record available at https://lccn.loc.gov/2022040690
LC ebook record available at https://lccn.loc.gov/2022040691

DOI: 10.1093/oso/9780197668160.001.0001

1 3 5 7 9 8 6 4 2

Printed by Sheridan Books, Inc., United States of America

For Charlotte and Abigail, who taught me a greater love.
And to all the brave mothers and fathers who endured losses and sacrificed
everything to cross their children to safety.

In the depths of darkness
On the verge of losing all hope
One still maintains a little glimmer of hope
Deep down inside
A tiny light
About the size of a speck
Like a distant star
Is spotted on the horizon this dark night.

Behrouz Boochani

Contents

Notes on Names and Terms

This book quotes and paraphrases many children and their mothers who spoke to me and my research team. At times, the book quotes women and kids who spoke to the press, sometimes identified by name, often not. The names of those families I met have been changed to protect their privacy and identities and to protect the children, siblings, spouses, partners, parents, neighbors, friends, and extended families they left behind or have in the United States. The locations and names of their Central American towns and villages have also been changed to guard against anyone being identified and exposed to reprisals from the very people who drove their loved ones into exile. What has not been altered are the gender, ages, or countries of origin of the persons who spoke to us. To place the stories in context, I add historical, political, economic, social, psychological, and legal commentary.

The only real names that are mentioned in this book are those of persons in public roles, such as experts, attorneys, and judges whose names appear on legal documents or news reports. When the names of my collaborators and colleagues appear, it is with their permission. There are some children and parents who have been identified publicly, but I chose not to disclose their names or other identifying information if it seemed that discretion was best.

In trying to present the stories accurately, I have stayed as true to the words of the speaker as possible and tried to convey the styles and manner of speech of the persons narrating the stories. In passages when I work from my recollection or my students' recollections of experiences with children or parents, I use paraphrasing or limited quotes if part of the recollection included words or phrases that stuck in our memories. Occasionally, I condense sentences for the sake of brevity. Sometimes, I resequence words and comments or correct the grammar to make their statements clearer and easier to comprehend. When a child or parent used a Spanish proverb, adage, colloquialism, or creative form that is striking, evocative, metaphorical, or simply engaging, I present it in Spanish with an English translation.

The families depicted in this book all sought asylum, the legal status which I use to refer to them. When referring to persons who entered the country without asking for asylum or without legal documents or permissions, I use the terms *undocumented immigrant* and *unauthorized immigrant*. They are persons who entered the country without permission or other legal documents or who entered with the proper documents but stayed beyond the time the permission allowed, such as after their visa has expired. Although my focus is on families, there are times when the term *unaccompanied children* appears. They are children who have no lawful immigration status in the United States and are not yet 18 years of age. They might not have a parent or legal guardian in the United States or anyone who can provide care and physical custody.[1]

When referring to nationalities I use the names of their countries and nationalities—*Salvadoran* for those from El Salvador, *Guatemalan* for those from Guatemala, *Honduran* for those from Honduras, and so on. They may also be described as being from Central America or from the Northern Triangle countries of Central America. When including them in the large segment of our population who claim ancestry and heritage in Latin America, I use the term *Latino* or *Latina* or *Hispanic*.

The term *maras* or *mara* will appear often in the stories told by families. *Maras* is short-hand for Mara Salvatrucha, sometimes known as MS-13, that originated with the Salvadoran gangs in Los Angeles in the 1970s and 1980s and became an international criminal organization. *Maras* has become the referent to any organized gang or local gangs. Whether a gang is part of MS-13 or its rival, the 18th Street Gang, or a group of village thugs, the people of Central America use *maras* to refer to any gang that terrorizes them. The Spanish word for gangs, *pandillas*, is used sometimes, primarily when the term is used by those I quote. Other common Spanish terms, some colloquial, also appear, such as *hielera* (icebox, freezer), *perrera* (kennel, dog pound), and *migra* (a reference to migration officials of any country). Using them offers a ring of authenticity to the speech patterns and idioms used by Latin American migrants.

Note

1. US Department of Health and Human Services, Office of Refugee Resettlement, 2012.

Introduction

It was the spring of 2014 when a surge of families appeared at the US–Mexican border, seeking safe haven in the United States, having run risks that could have led to their deaths. In response, under the presidential administration of Barack Obama and with the support of Congress, the United States began locking up thousands of asylum-seeking mothers and children from Central America in so-called family residential centers. This was not the first time that the border had adults, families, and even unaccompanied children coming in large numbers in search of safety and security. In 2010, for instance, migrants from the Central American countries of El Salvador, Guatemala, and Honduras accounted for about 10% of migrants apprehended at the southern border with Mexico. During the winter and spring of 2014, family units migrating together for safety began to appear more frequently. By the end of the decade, the proportion of Central American migrants apprehended at the border was 81%. While many were adults traveling alone, there were increasingly more family units taken into custody at the border.[1] In 2019, Customs and Border Protection reported the highest level of apprehensions since 2007—about 689,000 migrants from El Salvador, Guatemala, and Honduras. Of the total, 62%, or 430,546 individuals, were traveling as family units, and just under 10%, or 62,748, were unaccompanied minors.[2]

Unique about 2014 was the arrival of the largest single surge of families, mothers with minor and tender-age children—showing up desperate, tearful, hungry, tired. The vast majority came from the Northern Triangle countries of Central America of El Salvador, Guatemala, and Honduras; but there were also mothers and children from Mexico, the Caribbean, other parts of Central and South America, even eastern Europe, the Middle East, Africa, and Asia. It was unlike anything that the United States had ever seen.

It was also not the first time that the federal government had put mothers, fathers, and children in immigration prisons, or "baby jails" as many called them. But the spring of 2014 ushered in the most extensive and longest-running era of family detention. Pictures from this national disgrace showed

Through Iceboxes and Kennels. Luis H. Zayas, Oxford University Press. © Oxford University Press 2023.
DOI: 10.1093/oso/9780197668160.003.0001

desperate mothers with children surrendering, with tears of fear and gratitude, to US border agents. The children's faces were blurred, or the cameras were trained on their feet or hands to protect their identities and innocence as minors. Adult men weren't offered the same anonymity, especially under Donald Trump. Their faces were shown by newspapers and other media, playing into Trump's efforts to stoke fear of them as *bad hombres*, a term he first used in an October 2016 presidential debate with Hillary Rodham Clinton. Trump added more slurs to this growing glossary of rhetorical devices he slung at immigrants—Mexicans as "rapists," Haitian immigrants as "all have AIDS," Nigerian immigrants who wouldn't "go back to their huts." Other terms included "chain migration" and "shithole" countries.[3]

Trump harbored no empathy for children and mothers traveling alone or poor people fleeing violence. His misleading rhetoric about the nature of migrants traveling north coarsely claimed too that the caravans were rife with hardened criminals. Without any evidence, Trump warned in an immigration speech on November 1, 2018, of brown hordes coming north:

> At this very moment, large well-organized caravans of migrants are marching towards our southern border. Some people call it an invasion. . . . These are tough people in many cases; a lot of young men, strong men and a lot of men that maybe we don't want in our country. . . . This isn't an innocent group of people. It's a large number of people that are tough. They have injured, they have attacked.[4]

Disingenuous rhetoric, unsubstantiated statements, and false alarms were Trump's tools. The reality was that amid a global refugee crisis that sent people fleeing their home countries on virtually every continent, Central America was seeing its own share of women fleeing violence, extortion, rape, and murder in their motherlands. They weren't bad hombres, criminals, murderers, or rapists. With little to no protection from the government or law enforcement to handle the surging waves of violence and corruption in their home countries, Central American women had few options but to leave behind parents, siblings, and other loved ones to protect themselves and their children. They left familiar lands, ancestral homes, and cultures and rituals that filled their spiritual and emotional needs. Poverty and economic hardship had already reached into every aspect of their lives. Now the civil instability brought devastating effects on them, their families, and their communities. In 2014, tens of thousands of women and children came seeking safety—asylum—in the United States.[5] The number of women crossing the US border was nearly three times higher than in 2013, only 1 year prior.[6] An alarming feature of this refugee crisis was the number of children fleeing home, with their mothers or alone. Over 66,000 unaccompanied and separated children from the Northern Triangle reached the United States in 2014.[7] Others sought safety, refuge, or asylum in neighboring countries, such as Mexico, Belize, Costa Rica, Nicaragua, and Panama—countries that saw the number of asylum applications from Northern Triangle countries grow about 13 times over the previous 6 years.[8]

"Fleeing is an ordeal in its own right, and for most women, the journey to safety is a journey through hell." That is how a 2015 report by the United Nations High Commissioner for Refugees described the plight of women migrants from Central America.[9] In this book, I tell about that hell, its origins, and the aftermath in US immigration systems. The book examines the experience of Central American children and parents migrating to the United States in search of asylum. It tells about the detention and sometimes forcible separations that have become a tableau of our time. I trace the arc of immigration detention that began under the Obama administration and continued through the Trump administration and into the early days of the Biden presidency, including the family separation policy that took children from the tenderest ages from their parents at the border. At the heart of this book stand the stories of families who were forced to leave their countries, journeyed through treacherous terrain, and ultimately landed in the hands of an American immigration apparatus that is a part of the profit-driven *prison-industrial complex* of the government, private prison companies, and other groups.[10] These are the true stories told by just a few dozen of the thousands of parents and children held in the US immigration detention centers during the period between 2014 and 2021.

"Scarce few of their stories have been told. Most will never be," writes NBC News correspondent Jacob Soboroff in *Separated: Inside an American Tragedy*. "There are families who were quickly put back together, and children who were, as predicted, permanently orphaned. My one little blue [reporter's] notebook could never do all their stories justice."[11]

True, no one book can convey the suffering of families and children in detention and those who were separated. Still, I wanted to tell the stories of the families I met to add to the scarce few that have been told. Without a doubt, these stories must be heard and understood and placed within proper contexts—their countries, the migration journey itself, and the appalling experience of being incarcerated just for seeking asylum. Readers, I thought, need to hear the stories of detained and separated families—mothers and children who had left their countries; braved their way across rugged land and international borders; felt cold, heat, hunger, and thirst; suffered kidnappings and ransoms, violence, rapes, assaults, and humiliations; and saw death, cadavers, human remains, and other unimaginable horrors. Readers need to know about the effects of the detention that President Obama started and that Donald Trump took to an extreme with his family separation policy, adding untold misery to hundreds of already traumatized children. I want readers to hear from the detained and separated mothers and children themselves, about how their lives, minds, and souls were permanently wounded and scarred, effects that have been seen few times in American history. Through the voices of mothers, fathers, girls, and boys we can know the cruel and callous policies and actions of officials of the US government and the private prisons that engorge themselves on government dollars by holding mothers, infants, toddlers, school-age children, and teenagers as prisoners for simply setting foot in the United States and asking for asylum.

In 2014 and several years after, the public's attention was not on the detention of mothers and children. We can forgive Americans for not knowing. After all, much of the American media was concentrated on the misery of hundreds of thousands of people crossing the Mediterranean Sea from North Africa and the Middle East into Europe. It was capturing the stories and blistering images of rickety vessels operated by unscrupulous people with more human cargo than the vessels could reasonably bear. The huddled masses were fleeing decades of civil conflict, genocide, famine, corruption, and repression. The riveting picture of Aylan Kurdi, the Syrian toddler whose lifeless body washed up on Bodrum Beach in Turkey, rocked the globe.[12] Americans were profoundly moved by that haunting image, as they should have been.

It seemed that Latin American news sources— *Univision* and *Telemundo* and regional networks—and local news outlets in the Southwest United States were paying attention to our southern border. These news sources were showing, almost nightly, the travels and travails of Central Americans coming to the border with children, some infants, begging for help. The images were no less compelling than those from half a world away. Then, two events drew the US media's and the American public's greater attention to the situation of Central American migrants.

One was pictures and videos of children and mothers during the summer of 2018 when the family separation policy was at its peak, images accompanied by the sounds of wailing children and crying parents. The American public responded and forced an unemphatic president to stop the atrocity. The other event was the June 24, 2019, photograph of the drowned bodies of Salvadoran migrant Oscar Alberto Martinez Ramirez and his toddler daughter, Valeria, on the bank of the Rio Grande in Matamoros, Mexico. First published in a Mexican newspaper, the picture by Julia Le Duc, a Mexican photojournalist, was sent around the world via social media.[13] The picture

shows a migrant and his less than 2-year-old daughter lying face down in the murky waters on the Mexican side of the Rio Grande. The girl's right arm rests across the back of her father's neck. . . . The image encapsulated the grim reality of the border amid the growing desperation of migrants fleeing poverty and crime in Central America and elsewhere who are willing to face great dangers—at times with children—for a shot at a better life in the United States.[14]

That image of a child holding on to her father even in death gave the US public a better understanding of what was happening in their own backyard.

This book is not an anthology of family stories, although I wanted to pay tribute to the stories of the many children and parents I met. But there is, we can agree, no more powerful means to illuminate than through storytelling. The tradition of telling the stories of detained, interned, and jailed people who committed no crimes or who may have been guilty of minor misdemeanors and were persecuted by their governments is a long one. It is a literary tradition that has always fascinated me. In this book, I wanted to cast a light on the atrocities that government systems can commit on people—citizens or non-citizens—by telling the stories of those who were the victims of such brutality and inhumanity. Some of the stories included in this book were told by others, in newspapers, documentaries, and reports by human rights organizations. Others were told to me and my research team, first-hand, using the tellers' own words, glimpsing the insider's view. The words are of the children and parents who spoke to us in simple, everyday vernacular Spanish. Every one of the mothers and fathers who let me into their lives is a humble but proud person. They came from small towns in the countryside of El Salvador, Guatemala, and Honduras. All knew poverty and had worked hard to feed, shelter, and protect their children but could no longer do so. A fraction of those I met had more than a high school education, but most were semi-literate or illiterate. Regardless, they are people reverent of the written word, not just the spoken one. They know of the world of books but have, for the most part, not been trained to read them, absorb their knowledge, and expand their worlds. They were pushed into exile by conditions of violence, threats, poverty, climate change, and no protection from anyone.

The brave people I met or read about will probably not be the ones to chronicle the events of their migration and the aftermath. More than likely, only a few kept diaries or wrote letters or poetry. If they have confided about their lives in their diaries or letters written to others, then those writings must be found and brought to publication for others to understand the trajectories of their lives. (One exception is the letters collected by Grassroots Leadership, Inc., in Texas, that appear in Chapter 5.) Whatever they have written in their own hand, told in their own words, or recorded for or passed orally to their children and grandchildren, as well as what has been written by others about them, will form a body of writings chronicling the first three decades of the 21st century when they were the targets of the paroxysms of hate that poisoned US policies. Their children, we pray, will write memoirs of the time they spent on the road and in detention and of life after detention. Until then their lives must be recorded as best as we can for the world to grasp the human agony. I hope that this book adds, however modestly, to the collection of stories from this period in American history.

With this in mind, one objective of this book is to describe the conditions that drive desperate families to take flight and endure the difficulties of coming to the United States. A second objective is to portray the migration itself, the human costs of a perilous, possibly deadly journey, and the resilience and triumph of so many people. A third objective is to expose the experiences of children and parents at the hands of the immigration system of the United States, where cruelty, harshness, and punitiveness often stood side by side with kindness, compassion, and professionalism. I wanted to highlight the immorality of incarcerating children and mothers, sometimes separating them as if they were petty criminals and, in the process, causing untold human damage. It is an unfair, inhumane attack that continues through the time of the writing of this book. The fourth objective is to pull together what I had learned into a conceptual model or explanatory framework to inform our understanding of Central American migration to the United States from the perspective of parents and children who made the trek to find asylum. My intention is to inform. But my deeper motive is to ignite thinking, conversation, and reflection that might change minds and influence how immigration enforcement is debated at the federal and state levels and the way immigrants are treated by the government's enforcement systems. Perhaps a reader or group of readers will take some of the ideas proposed in this book and be the change they want to see.

In Part I of the book, titled "The State of Affairs," I tell of my first encounter with families in detention and my subsequent interactions with detainees—children and adult women—and with government employees as well as prison guards. I tell about how private prisons have been licensed as child care centers and about the ignominious separation of children in 2018. I try to shed light on how the Office of Refugee Resettlement held teenage immigrant boys in a therapeutic residential center away from the prying eyes of the news media. Part II analyzes the human costs of detention and separation; hence, it is titled "The Human Costs." From information and data that I gathered first-hand and pulled from history books, scientific journals, legal documents, photographs and videos, news media reports, and anything I could learn from, I formed impressions about the stages of the Central American migration process. These impressions led to the development of a model to explain and describe Central American migration since 2014 (and possibly before). Part II reviews the science of stress and trauma, informed by research on immigration and detention, child psychiatry, neuroscience, and human development, as well as my personal accounts from working in this area of the immigration enforcement system. To add the human dimension to these chapters, I draw on the many illuminating descriptions, clips, and full-length stories that cover, to some extent, the range of stages of the migration process.

This book does not examine immigration as a global phenomenon. Instead, it focuses on a sliver of the world's migration: the crisis of women and children, sometimes fathers, who fled the Northern Triangle of Central America as family units and applied for asylum in the United States. I focus on children because, as a developmental psychologist, I understand the long-term impact of adversity on their lives. The events that began before 2014 drew my compassion and abiding interest. These happenings escalated that year into a national crisis and a national disgrace, a cruel multi-pronged government attack on the next generation. Although it is possible to see families as stories in a long procession of stories, it is not possible to write a book that explores the migration of families from all countries, continents, cultures, economies, and forms of government. I don't attempt to do so in this book, not because the many migrants seeking asylum from Africa, Asia, and other South American countries matter less. Nor is it because fleeing persecution for one's religion, ethnic group, sexual orientation, or sexual identity does not have a place in broad, global immigration trends. I stay within the field that I know and study and leave the description of other migrants in the capable hands of writers who are far better informed about them than I am.

Notes

1. Congressional Research Service, 2019.
2. US Customs and Border Protection, 2020.
3. Finnegan & Barabak, 2018; Hirschfeld Davis & Shear, 2019.
4. Yen & Long, 2018.
5. Retrieved from the United Nations High Commissioner for Refugees Population Statistics Database, https://www.unhcr.org/refugee-statistics/.
6. Galvan, 2014.
7. US Department of Homeland Security, 2015. Between 2008 and 2015, the US Customs and Border Protection recorded a 561% rise in unaccompanied and separated children apprehended at the border.
8. United Nations High Commissioner for Refugees, n.d.
9. United Nations High Commissioner for Refugees, 2015.
10. The others in the prison–industrial complex include suppliers of goods and services such as construction companies, surveillance and corrections technology vendors, food service companies, for-profit medical companies, unions, and lobbyists. For more on the prison–industrial complex, see Alexander, 2010. For details on immigration detention, see Ebert et al., 2020; Haberman, 2018; Young, 2021.
11. Soboroff, 2020, p. xix.
12. Vinograd & Omar, 2015; Katz, 2021.
13. Le Duc, 2019.
14. Linthicum, 2019.

PART I
THE STATE OF AFFAIRS

1

The Poet, Heroic Mothers, and Cash Cows

The southerly drive from Austin to Karnes City, Texas, takes about 2 hours. The first half-hour or so is on Interstate 35, traveling past car dealerships, fast food restaurants, and outlet malls. Leaving I-35 around about San Marcos, you take State Route 123 past front yards, farms, ranches, and "the graveyards of rusted automobiles," as Johnny, Arlo, and Willie sang.[1] Small towns along the way are steeped in Texas history. One of them is Geronimo, known for its annual barbecue and chili cook-off. Then comes Seguin, established in 1838, once a frontier stop for the then-12-year-old Texas Rangers patrolling a three-county area. After Seguin, you go past Stockdale, which describes itself as a "friendly little town" and host to the annual Watermelon Jubilee since 1937, one of the oldest watermelon festivals in Texas. Route 123 brings you straight into Karnes City, a town occupying a more recent seat in Texas history.

Like any drive I have taken on unfamiliar country roads, the first trip to Karnes City was slow; it took longer than any other time that I drove there. It all started with a call from a lawyer with the National Center for Youth Law in Oakland, a non-profit law firm with a 30-year history of advocating for immigrant children in federal immigration detention. She was leading a group of legal advocates from Oakland, California; Austin, Texas; and other parts of the country to visit a family immigration detention center in Karnes City. The call had come unexpectedly, without a lot of detail; but it was urgent. The information I could gather from the conversation was that the group had filed a request with the US Department of Homeland Security to look at and assess the conditions of the immigration detention center in Karnes that held asylum-seeking mothers and children. The lawyers' group had been granted permission. Someone who knew my work with immigrant children had recommended me as an experienced mental health professional who had worked for years with immigrant children and parents. Could I join them in 2 days? Was I in or not?

Truthfully, I did not know what it was I was supposed to do when I got to the detention center at Karnes. I was full of anxiety about entering an

Through Iceboxes and Kennels. Luis H. Zayas, Oxford University Press. © Oxford University Press 2023.
DOI: 10.1093/oso/9780197668160.003.0002

immigration detention center to see incarcerated families and children. I had visited a state maximum-security prison once. But a prison for families with children? Never. This would be my first.

I signed on. I just wasn't quite clear of what it was I would be expected to do or contribute, but I knew this was important. It left me a little nervous but undeterred. I joined the group made up of human rights and immigration lawyers as the mental health and child development specialist. The only red tape required to enter the detention facility was that I furnish a copy of my driver's license, social security number, and other contact information to US Immigration and Customs Enforcement (ICE), a division of the Department of Homeland Security that is responsible for enforcing immigration laws at the border and within the interior United States. ICE has authority to investigate border violations and apprehend, detain, and remove anyone who enters the United States without permission.[2] Two days later I hit the road at 6:00 in the morning, just to make sure I arrived by 9:00. Besides being a maiden trip on new roads and towns, my anticipation made the drive feel longer.

I drove down I-35 and Route 123, fueled by caffeine, anticipation, and anxiety. Thoughts, ideas, questions, scenarios, and plans sped across my mind faster than usual. My brain was doing what brains do in the absence of facts: fill-in the gaps, hypothesize about uncertainty, concentrate attention, and prepare with conjured scenarios and questions. The answers that formed to close the holes vanished as quickly as they appeared. What I could hold on to was the humanitarian operation, vague as it was, but one that was nothing less than a call to duty. Only the confidence in my expertise on the psychological conditions of immigrant kids and parents calmed me that day, and every visit after. On August 19, 2014, I didn't know that this 2-hour drive would be a trip I would take many more times, much less that it would change the direction of my life. Still less known to me was that this and subsequent visits, meetings, interviews, conversations, investigation, readings, teaching and public speaking, and musings would lead to a book examining the plight of asylum-seeking parents and children. The book that emerged would present a framework through which we could understand the stages of migration and reveal the layers upon layers of stress and trauma heaped on migrants, a process that began in their home countries and spanned several thousand miles.

Karnes became the place in which I saw first-hand how the mental health of children and mothers was incubated, damaged or exacerbated, and set into unhealthy trajectories. It was at Karnes County Family Residential Center, and later at the South Texas Family Residential Center in Dilley, that I would truly understand how an environment of fear and deprivation worsens the stresses and traumas of home-country violence and migration. In *Baby Jails: The Fight to End the Incarceration of Refugee Children in America*, Georgetown University law professor Philip Schrag captures how different the Dilley detention center was in comparison to Karnes.

> [P]rivacy at Dilley was worse than at Karnes. . . . The housing at Dilley consisted of trailers, each of which had beds for more than one family, as well as a couch, a television, and a phone, but no bathroom or other private area. Children from one family were therefore housed in the same quarters as adults from other families. . . . (This intermingling of adults and unrelated children would not be allowed in a licensed child care facility). To change clothing in the living area, adults or children had to pull a curtain around themselves; to use a bathroom they had to go outside of the living area and down a hallway.
>
> The families were reportedly awakened by middle-of-the-night bed checks, and the wait for medical care could "exceed five hours," after which the staff nurses "prescribe[d] a mixture of honey and water for a wide variety of ailments." When children misbehaved, they were sent with their mothers to solitary confinement for several hours in a "cold room."[3]

Karnes City, with a population of about 3,000, is the seat of Karnes County and is located on the Eagle Ford Shale, at the time one of the top oil-producing areas of Texas. Karnes County saw a boom in the gas and oil industry in 2011, driven by the advancements in hydraulic fracturing, more commonly known as *fracking*. When I visited, there were more than 2,300 active wells in Karnes County that spewed pollutants associated with cancer, brain damage, and respiratory problems—just about one well for every six county residents. Hundreds of immigrant mothers and children were being held in a detention center in the midst of this poisoned environment. It was worse for those confined at Dilley, according to Schrag.

> [They] were also concerned about the water. Fracking in other areas of Texas produced "millions of gallons of contaminated wastewater" that was trucked to the town of Dilley and dumped into abandoned wells that were "repurposed as 'disposals' for the toxic mix." The officers and medical staff reportedly drank bottled water, and volunteer lawyers were also cautioned

to drink only bottled water, but the mothers and children had to drink tap water.[4]

Finding a hotel room in Karnes on my first visit and the times after took planning. Nearly every motel and hotel room within miles was booked months in advance by the fracking companies to house the hundreds of young men in search of fast money and adventure. Outside of every restaurant and bar there were pickup trucks with large, muddy tires. Inside the bars and restaurants were the strong young men who drove the pickups—making brisk fortunes and spending them almost as quickly, much like the thrill-seekers of the California gold rush of 1849 or the oil wildcatters of the 1870s.

When I arrived and met up with my fellow visitors, I learned that we would be toured through the facility by ICE and the GEO Group (GEO) prison officials, allowed to question some staff, and permitted to interview the detainees, both mothers and their children. As the only mental health professional in the delegation, my job was to talk to mothers and children, to hear their stories, and to gauge how they were coping. The detainees could also tell me how the government and prison operator were treating them.

The Karnes County Family Residential Center, as it was called at the time, is a prison, plain and simple. Calling it a "family residence" to evoke the image of a quaint lodge didn't fool anyone that it was anything but a prison. From the parking lot, you see a large entrance painted blue with 20-foot walls stretching left, right, and back to enclose the part of the 29-acre facility that is actual prison space. You can't see in. Detainees cannot see out. There are no windows for those inside to watch people walking their dogs or jogging or cars speeding by or even see the sun rise or set on the horizon. The walls confirm that Karnes is a prison for families.

In July 2014, ICE decided to convert what was originally a county prison into one that would house women and children who had arrived at the US–Mexican border asking for asylum. Karnes was the first ICE detention facility built from the ground up, according to ICE's online Key Facts.[5] The building forms a large rectangle, with the front section of the interior taking up the largest portion of its space. It has three wings that run perpendicular to the front section, each two stories tall and with outdoor spaces in between where detainees can walk and play. Operating Karnes at the time involved a series of contracts. ICE contracted with Karnes County government to run the detention center under an intergovernmental service agreement. In turn, Karnes County subcontracted the day-to-day work to GEO, a private prison company that has been in the corrections field for over 30 years, not all of these with a clean record.[6] Except for fracking there aren't many jobs in Karnes City and County. Through GEO, locals find steady employment. Working for GEO in the detention center was the only good employment available, and, it seemed, not a lot of training was needed.

As recently as February 2019, the ICE web page boasted that the Karnes detention center is "a significant milestone in the agency's long-term effort to reform the immigration detention system," a dubious assertion since reforming the immigration detention system is not a mission that we commonly associate with ICE. Its family residential facilities are described as an "effective and humane alternative to maintain family unity as families await the outcome of immigration hearings or to return to their home countries." ICE asserts that its residents have freedom to move about from 6:00 in the morning to 10:00 at night and use the outdoor recreation areas and indoor playrooms. I heard stories of headcounts and demerits if teenagers were in their mothers' cells rather than their own in the adolescent wing. It didn't feel like freedom to them.

The Karnes cafeteria provides three meals per day and is open from 6:00 in the morning to 7:00 in the evening, according to ICE. But the detainees did not like the food. They would instead go to the commissary where a 10-ounce package of powdered milk sold for $5—contrast this to $8 for 26 ounces at the local supermarket. At every visit to the commissary, mothers and children were snapped at by the *grosera* (rude) lady who ran it. One mother told me of an incident in the cafeteria when she was about to place bread in a toaster for her child. A female prison guard pushed her aside to get to the toaster for her own bread, saying to the woman and others waiting their turns, "Muévanse, muertos de hambre," which translates roughly as "Move aside you starving wretches."

The women and children we would meet, mostly from the Central American countries of El Salvador, Guatemala, and Honduras, were seeking asylum, a perfectly legal act. Every mother I met knew she had to request asylum.[7] They were under no illusion that they could enter the United States with impunity. If they entered through an official checkpoint, such as a bridge, road, airport, or seaport, they could request asylum with ICE officers. If families crossed the borders with Mexico or Canada or entered the United States by sea at a location that was not an official checkpoint, they were more likely to encounter a Customs and Border Protection (CBP) officer. Either way they were passed on to ICE when apprehended.[8]

To be eligible for asylum, individuals must meet the definition of *refugee* as described in the Immigration and Nationality Act of 1965 (INA). Section 101(a)(42)(A) of the INA defines refugees as individuals who are outside of their home country and are unable or unwilling to return to it because of persecution or a "well-founded fear of persecution on account of race, religion, nationality, membership in a particular social group, or political opinion." An *asylum seeker* is a person who may meet the definition of refugee but is already in the United States or at its border or other port of entry seeking recognition.

After an asylum seeker arrives in the United States, immigration authorities take them into custody and begin the process of establishing the person's eligibility for asylum. Parents undergo a credible fear interview (CFI), which is conducted by an asylum officer who asks formal questions and other questions that might arise during the interview in response to information given by the asylum seeker. With the information in hand, the officer determines if the individual and their family can apply for asylum protection. In recent years, many of these interviews have been conducted by telephone or online video conference with an asylum officer at some distant place, perhaps in an office several states away. The number of asylum applicants has far outpaced the number of officers available to conduct CFIs. Sometimes, a Spanish interpreter may participate in person or by telephone if the officer is not fluent. In other increasingly common situations, the need for an interpreter skilled in a rare Indigenous language may be needed, invariably provided by telephone or video conference. This need may delay the process until an interpreter is found. Essential to the CFI is that applicants share any information that can support their asylum claim. While US immigration laws allow the mothers I met to ask for asylum, they bore the burden of proving that they had a credible fear of persecution or torture to qualify for asylum. Communication and cultural differences sometimes created chasms between interviewers and migrant women, especially on discussions of rape, incest, and sexual abuse. This is especially acute in interviews with male officers. Even when asked directly and assured that it was a difficult but necessary topic, the women might not confirm their experiences. This was compounded when there was more than just the interviewer, such as an interpreter, male or female. Often, both women and men who have been the victims of sexual assaults and rapes feel ashamed and do not provide detailed information out of a sense of humiliation. Omitting critical information about rape and sexual assaults could result in a negative ruling and necessitate an appeal if time and legal representation allow. The dynamics are fraught with power, vulnerability, humiliation, and inequality.

Nearly every Central American asylum applicant mentions the harms they suffered at home that constitute persecution in the US legal system. Most often, the mothers, fathers, and even unaccompanied minors who enter the United States cite serious physical attacks and criminal extortion or robbery that occurred in their countries. In the case of adolescents, families will also mention coercion by gangs that adolescent males become gang members through cruel, sometimes deadly initiation rites and that adolescent females become the physical and sexual property of gang members. In their asylum hearings, parents will mention the inaction, ineffectiveness, or complicity of police to the complaints they filed back home. They have claims of persecution carried out by governmental actors (e.g., police, corrupt officials) and non-governmental actors (e.g., gangs, abusive partners, rapists) that the government is unwilling or unable to control. Corroborating evidence and documents are allowed to be presented, but even without them, a mother's testimony, if deemed truthful by the asylum officers, may be enough to support a showing of credible fear.

If the asylum officer deems the person's fear as credible, the law protects the individual from being returned to their home country. The usual next step is the presentation of the asylum request to an immigration judge, who will determine if asylum will be granted. Since 2014, detention has been used to hold individuals rather than release them into the community while they await a hearing in immigration court. According to immigration laws, asylees have the right to remain in the United States indefinitely (or, at least, until conditions in their home country return to normal). Asylees can work as soon as their asylum is approved. Some can apply for a work permit while they're still in the asylum application process, depending on timing. Sometimes, a case may take a long time for reasons that are outside the asylee's control. After obtaining a grant of asylum and holding asylee status for a year, the individual can apply for US legal permanent residence (the so-called green card).

Entering the detention center in Karnes with a group of immigration and human rights attorneys gave me some comfort. The legal advocates had been here and places like it before. They spoke the language of law and knew how to litigate and respond to private prison guards and government officials. They were far more perceptive than I was about jail conditions and the slippery answers of the ICE officers and the prison guards. We were there to see the conditions of the newly jailed refugees. ICE and prison personnel were not going to be gracious or forthcoming. They did not like to have outsiders, especially advocates opposed to detaining families, entering the domain where they held authority and might over powerless women and children.

The morning began with a lesson on how to enter a federal detention facility. From the moment we met them, ICE officers and GEO employees let us know that they were in charge even though we had the right to be there under orders of the Department of Homeland Security. No recording devices. No cell phones. Attorneys could bring in laptops for notes. The rest of us—behavioral health professionals, volunteers representing non-profit advocacy groups, representatives from religious human rights organizations—were permitted only paper and pens. Lockers in the lobby were there to store anything else you didn't need. Briefcases, backpacks, and other bags were scanned the way they are at airport security points. Then we walked through metal detectors. To get to our first meeting, our escorts signaled to guards in a control center near the entrance to unlock electronically operated doors. Even with new technology operating the doors, the loud clang of metal doors striking doorframes transported me back in time to a prison built in the 19th century.

At our first stop, we sat around a large conference table with ICE heavies from Washington and GEO. The facility had just opened 4 weeks before, and it would remain open for much longer than anyone would have thought at the time. The ICE officials did most of the talking, chattering on and on to slow the progress of our visit. The immigration and children's rights attorneys asked smart, incisive questions, which were often dodged or finessed by our hosts. It was cordial but clearly tense since neither group trusted the other's motives. The detention officers answered in government lingo, citing sections of obscure rules and invoking impenetrable acronyms so common in government, the military, and prisons. The attorneys spoke assertively, knowledgeably, challenging those answers from ICE that hid the facts the delegation was seeking. It was impressive. I was simply eager, probably impatient, to get a tour and talk with children and mothers. Talking to cruel prison guards was distasteful, and I did not trust much of what I could understand of the ICE and GEO answers. The ICE and GEO officials were in no hurry; in fact, the more questions and concerns the attorneys raised, the less time we would have to visit with detainees.

Before we met with detainees, we were toured through much of the facility. We saw the visiting area and small offices that attorneys used to meet with clients in Karnes and the play area for children. The prison officials showed off the center's medical office and infirmary, cafeteria, computer center and library, commissary, and recreation areas with a soccer field and basketball stanchions.

The most striking aspect of the tour were the cells that families were held in. Each cell was large enough to house eight persons, usually three families with young children. ICE calls these cells "suites," where families can watch cable television. The dubiously named "suites" commonly had four bunk beds and one bathroom. In one cell, I saw a mother sitting in the bottom bunk as her school-aged son rested on the bed. The entourage had interrupted an intimate moment, a conversation. The mother's sad eyes met mine. I smiled and greeted her in Spanish. She smiled back shyly.

We were witnessing one of the most troublesome elements of detention: the loss of privacy and family identity. In jail, mothers cannot parent. They cannot discipline their children, cook their favorite meals, or take walks as family units. If a mother wishes to have her children in bed early, her efforts are thwarted by the many people in the cell with different practices and schedules. Mothers reading children bedtime stories or gathering for nighttime prayers must do so, if they can, with other parents and children milling about. Children see their mothers' powerlessness in the face of the authority of prison guards. Parents cannot act as the protectors, disciplinarians, or decision makers for their children. Those responsibilities are taken from them by the institution. Seeing their mothers in such impotent positions can frighten children. They detect the erosion of the parent's strength and authority. Other children seize on parents' diminished roles to upend the parent–child relational subtleties. None of these effects are good for children.

Detention centers like Karnes are not the detainees' first traumatizing exposure to the immigration system. Before the cells, bunk beds, showers, regular meals, medical care, commissary, and library of family residential detention, detainees will have spent time in *hieleras* and *perreras*, terms that pepper any conversation with immigrants who crossed the border in search of asylum.

The term *hielera* refers to an icebox or freezer in Spanish, but colloquially it is a descriptor for the holding cells where asylum seekers are placed after being apprehended by CBP. The holding cells are cramped facilities that often hold 30 or more people. Most often, they are fitted with tile walls and concrete floors and have one toilet for everyone to use, separated by a pony wall that rises about 4 feet from floor to ceiling. There is typically only one sink for the more than two dozen occupants. Too often there is no soap or paper towels, the absence of which causes sickness among the migrants, individuals who were tired but otherwise healthy at the time they were arrested at the border.

Women and children, including infants, are held in these overpopulated cells, usually for 48 hours but sometimes longer. The most notable characteristic of the *hieleras* is the intense and intentional cold, with temperatures hovering in the range of 50° to 60° Fahrenheit, which is how they earn the moniker. Mats are seldom, if ever, available; and mothers and children must sleep on the concrete and tile floors. They may be provided with sheets of Mylar foil, paper-thin and metallic, to stay warm, the same way that marathon runners do after a race.[9] An immigration rights activist told me of young girls sleeping at the foot of the toilet because the floor was warmer there. It has been argued that the rooms are kept cold for the benefit of the Border Patrol officers who must wear thick, warm uniforms and bullet-proof vests. Migrants know better. It is punishment for coming to America.

Other characteristics of the *hieleras* are inhumane and certainly unnecessary. Overhead fluorescent lights are kept on 24 hours a day, all week. Tired, unwashed, and hungry after a grueling trek, the children and mothers are kept cold and deprived of healthy, restful sleep. The activities by guards and other staff overseeing the *hielera* disturb what little sleep mothers and children can get.[10] There are noises outside the cells from other parts of the building. Announcements are heard and names of migrants called out loudly at all hours of the night, as they are told to report to someone somewhere for some unclear purpose. They may be awakened brusquely by agents to sign release papers. It all seemed so intentionally retaliatory to the women and children I met.

Perrera is the Spanish term for a kennel or dog pound. The *perreras* that are so often mentioned by migrant parents are typically chain-link fencing of galvanized steel wire that separate large indoor areas, such as refitted empty buildings that once housed "big box" stores. Even a sitting US senator, Jeff Merkley of Oregon, described the enclosures he saw on a visit to a border detention center as "Cyclone fencing and fence posts that look like cages. They look like the way you would construct a dog kennel."[11] The fences separate parents from their children or children from each other by age and gender.[12] Pictures of *perreras* were published by newspapers and magazines and shown on television and online, especially during the family separations of 2018.

Most often, the pictures were of groups of children or adults behind cages, segregated by age and gender, in rows, each cage separated by the chain-link fence. The detainees can be seen reclining, looking through the fences, talking with others, asking questions of the guards. One mother, quoted by Reuters, described watching young children trying to touch their parents through the metal fences: "The mothers tried to reach their children, and I saw children pressing up against the fence of the cage to try to reach out. But officials pulled the children away and yelled at their mothers."[13] Semantic differences have been parsed in debates about the term *perrera* after pictures of children and adults in them became ubiquitous in the media. Are they "cages," "kennels," or "pens"? Or are they "chain-link fenced holding areas," "chain-link partitions," "enclosures," or "walls of chain-link fences"? The people having the debates were not migrants, had never been held inside one of these structures, never spent any stretch of time in them. From outside, the terms could be debated. From inside the chain-link enclosures, there was no debate: Migrants were like dogs in kennels.

Human Rights First, an independent human rights advocacy and action group that believes that the United States must be a beacon for freedom and that America should live up to its ideals, toured Karnes in December 2015 and wrote that

> Children do not want to eat, they are clingier and more aggressive, cry frequently, and are fearful. Women spoke tearfully of their own anxiety, feelings of desperation, and confusion over the legal process, and confirmed the doctors' concerns that being held in detention was re-traumatizing.[14]

Our delegation's meetings and tour ended just before lunch. Immediately after lunch, we re-entered the facility, and I began my meetings with detainees. I was assigned a small office, one of the five or six that opened into the waiting room and play area. I asked the ICE officer assisting the delegation to bring me mothers with children ages 7 and above, although I would judge if I needed to interview a younger child. The large visiting room was clean, brightly lit, colorfully painted, and furnished with several tables and chairs for parents and children to sit while they waited for someone in their family who was meeting with either legal counsel or me. The office was small; four could fit comfortably, but it would be snug. Removing this area from the context of the detention center, it could have been a room in a school or community center anywhere in America.

A door off the main visiting area with a glass window next to it led into a small foyer, a waiting room, that could fit about six mothers and children at a time. Here, mothers and children marked the time until it was their turn to meet with an attorney or me. A GEO guard controlled the entry and exit through that door. Only families could come and go and only when the guard allowed them. Beyond them, at the other end of the narrow foyer, was a door with a glass window that led into the prison courtyard and recreation areas. Mothers waited expectantly for their names to be called.

The officer came back to me with a list of 10 families, mothers ranging in age from 24 to 47. Eight were Salvadoran, one Honduran, and one Guatemalan. They each had from one to three children with them in detention. The women on my list had a total of 13 sons between the ages of 2 and 17 and 10 daughters ranging in age from 9 to 17. The team of visitors knew that many of the mothers had left other children behind or had children already living in the United States. The families we were seeing were not the entirety of their family units.

Finally, after the long drive and morning meetings, I called out the first name on the list. Opening the door to the holding area, the guard repeated it to the people outside. From the door of my cubicle, I saw movement in the waiting room, a mother rising from a chair. I could make out the mother moving hastily to get her child up from the floor. The guard let her into the visiting room with her child and pointed them in my direction. As I greeted the woman, my eyes were drawn to the left side of her face. Her eyebrow drooped noticeably to below the left eye. It didn't quite reach her cheek and mouth the way a stroke affects the face, but it was noticeable.

The 34-year-old Honduran seemed relaxed as she entered, confident that the lawyers and I were there to help and that I was interested in her psychological health. She told of her husband's abandonment when their first child, a girl, was 3. At the time, she was pregnant with the now 6-year-old son who played in the visiting area, in sight of his mother. After her son was born, she met a man who romanced her. She learned he was involved with narcotraffickers, and shortly after they began their relationship, he became physically abusive, resulting in incidents that her daughter twice witnessed. Pregnant with his child, she escaped with her daughter and son. Then the stalking began, and soon after the man kidnapped and tortured her, the same man who once promised her a good life. For 24 hours, he brutalized her with punches and kicks to her body, pulling her hair, and repeatedly raping her. He poured water into her mouth until she choked. During the beating, she miscarried their unborn son. The countless blows to the head with fists and all kinds of objects, she surmised, are what caused her facial paralysis. She confirmed that she was still numb from brow to cheek. When he finally released her, she escaped with the son who was in detention with her. The daughter stayed in Honduras, refusing to leave her grandmother.

Upon entering ICE custody, she and her son spent the first 72 hours in a *hielera*. She complained that the lady who ran the commissary "is rude and makes us wait in line in the hot sun for a long time." Guards conduct headcounts twice a day; these ordeals last 2 hours in the morning and 2 hours in the afternoon before dinner. During the slow headcounts, everyone had to remain in their cells, something that other mothers confirmed. Why 2 hours twice daily? Prison staff denied, downplayed, and then admitted to the headcounts. Their rationalizations were as thin as onion skin. Power was the real reason.

With barely time to check my notes for legibility and accuracy, I met the next family, a Guatemalan mother with two sons, aged 5 and 2. I scribbled hastily as much as I could of what she said. In scratched handwriting, my notes read,

> Molested by father from 13 to 18 or so. Father came home drunk, they (?) would go to the mountain to sleep the night and return home in the morning. Beat her, causing trauma to her head. Quote: "beaten by him with whatever he had at hand." Father rejected her when she had boyfriend. 1st child result of rape by neighborhood boy. Child's father beat her. Father of 2nd child in U.S. as is her mother (Cincinnati, undocumented). Father threatened her. "I will not rest till you & your mother are dead." She feared for younger sister still in Guatemala; can't return for her; would be killed. 2 men told her & mother they would be killed—They think father put them up to it. Crossing Rio Grande, older son nearly drowned. Saved by CBP. (2 yo son distressed when mother crying in interview.)

The third mother I spoke to had been in Karnes for 3 weeks but had spent 3 days at another facility before being transferred here. The journey from El Salvador with her 9-year-old daughter had taken 8 days without incident. The 33-year-old woman had left two sons with her parents. Her cousin had been killed by *maras* in a home invasion, and a day or two later, three *maras* walked past her home and saw her outside. Their words to her were few but clear: "Mirar. Oir. Callar." ("Look. Hear. Keep quiet.")

After the third family, I was aware of feeling increasingly uncomfortable from the pressure I was putting on myself to see as many families as possible in the 2 days that I had at Karnes. Choppy, scribbly notes from the last interview were evidence enough. Before calling the next name on the list, I paused. Three minutes, probably, and some deep breaths. I asked to be let out to go to the men's room. The guards called the central control unit to open the door, providing a number indicating which door it was. The request was repeated as I went through a second door, hearing it shut loudly behind me. Splashing cold water on my face helped. Looking in the mirror I told myself, several times, "Depth. Quality." Maybe I'd see fewer families, but I would get a better grasp of each of their lives and show them the respect they were not accustomed to getting in a place like this, respect they fully deserved.

"The *maras* arrived in our town in 2013," the Salvadoran women, aged 47, said. She was joined by her daughter, who would turn 18 the next day, and an 8-year-old son. Her 14-year-old son preferred to wait in the visiting area, playing with toys that were for kids below his age but were, at the very least, entertaining. After the arrival of the *maras*, the reign of terror began with threats, extortions, and beatings of townspeople. At least one body was hung from a pedestrian overpass, sending a deadly signal to everyone. Within the year, her turn came. The elder son was threatened with death if he did not become a gang member. He refused but didn't tell his mother, knowing that it would upset her. It was not long before his mother found out and decided to escape the country. She paid an organized group of smugglers $13,500 for safe passage from El Salvador on July 10. Terror would follow them well beyond that date.

By the second day, the family and a group of about 20 others were well into Mexico, the Guatemalan border behind them. Their hopes of safe passage were dashed when the group was beset by a group of rival smugglers. Their trusted *coyote* (human smuggler) was killed. Abruptly, the travelers became hostages.

"We were held in an empty *bodega* [warehouse] for 12 days," until everyone could raise their ransom from families in their countries or the United States. For nearly 2 weeks, they lived in squalor, little food, no electricity, no potable water, and no place to sleep comfortably. Escaping wasn't an option. By July 28, all ransoms had been paid, and the group completed the rest of the journey in 4 days, crossing from northern Tamaulipas, probably Reynosa, to McAllen, Texas, on August 1. The level of terror dropped but did not end, even in the hands of US officials. The three children and mother spent 4 days in a *hielera* wearing the clothes they had worn for weeks, unbathed, tired, and hungry. They huddled together for warmth and shared what little food they were given.

After their transfer to Karnes, they were subjected to threats of deportation or separation by GEO staff, Karnes County residents who now had a job and some power. Their cruelest words were reserved for the eldest child, who they knew was turning 18. "You will go to an adult detention center away from your mother and brothers," the guards would say. "You will be treated like an adult and deported alone." Terror that once came from *maras* and kidnappers was now coming from the mean-spirited employees of the prison company who were entrusted with the safety and security of detainees.

Retelling their ordeal took an hour, and all along the girl sat slumped; there was no excitement in turning 18. Instead, it was all fear and apprehension. The boy would not leave the room and join his brother in the play area. "I want to get out of this place," he said, tears carving tracks on his dusty cheeks. They were the only words he spoke during our meeting.

There was a knock at the door. It was firm and unexpected. Startled, the girl gasped, shot up from her slouch, now sitting upright, her face pale with fear. She did the best she could to shake off the dejection and act more alert, though it was clear she was frightened. The mother looked alarmed, and the little brother confused. I was irritated. Was it a deliberate attempt to interrupt our meeting? Guards were known to play mind games with detainees, attorneys, and other visitors, just to show they were in charge and to make our jobs harder. Through the window, I could see it was an ICE officer I had met earlier in the day. I opened the door fully, holding back the urge to argue. There wasn't room for another person in the space. The officer stood at the door. His Spanish was pretty good.

"I have some good news," he said, speaking directly to the girl, using her first name. "You will be able to stay here with your mother. You will not be transferred to an adult facility."

His tone was kind. The teenage girl, who feared being separated from her family on her 18th birthday, let out a muffled scream and wept with relief and joy. Her mother, still sitting, leaned over and wrapped her arms around the girl. The teenager reciprocated, melting into her mother's arms. Wanting to be a part of the family hug, the boy locked his short arms as far around his mother and sister as he could. The officer asked the family if they understood what he was saying. They understood. He didn't need to ask further. So unexpected was that moment that I was left speechless. The family needed to celebrate this intimate moment without a stranger present. I gave them the office. Minutes later they emerged. Mother thanked me. The girl's face now had color, the muscles that only minutes before seemed frozen in fear were now relaxed, almost radiant. I watched them go into the waiting room past other waiting families and through the second door into the recreation area. I noticed how bright it was outside. The unforeseen moment left me wary: Had the announcement been staged as a grand gesture, to show ICE's magnanimity and earn my respect, or was it a sincere, spontaneous moment? There wasn't much time to process what I had just witnessed or take in the misery that this family had been through to get to today.

The next meeting started right away. It was with a teenage boy, the only one who spoke with me alone without his mother present. At 16, he was tall and slender with a serious and handsome demeanor and carriage. In the course of the conversation, he became one of the most memorable of the youth I would meet. His reverence for the written word, great literature, and poetry was gloriously displayed by the stanzas and passages he quoted at just the right moment in our conversation. Later, when I marveled about him with others in the delegation, he became known to us as *The Poet*.

Speaking slowly, The Poet told of the dangers that *maras* had brought to his small town and his neighborhood. What did the *maras* do in his town? I asked. He told of shootings, rapes, dead bodies found in the morning by someone leaving work at daybreak or a person walking their dog. Families like his would remain inside with shutters drawn as groups of heavily tattooed and armed boys—teenagers like him, many drunk or high from sniffing glue and other cheap but deadly inhalants—fired their guns into the air or at buildings. Anyone caught on the street at such a moment would very likely die. They would certainly be robbed and maybe beaten.

He was a good narrator, adding words that provided depth, nuance, color, and gravity to the stories of the residents forced into isolation, their freedom of movement now circumscribed. I remarked on the fear that everyone must have been living in. Indeed, he said, the town was terrorized.

"Well, sir, everyone was in fear. Some men in town, I don't know who, found it necessary to take actions that the police would not. They must have felt they had no alternatives." Vigilante justice was born in this town, as in other places, of frustration, fear, anger, and revenge. The bodies of gang members began to appear in the streets at daybreak, no longer just those of

innocent people. The Poet could not say if the vigilantes were formally organized or were townsmen in twos and threes, or even solo, who were just
fed up with the thugs and their terror. They were sending signals back to
the *maras*. The Poet said that his neighbors and others took to calling the
vigilantes *La Sombra Negra* (The Black Shadow) because it all happened at
night and the people who served out this justice remained unknown, unseen in the shadows of darkness. Many in town lauded the unnamed men,
whether working alone or in concert, who formed *La Sombra Negra*. Others
feared an escalation, a local civil war.

It was a moral dilemma, according to The Poet, between being killed and
killing. He saw both sides and admitted that the way the gangs had wanted
him to join, their ruthless words and actions, gave him an understanding of
the perspective of the vigilantes. I had many more questions, but The Poet
could not answer them; he just didn't have the information and would not
infer, deduce, or speculate. He only knew what he had seen and heard and
had no knowledge of the inner workings of *La Sombra Negra*. Besides, he
reminded me, his family had left it all behind. He would not dwell on trying
to connect the links or fill in the blanks. He was looking ahead. He and his
family knew little else of what was happening. Perhaps they didn't want to
know. They had set out on their quest to come to United States, Denver to be
more specific, where family awaited them.

At Karnes, teenagers occupied cells with other teenagers, away from
their mothers and younger children. Adolescents were housed in the
western wing, one of three that comprised the facility. On one floor were
teenage girls and on the other, teenage boys. From a top bunk, The Poet
shared the cell with five other boys. He told me he spent a great deal of
his time in bed reading. Sometimes he would find a shaded spot in the
outdoor recreation area to read and immerse himself in the words of the
authors. Confined to a cell with a group of teenage boys, I imagined, must
have been a challenge for a young book lover. They could go from friendly
ribbing and teasing to outright ruthlessness—maybe more so given their
backgrounds of hardship, truncated education, and probably homes with
few books or very little modeling of the life of the mind or the world of
written words. They were not the sons of wealthy families steeped in a
tradition of education and erudition, spending academic years in elite
boarding schools or just good public schools. He was among boys from
small towns. I asked him what it was like being a reader in a cell with
other boys.

Well, you know, Doctor, when I was first put in the cell with them, they made fun of me. They weren't really trying to hurt me but just pointed out that I was *libresco* [bookish] and they were having fun. It really didn't bother me; it was just teasing, and I was used to it. I just kept reading.

But then they asked me about what I was reading. And I told them the stories and novels that were in the books I borrowed from the library. I even read stories to the guys. That happened a few times, and one of them said he wanted to read the stories himself and got a book. I helped him a little bit with words here and there. Then we got to talking about the stories and what they meant. The other guys listened to us talking and became interested in the stories. It was almost like they didn't want to be left out of the conversation. After a few weeks, some of them were reading books in their bunks. Not all the time; mostly when we had to be in our cell at night or for a headcount.

His love of Spanish novels, short stories, and poems made him influential with his peers and helped him survive, maybe even thrive, in Karnes. His ability to quote from memory great Latin American writers was extraordinary. He seemed to have quotes that were exquisitely attuned to the moment or topic our conversation had wandered into. One of those topics was how senseless, backward, maybe even barbaric it was to imprison children and mothers for simply crossing politically created boundaries. With a look of patience and wistful hope that the world would change, that life would get better, he quoted Romulo Gallegos's *Doña Barbara*.

Algún día será verdad. El progreso penetrará en la llanura y la barbarie retrocederá vencida. Tal vez nosotros no alcanzaremos a verlo; pero sangre nuestra palpitará en la emoción de quien lo vea. [One day it will be true. Progress will penetrate the plain and barbarism will retreat defeated. Perhaps we will not be able to see it; but our blood will throb in the emotion of those who see it.][15]

It was impressive how easily he pulled the quote from thin air to apply to the moment. I asked him to repeat it several times to make sure I got it right. It was applicable to the moment but showed profound knowledge that a time would come when things would be better, even if he would not be there to witness it. Like most adults impressed with the literary prowess of such a young person, I asked if he wanted to become a writer. As he had in several other instances during our conversation, The Poet replied with an elegant and pointed quote, this time from Jorge Luis Borges: "Uno llega a ser grande por lo que lee y no por lo que escribe" ("One becomes great by what one reads and not by what one writes").[16] Before we parted, I handed him my business card, saying, "When you are ready to go to college, call me. I will help you." He smiled.

Later that night in my hotel bed, it was a long time before I slept. My mind was in overdrive, replaying the sounds, words, looks, faces, sights, even the smell of detention. My thoughts were on The Poet and the families back at Karnes.

In November 2015, little more than a year after my first visit to Karnes, I was in San Angelo, Texas, to address a group of alumni of the University of Texas and local leaders. My talk was about the social problems besetting Hispanic American adolescents caused by poverty, substandard housing and schools, and low-paying employment, among other issues. The topics were of little interest to an audience of wealthy and middle-class White, rural, small-town Republicans over age 65. They applauded politely. Mostly, they were pleased that a dean from the University of Texas had bothered to come to see them.

Back at the hotel after dinner, I met up with two friends who had come from Austin and Amarillo for the luncheon talk. Like my audience a few hours earlier, they really weren't much interested in the topic of my talk either. They just wanted to hang out, friends with a free night. They are both typical native Texans, friendly, gregarious, and funny. Sipping drinks and smoking cigars at the hotel patio, we bantered, our feet on a low-set rectangular firepit, a structure of polished concrete with shimmering pebbles through which little flames warmed the cool night.

Soon a middle-aged man entered the patio and sat at some distance drinking his beverage. It was a quiet night; he could hear our lively give-and-take. As I said, my friends are friendly Texans, and it took no time for the one from Amarillo to greet the newcomer.

"Well, what brings you to San Angelo?" he said in a pleasant-to-the-ear Texas drawl, the kind that makes you feel comfortable, welcomed. The man said he was a regional manager for GEO. Pointing in no particular direction, he said that GEO operated a prison just outside of town through a contract with the county or state. I had seen signs for a prison when I drove around the area after the luncheon. He confirmed to me that it was the one he had come to inspect and meet with his staff.

"GEO," I mused before asking, "Isn't that the same company that operates the immigration facility in Karnes with all the children and mothers?"

The man replied with no apparent pause.

"Cash cow," he said coolly. As if once was not enough, he crooned, "Cash cow."

Notes

1. Johnny Cash, Arlo Guthrie, and Willie Nelson each recorded the song "City of New Orleans," written by Steven Goodman, 1972.
2. US Immigration and Customs Enforcement, 2019a.
3. Schrag, 2020, pp. 146–147.
4. Schrag, 2020, p. 147.
5. US Immigration and Customs Enforcement, 2019b.
6. For examples, see Earthjustice, 2022; GEO Group, Inc., 2021; Plevin, 2020.
7. See section 101(a)(42)(A) of the Immigration and Nationality Act. US Department of Homeland Security, 2022b.
8. Children who arrive at the border unaccompanied or are separated from their parents or other family are transferred from CBP or ICE to the Office of Refugee Resettlement, which is part of the Department of Health and Human Services.
9. Mylar is a flexible and strong polyester film that reflects heat and prevents heat loss.
10. Alfaro, 2018; Cantor, 2015.
11. Hirschfeld Davis & Shear, 2019, p. 269.
12. Carpenter, 2015.
13. Levinson & Cooke, 2018.
14. Byrne, 2015.
15. Gallegos, 1929/2000, p. 178.
16. Attributed to Jorge Luis Borges in a 1980 interview with *La Nación* (daily newspaper), Buenos Aires, Argentina.

2
Ordeals and Histories of Immigration

The next morning, August 20, I found mothers chatting in the holding room between the outdoor space and the visiting room, their kids impatient to get to the toys in the play area. I returned to my list and called out a name. The guard looked at her list, looked into the anteroom, and turned to me to say the person wasn't there. I called the next name, and the first meeting of the day began.

"Doctor," the mother said, "nosotros vivíamos bien. No carecíamos de nada. Nunca habíamos pensado venir a los Estados Unidos. Éramos felices en nuestro país" ("Doctor, we lived well. We lacked nothing. We had never thought of coming to the United States. We were happy in our country"). But it was the gangs that drove her and her two sons out and left behind her husband, the boys' father. Her words, tone, and expression were imploring, as if addressing listeners in a larger audience beyond me: the American people, maybe the president, or that great democratic experiment known as the United States. It was a sincere appeal that was as apologetic as it was pleading, explaining to the invisible audience that she had no choice, that she didn't mean to intrude on us but needed to save her sons. It was the voice of a thousand mothers.

"I was a businesswoman living with my life partner," she said. Her business was a successful restaurant in town that many of the locals visited daily. The family lived upstairs from the restaurant. Her husband was a respected farmer and rancher, a substantial landholder with a grain mill that gave him the independence to feed his livestock and a hundred head of exotic cattle, each carrying a high price. Together, they owned three cars. The boys, both young teens, ages 14 and 15, attended the local school and helped on the farm and in the restaurant. They lived a middle-class life by the standards of a small Salvadoran town.

They had no reason to leave their comfortable life, the mother reminded me. At least not until the *maras* and other gangs began their activities. First came the threats. The *maras* threatened to kidnap one of her sons. They tried to coerce them into joining the gangs. Refuse and the boys would be

Through Iceboxes and Kennels. Luis H. Zayas, Oxford University Press. © Oxford University Press 2023.
DOI: 10.1093/oso/9780197668160.003.0003

beaten, maybe killed. "We know your boys' movements. And we admire your husband's beautiful cattle, so many of them that it would be a shame to see them die." Then, her husband was robbed of $700 by eight armed men. The *maras* left him with a message: "We are looking for your two sons." Days later, a group of *maras* entered the boys' school and found the younger son's classroom. There, in the presence of horrified classmates and teacher, they threatened him with death. Everyone knew that the gang meant what they said. Just a year earlier, they had abducted a 12-year-old girl from the same school as her son. The pre-teen girl was taken to a river in a national park that bordered the town. Valiantly, the girl refused to be the consort of a gang leader. It was a refusal that ended her life. She was found by the river, her head cleaved from the crown of her head to just below the nose, her torso disemboweled. A bloody machete was cast near her lifeless body.

Then the extortion and the spiraling terror campaign came for this family. *Maras* invaded the mother's restaurant, asking for $7,000. She tried to explain that she did not have that kind of money and was led upstairs to her home and bound and gagged. In frustration, the *maras* took some money but not the thousands they demanded. They stole some landscaping equipment and family valuables for good measure. One of the bastards cut her throat, just enough to draw blood and instill fear. This courageous woman refused, but she was scared. She knew the gangs would not stop their threats, nor their menacing words, glances, and gestures as they walked past her eatery.

The family could no longer resist the *maras*. The parents decided to find their way to Virginia where they had family who were US citizens and legal permanent residents. Immediately, her husband sold 20 of his prized cattle to finance his wife's and sons' escape. Once they were on their way, he would sell all his cattle, cars, possessions—anything he could—and follow them north, even if it meant abandoning his land. In an act of supreme generosity, the father also paid for his wife's sister and her three children—10, 8, and 2—to take flight together. His wife drove one of the family cars to the capital, San Salvador, where she quickly sold it; and the group boarded a bus to Guatemala and then on to Mexico. They felt relief that it was all behind them. That was July 14, just weeks before our meeting in Karnes.

It took a few uneventful days by bus to cut through Guatemala and into Chiapas, Mexico, until they reached Veracruz. There, Mexican immigration held the family group for 6 days and then repatriated them to El Salvador. Undeterred, the women headed back north the next day, passing the same terrain as they had before; only this time no one stopped them.

They continued north almost without incident until, she said, they were 3 hours from the US border. It was then that sisters and children encountered what the mother said were *otros terroristas* ("other terrorists"), the Mexican federal police. Dressed in camouflage uniforms, the police officers took her teenage sons to a waiting van with tinted windows. The *federales* never asked her sons any official questions. They asked, instead, if the boys had money. When the boys said that they did not, the police threatened to take them and sell them. The *federales* were bluffing, though, and let the boys walk back to the waiting bus and their family. Quickly, the sisters left the bus with their brood and hired a taxi to bring them to the border. They waited several hours in a small building near the border before crossing and turning themselves in to border agents. It was August 1, and the ordeal wasn't over yet. The seven of them spent 6 days in a *hielera* and a day and a half in a *perrera*. They were subjected to the abusive attitude and the slurs of US border officers. The families were transferred to Karnes from there.

I heard it said scores of times: "We left our homes because of the violence." Leaving a place called home took a grim but fairly easy calculation: Live, maybe even die, with the known perils of migration or be killed staying. Families gambled on trekking together as a unit. Other researchers heard the same words from migrants. In *Witness to Forced Migration: The Paradox of Resiliency*, Mark Lusk and Georgina Sanchez Garcia of the University of Texas at El Paso articulate the words of the many mothers and children I met.

> It is rare to meet a forced migrant who did not undergo an ordeal. Everyone, even the few with resources, faced intense hardship. . . . Migrants spoke about the trauma, suffering and lack of protection that forced them from their homes. As we have been told repeatedly, forced migrants did not necessarily want to migrate. "This is not my country and I would have preferred to stay home, but I had no choice." "*Siento nostalgia por Honduras, pero no tuve opciones.*" ["I feel nostalgic for Honduras, but I had no options."][1]

Gangs make Central Americans feel that these are not their countries anymore; the presence of gangs pushes people to make the steep calculations of leaving. Two of the major gangs operating in Central America have ties with the United States.[2] Both were formed in Los Angeles. The *18th Street Gang* was founded in the 1960s primarily by Mexican youth who were excluded by other Hispanic gangs in the Rampart section of Los Angeles. It is believed to be the first Hispanic gang that did not discriminate by race or location; 18th Street Gang members came from all races and from outside of California. The *Mara Salvatrucha* (MS-13) gang was birthed in the 1980s by Salvadoran youth in Los Angeles. These young people had fled with their parents from the long-running civil war in El Salvador. When the United States began deporting illegal immigrants with criminal convictions to the Northern Triangle countries after the passage of the Illegal Immigrant Reform and Immigrant Responsibility Act (P.L. 104-208) of 1996, the presence of gangs in the region grew rapidly.[3] The gangs began recruiting or forcing youth from vulnerable backgrounds, mostly poor and squalid communities, to become gang members. It is not surprising that the combinations of poverty, family fragmentation, and slim to no opportunities for employment led youth to gravitate to the gangs for survival, money, food, and protection. The two gangs fought with other smaller, less-resourced gangs to claim their territories—turf—so that they could control the distribution of drugs, weapons, and humans.[4]

Central Americans use *maras* as a generic term to refer to the gangs that maraud their countries, regardless of the country they live in. In 2012, the US Department of State and the United Nations Office on Drugs and Crime estimated that there were between 54,000 and 85,000 members of MS-13 and the 18th Street Gang.[5] El Salvador had the highest concentration of gang members: There were about 323 gang members for every 100,000 citizens, twice the levels of Guatemala and Honduras.[6]

Violence has existed in Central America for decades, but since the 1990s, the region has been transformed by South American drug cartels into a path for getting their merchandise to hungry US markets. Violent gangs have overpowered, infiltrated, and bribed the police, making law enforcement efforts laughable. To build their drug superhighways, the criminal organizations used a lethal means of eminent domain, taking by force whatever they wanted. While governments acquire land by eminent domain and clear the path with bulldozers and other means, the gangs of Central America replaced the bulldozers with powerful weapons such as assault rifles and military firearms that are light and portable and can deliver a high volume of fire with reasonable accuracy. Other examples of "bulldozing and paving" by the gangs include beatings, maiming, threats, death, and symbols of death, such as dismembered human bodies and animal parts left in very visible locations as signals. The cartels' eminent domain mentality spans countries: It triggers bloody skirmishes and battles between organized transnational affiliates and local gangs. Small-time gangs of local thugs become subcontractors to the large gangs and pave the way by intimidating and assaulting citizens and bribing elected officials, government functionaries, and the police, often punctuating the extortion with beatings, threats to their families, and death. All told, gangs simply undermine the safety and security of the Northern Triangle.[7]

Under conditions like this, hopelessness brews and drives people to do desperate, courageous things, such as risking everything to leave the suffering behind or sending children to migrate unaccompanied, to save them. Behrouz Boochani, the Kurdish–Iranian journalist and poet who spent 6 years in Australia's notorious Manus Island prison in Papua New Guinea, said it eloquently and succinctly, speaking for the migrants we met: "This I know: courage has an even more profound connection with hopelessness/ The more hopeless a human being, the more zealous the human is to pursue increasingly dangerous exploits."[8]

I called out the next name on my list. The father of this family had left behind his wife and children to work in the United States and remit money weekly to provide for them, like hundreds of thousands of Mexicans and Central Americans have done for decades. When he left, it was not the *maras* he fled; it was unemployment and poverty. But during his sojourn in Baltimore, the *maras* took over his hometown, employing stark violence and imposing deadly curfews that everyone obeyed if they wanted to live. Their oldest son, 16, was coerced unsuccessfully to join a gang. The message they had passed on to other boys his age rang in his ears: Refuse and you die. The threats escalated, and guns were brandished. It was in May 2014 that his parents decided that the teenager, his mother, two brothers (14 and 13), and sister (10) had to leave El Salvador.

This family was like every other parent and child I met in Karnes and after, fleeing the worst of circumstances in their homelands. But that is where the similarities ended. Rather than hire a coyote or simply walk away without any help, the father hatched a plan for getting his family out. The escape plan was to guide his family *himself* from El Salvador through Guatemala and Mexico, but he would do it remotely from as far away as Baltimore and Dallas. He organized every minute detail to keep them out of harm's way. Father and eldest son set out to execute a finely engineered plan, and the rest of the family were to operate as a finely coordinated team. Everyone had to play their parts to perfection. A cell phone became their most guarded possession when they boarded buses from San Salvador to Santa Ana to Jutiapa in Guatemala and on to the capital, Guatemala City. The eldest son, who narrated much of the story in our meeting, was the handler of the cell phone. He took the instructions sent by his father via WhatsApp. His mother and siblings served as spotters as he read their next steps. The details, coordination, and ruses sent by the father, such as how to avoid being noticed by police and locals and how to shake anyone on your trail, rivaled those of a good spy novel. Messages would read—I fictionalize here—"Jutiapata, SW corner *avenidas* Obregón and Juárez. Bus #87 to Las Anonas." The son would text when they arrived at Las Anonas. Back would come precise coordinates and instructions for the next leg of their carefully plotted route: street corners, bus numbers, and even cautions (e.g., "There are two bus routes. Make sure you take the orange line").

Pilot, navigator, and spotters executed the plan flawlessly in the first 3 days. But in Veracruz, Mexico, the Mexican *migra* caught them and initiated repatriation procedures, but not before they took the cell phone and much of the money the family had. The Guatemalan *migra* and police did the same when they escorted the mother and four children to the Salvadoran border. Back in El Salvador, the son bought a new cell phone, paying for dozens of minutes and data in advance. They laid low for 2 days, informing the father of their new mobile phone number and establishing contact, before putting their game plan into effect again. This time they made it to safety, past *migras*, police, gangs, kidnappers, and other charlatans, using the same tactics as in their first attempt.

"We found our way to the border of Mexico and the US *without a coyote*," the eldest son proudly emphasized. His gloating tone revealed a prod at his family to recognize his daring heroism, maybe to be deemed commander of the expedition. Mother and sibling looked on proudly but would not indulge his vanity and bravado. Their facial expressions made it clear that the eldest son would not be their commander for long, if he ever had been in the first place.

The night before crossing the border they treated themselves with a night in a hotel in Reynosa, courtesy of the father who had paid by credit card from Dallas. Rested, washed, fed, and ready to face the US *migra*, the five members of the escape team walked across the Puente Internacional Reynosa-Hidalgo to McAllen, Texas, on a Wednesday in late July. On the US side, they were apprehended, just as they expected. All five agreed that they were treated well by the border agents. Then they were sent to a *hielera*, where they spent a night urgently trying to stay warm on hard, cold floors covered with Mylar sheets. The mother added a new term to the growing list of modifiers for the term *hielera*, the word *chiquero* (pigsty). From the *chiquero*, they were transferred to Karnes and now waited to be released to their father in Dallas, the mastermind behind the family's great escape.

My maiden visit to Karnes ended with a request from a team of trusted colleagues representing a young woman being held there. It was a special request to evaluate the mother and her child, not just to collect information that would help the delegation in its visit. They needed a formal psychological statement, maybe even with a diagnosis if I were to reach one, that could help the lawyers with the family's asylum application. They were added to the list of families for that second day.

Ms. Mercado was a 24-year-old mother of a 2-year-old boy who was still breastfeeding and refusing any form of solid food or other nourishment. The theme of her flight from El Salvador was much like that of the other women and children, except for the details. The month before her arrival in the United States, Ms. Mercado was handed two notes by gang members. These were 18th Street *maras*, the only time anyone I met had pinpointed another gang besides MS-13. The notes included identifying information about her husband, naming the business where he was employed, the town, and the times that he commuted home. Indeed, he worked in a distant town as a precision tool and parts maker for boats, cars, and firearms and commuted home on weekends and holidays. The first note stated that they were to pay the gang $100 every 2 weeks. The second note raised the demand: Her husband was to manufacture contraband implements for them, specifically, parts for their weapons. About a week after the notes were delivered, the same three gang members invaded her home, grabbed, punched, and tried to rape her. Ms. Mercado screamed as she fought them. Luckily, a male cousin who lived next door yelled out, asking her if something was wrong. Hearing a man's voice, the men ran off. That was the last straw for Ms. Mercado. Two weeks later, she arrived at the US–Mexican border, just 3 weeks before our meeting.

In the clinical interview, Ms. Mercado presented herself as lucid, alert, and of average intelligence. But she was highly anxious, shaking her legs and feet and holding her son with both arms. She reported some of the physical signs of depression: insomnia, lack of appetite, and difficulty concentrating. Until she could be out of Karnes, she felt hopeless. Her son's refusal to take any other nutrition but breast milk added to her distress. Ms. Mercado felt that she was to blame for his problems in leaving home. Weighing heavily on her too was her husband's safety in El Salvador. Her toddler showed no interest in the toys in the room. He clung to his mother, fussed, and insisted she give her full attention to him and not to the conversation with me. These were sure signs of separation anxiety. They also signaled that the boy's development toward independence had been truncated. With more observation and a full developmental history, he might have received a formal diagnosis of separation anxiety, very likely related to the sudden and weeks-long absence of his father, his cognitive immaturity to comprehend why, the disruption in the familiar setting of home, the strain of their travels, the deprivation of prison, and his mother's palpable anxiety and depression. Her symptoms could add up to diagnoses of major depressive disorder and post-traumatic stress disorder. To assign proper diagnoses, though, I would need more time—a valuable commodity we did not have.

Whether I heard it from immigration attorneys or read it in distinguished professional journals, I know that with competent legal representation the chances that asylum will be granted is far more likely than when not having representation. The Immigration Justice Corps (IJC) in New York City states that

> quality legal representation can make all the difference. . . . Without counsel, most immigrants face a complex and adversarial system alone. Those with representation are six times more likely to see a successful outcome. [IJC] counsel has a 92% success rate in completed cases, in contrast to a 3% success rate when a detained immigrant is without counsel.[9]

In 2014, the Syracuse University–based Transactional Records Access Clearinghouse (TRAC) analyzed 10 years of immigration court records on 60,000 cases and found that the presence of an attorney representing an unaccompanied minor made a world of difference in the outcomes.[10] Unaccompanied kids represented by lawyers were 47% likelier to be allowed to remain in the United States. Without legal representation, nine out of 10 unaccompanied children who appeared in immigration court without an attorney were ordered deported. Similar results are reported by attorneys Ingrid Eagley and Steve Shafer: Immigrants with representation are more likely to be released from detention (44%) than those without lawyers (11%). Moreover, those detainees with lawyers are far more likely to attend their immigration court hearings, avoiding arrest warrants and other legal complications. Eagley and Shafer show that 90% of unrepresented immigrants with removal orders were removed in absentia compared to only 29% of those with attorneys representing them.[11] The same is true in asylum cases. For asylum-seeking immigrants without representation, "the deck is stacked against [them]," says a 2017 TRAC report. "Statistically, only one out of every ten asylum claimants win their case. With representation, nearly half are successful."[12] Similarly, Emily Ryo, a law professor at the University of Southern California, found that detainees with an attorney at their bond hearings have about 47% lower odds of being deemed dangerous than detainees who lack legal representation.[13] In sum, having an attorney gives the asylees and detainees a far better chance of winning their claims.

One such case I worked on in 2016 was especially gratifying. That June, I got a call from Manoj Govindaiah, at the time director of Family Detention Services for the Refugee and Immigration Center for Education and Legal Services, based in San Antonio, about a teenager detained in Karnes with his mother and younger sister. There was a very short turnaround since the immigration court hearing was days away. I made the drive again to Karnes City without much planning. After 2 years, I was very familiar with the route and could get there in less time and with less expectancy.

Sixteen-year-old Romeo had entered the United States with his mother and sister, 12, on June 1. I learned from him, and his mother, that he had attended a highly regarded public school in his town, one that attracted students from across the economic spectrum. But Romeo was slowly going blind. Doctors in his country, Peru, had recognized their limitations and the scarce expertise and equipment in their country. Romeo needed advanced care not available in Peru, or at least not available to anyone without great wealth. Unable to afford a visa or airfare, his mother decided to take buses and walk with her son and daughter to the United States to get the medical care he needed. They had set out to join her brother in Maryland, where ophthalmic care could be found in its great universities and hospitals. In the United States, Romeo could request humanitarian parole, which allows individuals to enter and stay in the United States to seek medical treatment for illnesses such as Romeo's. Parole is discretionary, a decision of the secretary of Homeland Security, and is assessed by the US Citizenship and Immigration Service.

We sat diagonally from each other across a small table with molded plastic chairs in a tight interviewing room, close enough that I could see that neither of his eyes looked healthy. It appeared to me that his left eye was more damaged than the right eye, the impression of an untrained observer. In our conversation, I soon learned that his vision was his only disability.

Romeo had felt the blunt force of taunts at school because he was different and vulnerable, part of the cruelty of childhood. He was mocked by schoolmates as "four eyes" or "blindy" for his thick glasses. The insults were followed by laughter in the classroom when he had to put his face close to the chalkboard to write or do arithmetic. Seizing on the possibility that the blind kid might be a very useful stooge, some of the older boys who sold drugs at school wanted Romeo to sell for them. A blind kid would not draw the attention of teachers or the police. By refusing, Romeo became the merciless target of the older boys. When higher-level drug dealers learned of the blind kid's refusal, menacing telephone calls came into his home from voices of men, none of whom his family recognized. His mother said, "I need to save my son and save his vision."

By Romeo's estimation, the vision in his left eye was "three on a scale from 1 to 100." Surgery had helped correct his right eye but not entirely. Missing the range of peripheral vision that was about half that of a fully sighted person made Romeo feel vulnerable. As he confided his defenselessness, I thought how extraordinarily hard it must have been to endure the long journey with his mother and sister when he could not see enough of his surroundings. He could not know easily if danger was near or far, coming from one side or another. Although Romeo wasn't seeking sympathy, I could not help feeling my helplessness. But our rapport revealed strengths: His only disability was in his vision. Romeo's character, intelligence, personality, insight, and determination more than made up for what he could not see. Despite a serious visual impairment and painful experiences back home, Romeo spoke with the grace, earnestness, and seriousness that few teenagers of his age possess.

"I must save my left eye." Across that table, Romeo faced me, saying that he wanted to study law because it requires "careful thinking, provides order to the world, and I can use it to help others." With his precarious hold on eyesight, using what remains of it to navigate in a complex world, Romeo's reasoning seemed perfectly normal. He was gifted with a fertile, active intellect.

"I have listened to a lot of radio and television shows, and tried to read, to learn about the United States," he told me. "I like what I have learned. And, you know," he said, leaning in slightly closer as if to make sure I understood that even under the conditions of detention he had arrived at his conclusion after careful deliberation. "I like what little I have seen since coming here. I like that everything is clean and safe. People follow the rules and laws here."

With his self-described vision limited to about 3%, he needed order to get through life.

His intelligence and determination could not erase the fear and sadness that were close to the surface emotionally. Every day that he sat in detention was 1 day further away from protecting his eyesight and fulfilling his dreams. The psychological assessment I wrote for Manoj concluded,

> It is imperative that every effort be made to save this young man's remaining vision. On purely humanitarian grounds, Romeo and his mother and sister should be permitted to enter the United States for the ophthalmological care he needs. Not only is this essential to his visual health but to his emotional and psychological health. It is my professional opinion that Romeo should be provided with the advanced care that is available to him in the United States as soon as possible to prevent any further deterioration in his vision. It will not only improve his vision but his mental health.

Five days later, I received a brief email from Manoj that read, "wanted to let you know that for Romeo, his family ended up getting a positive [court] decision and has been released to Maryland, which is great news." Great news that clouded my eyes with tears.

Meeting so many children and families in detention, like Romeo and Ms. Mercado and her son, and hearing their stories, seeing the look in their eyes, brought to life the how and why migration has existed since the beginning of time. For millennia, people have migrated from one place to another, often escaping droughts, floods, wars, tribal rivalries, famine, genocide, and ineffective governments—conditions so unbearable that they are left with no other option but to take flight, leaving home for a vague but hopeful future. For the same millennia, the people in the receiving countries have asked, "Why are they coming here? Why can't they stay in their own countries? Why not go somewhere else?" It is not just Americans who ask these questions in the 21st century. People of western Europe, Asia, Africa, Central and South America, and the Caribbean are asking as well. For Americans, immigration is not a new phenomenon. Individually, people recall their immigrant ancestors with pride. But collectively, it seems, Americans omit from the stories and legends of their ancestors the fact that many of their forebears made similar decisions in which they risked everything to come to the United States, even by illegal means.

As callous as the immigration debates appear to be in our day and time, it is not the first time in American history that hateful vitriol has been spewed in the public square and in the press. In fact, immigration has been a major battleground in the United States since the founding of the republic. As far back as 1751, Benjamin Franklin bemoaned the immigration of French, Swedes, and others as insufficiently White. Franklin questioned if German immigrants would "Germanize us instead of our Anglifying them," predicting that they could never adopt the language and customs of the previous British colonists any more than they could acquire our "complexion."[14]

The 1800s saw massive numbers of immigrants coming to America, a land of dreams and a place to settle. Seventy percent of immigrants to the United States between 1820 and 1840 were German, British, and Irish. By the end of the 1800s, they had decreased to 50%; the influx was now coming from eastern and southern Europe. Not everyone was happy to receive immigrants from any part of Europe. None were as vilified in the media and public discourse as Asians. In 1882 anti-immigrant sentiment was enshrined in two landmark laws. In May of that year, President Chester Arthur signed into law the Chinese Exclusion Act of 1882, a law that prohibited immigration from China and did not allow legal residents of Chinese origin to become US citizens.[15] As happened in other eras, Americans, in this case residents on the West Coast, blamed the decline in wages and the economic malaise of the time on the Chinese, who were perceived as taking their jobs for lower pay. Despite comprising only 0.002% of the US population at the time, the Chinese were targeted by the Exclusion Act to appease workers and—may this reality not be lost to history—assuage Americans about keeping White racial purity and power. Driven by China's national debt after the Opium Wars with Great Britain (1839–1842, 1856–1860) and complicated by floods and drought in their country, many Chinese left farms to find work. When the California gold rush began in the Sacramento Valley in 1848, Chinese immigrants entered the United States to seek their fortunes. A Supreme Court case, *People v. Hall* in 1854, determined that the Chinese, like African Americans and Native Americans, could not testify in court. The decision meant that Chinese people could never seek justice for the violence they faced. In 1870, Chinese immigrants in California had paid $5 million to the state as called for in the Foreign Miners Tax. The discrimination at work and in society continued unabated.

The Chinese Exclusion Act of 1882 suspended Chinese immigration for 10 years and declared Chinese immigrants ineligible for naturalization.

Chinese Americans who were already in the country filed challenges to the constitutionality of the act, to no avail. They remained disenfranchised. Ten years later, the Geary Act, named for a California congressman, took effect and extended the ban on Chinese for another 10 years.[16] Chinese residents in the United States had to carry special documentation—certificates of residence—issued by the Internal Revenue Service.[17] Anyone caught without a certificate was sentenced to hard labor and deportation. Bail was an option in these situations, the only option, in fact, and it came only if a "credible White witness" would vouch for the Chinese person. Chinese immigrants and their US-born children remained ineligible for citizenship until 1943 when the Magnuson Act was passed. By that time the United States was at war in Japan and Europe.

The Immigration Act of 1882 taxed each new migrant 50 cents, barred convicts and other "undesirables" from entering, created the first requirements for national origin, and denied admission to anyone over the age of 16 who was illiterate.[18] As historian John Dower points out,

> the vision of the menace from the East was always more racial rather than national. It derived not from concern with any one country or people in particular, but from a vague and ominous sense of the vast, faceless, nameless yellow horde: the rising tide, indeed, of color.[19]

Another restrictive immigration policy in US history came with the signing by President Calvin Coolidge of the Immigration Act of 1924, which reflected America's legalized racial discrimination of the time. As seems to occur throughout US history, the objection to immigration was due to the fear of unfair competition for jobs created by the immigration of largely unskilled, uneducated people in the early 1900s. Immigrants with a college education or special skills could enter the country but not if they were Mexican, Japanese, eastern European (e.g., Polish, Ukrainian, Bulgarian), or southern European (e.g., Italian, Greek, Spanish). Permitted into the country were immigrants from northern Europe, such as Britain, Ireland, and the Scandinavian countries. Across nearly three centuries, the sentiment has remained alive in America, often bringing national disgrace by our treatment of immigrants and people who appear to be of a different "complexion," as Ben Franklin said.

The idea of an Asian menace was kept alive in the early 20th century by Japan's defeat of Russia in their war of 1904–1905. If suffering discrimination through the Immigration Act of 1924 was not enough, Japanese Americans—and not just *issei* born in Japan who immigrated but also US-born *nisei* children of Japanese immigrants—would be singled out for one of the harshest treatments implemented by the US government: ostracized and relegated to internment camps for no other reason than being Japanese and Japanese descendants. When Japan attacked Pearl Harbor on December 7, 1941, there were approximately 125,000 Japanese Americans living on the mainland, mostly on the Pacific coast. Hawaii, at the time a US territory, had about 200,000 Japanese immigrants. After the Pearl Harbor attack, more than 1,200 leaders in the Japanese community were arrested. Japanese banks with branches in the United States saw their accounts frozen. The federal government, through the War Department, suspected Japanese Americans of sabotage and spying for Japan. No hard evidence ever came to light. Still, politicians and many in the public wanted Japanese Americans to be rounded up, particularly those living in California and on the West Coast. Despite opposition by the US Department of Justice, the War Department prevailed on President Franklin Roosevelt to sign Executive Order 9066 on February 18.[20] Immediately, the War Department created 12 "restricted zones" on the Pacific coast. Nighttime curfews were set that applied only to Japanese Americans within those zones. Anyone who broke curfew faced immediate arrest. Soon after these intrusions, the Federal War Relocation Authority was created to "take all people of Japanese descent into custody, surround them with troops, prevent them from buying land, and return them to their former homes at the close of the war."[21]

In late March of 1942, Japanese Americans along the Pacific coast were ordered to find their way to control stations where they were to register all family members. At the control centers, families were assigned dates and locations from which they would be transferred to internment camps. While *internment* was the term used by the government and others, many argued that the terms that were most fitting were *incarceration* and *detention*. (Similar arguments have been made about the immigration detention centers during the Obama and Trump administrations.)

The location of the first internment camp was Manzanar in southern California. From 1942 to 1945, 10 camps in Arizona, Arkansas, Colorado, Utah, and Wyoming held approximately 120,000 Japanese Americans for varying periods of time. The photographs of the internment camps by Dorothea Lange and Ansel Adams seared the dispossession of Japanese Americans in US memory for generations to come. The pain, suffering, dislocation, and loss were captured movingly in their pictures. So too were the heroic efforts by Japanese Americans in internment to retain their dignity, communities, and American traditions. They lived in family groups and set up schools, newspapers, gardens, and churches. The pictures by Adams and Lange, as well as many written accounts, laid bare the sparse living conditions of the camps: uninsulated barracks, cots, coal-burning stoves, and surrounding barbed-wire fences with armed guards who were instructed to shoot anyone who tried to escape.[22]

In December 1944, the government determined that all internment camps would close within a year, at the end of 1945. But it was not until March 1946 that the last camp, a high-security facility at Tule Lake, California, was closed. When internment ended, Japanese Americans began rebuilding their lives. Those who still had homes returned to them. Still, 3 years of internment had stamped its impact on American society and Japanese Americans. Not just tension, suspicion, and despair but disrupted lives, upturned family structures, depression, and other human problems took their toll on the lives of Japanese Americans. The detention of Central American women and children by the US government in contemporary times is often compared to the internment of Japanese Americans in the 1940s. The parallels are striking.

The history of immigration to the United States shows that each successive wave of immigrants faces mistrust, resentment, rejection, xenophobia, outright attacks by the public, and the threat of exclusionary legislation. Fear motivated the anti-immigrant, racist beliefs and actions of many Americans—themselves the children and grandchildren of immigrants. Even when a line of presidents tried to repeal laws and make America the welcoming nation it was thought to be, public opinion thwarted them. There was President Woodrow Wilson in 1915 arguing that a literacy requirement was bad for the United States and simply ironic: "Those who come seeking opportunity are not to be admitted unless they have already had one of the chief of the opportunities they seek, the opportunity of education."[23] He opposed legislation that favored people who already had a privileged, educated life. Wilson believed that everyone, including the less privileged, could add to the greatness of the United States. The literacy requirement was ultimately repealed.

However, the planting of seeds for national origin quotas found fertile soil in the Immigration and Nationality Act of 1952, the first major act on immigration. Abolished from the bill was the exclusion of Asians, but it kept the overt preference for immigrants from northern and western Europe.

It placed limits on immigrants from the entire "Asia-Pacific Triangle," including individuals of Asian descent living anywhere in the world. President Harry Truman reminded Americans of its venerable traditions.

> Today, we are "protecting" ourselves as we were in 1924, against being flooded by immigrants from Eastern Europe. This is fantastic. The countries of Eastern Europe have fallen under the Communist yoke—they are silenced, fenced off by barbed wire and minefields—no one passes their border but at the risk of his life. We do not need to be protected against immigrants from these countries—on the contrary we want to stretch out a helping hand, to save those who have managed to flee into Western Europe, to succor those who are brave enough to escape from barbarism, to welcome and restore them against the day when their countries will, as we hope, be free again. . . . These are only a few examples of the absurdity, the cruelty of carrying over into this year of 1952 the isolationist limitations of our 1924 law.[24]

The masterful negotiator and deal maker President Lyndon Johnson managed to work with Congress to amend the Immigration and Nationality Act of 1952. In 1965, the law shifted preference from northern and western Europe to immigrants who already had family in the United States, prioritizing family unification. Johnson reflected on prior injustice in the quota system and its violation of American values, stating, "We can now believe that it will never again shadow the gate to the American Nation with the twin barriers of prejudice and privilege."[25]

The 1970s saw a shift in the refugees and immigrants coming to the United States from Latin America without visas or other documents. The immigrants were propelled to leave by the repressive dictatorships and authoritarian regimes ruling their countries and disastrous economic conditions. Now the cultural fear generated against Asian immigrants in the past re-emerged but this time against Latin American immigrants. Legislation tried to limit immigration from countries in our own hemisphere. And while he voiced concern about legislation that might affect the US–Mexican relationship, President Gerald Ford signed the Immigration and Nationality Act Amendments in 1976.[26]

It took four decades before a formal apology and compensation were issued to Japanese Americans, an apology from the American government to its own citizens. In 1976, President Gerald R. Ford repealed the executive order that had started the roundup and detention of Japanese Americans

after the attack on Pearl Harbor. His statement expressed the regret of the nation for a policy that should never have been.

> February 19th is the anniversary of a sad day in American history. It was on
> that date in 1942 . . . that Executive Order 9066 was issued . . . resulting in
> the uprooting of loyal Americans. . . . We now know what we should have
> known then—not only was that evacuation wrong, but Japanese Americans
> were and are loyal Americans. . . . I call upon the American people to affirm
> with me this American Promise—that we have learned from the tragedy
> of that long-ago experience forever to treasure liberty and justice for each
> individual American, and resolve that this kind of action shall never again
> be repeated.

Six years later, a presidential commission concluded that racism, hys-
teria, and lack of political will brought about the disgraceful period of
Japanese American internment. It was another 6 years later, in 1988, that
Congress through the Civil Liberties Act awarded more than 80,000 Japanese
Americans compensation of $20,000 each for their ordeal. Perhaps more sa-
lient was a formal apology issued by the government for its policy toward
Japanese Americans. President Ronald Reagan, in contrast, recognized
that Mexican migrant workers in the United States were a benefit to both
countries: sending money back home and providing a large labor force for
the United States. Reagan argued that this important contribution justified
the reward of citizenship, a point of contention that quickly emerged at the
forefront of the next major comprehensive immigration reform. Family
unity and reunification was reinforced in 1981 by the Select Commission
on Immigration and Refugee Policy, a group appointed by Congress to
study immigration policies and recommend legislative reform. The Select
Commission stated that

> Reunification . . . serves the national interest not only through the humane-
> ness of the policy itself, but also through the promotion of the public order
> and well-being of the nation. Psychologically and socially, the reunion of
> family members with their close relatives promotes the health and welfare
> of the United States.[27]

In 1986, Congress passed the Immigration Reform and Control Act (IRCA).
The bill made it illegal for employers to knowingly hire undocumented

immigrants and imposed sanctions on employers who failed to make a good faith effort to verify the legal status of their workers. In an attempt to control the border, the IRCA increased Customs and Border Patrol personnel by 50%. But the IRCA also awarded amnesty to 3 million undocumented individuals.[28] Nonetheless, the Reagan administration saw detention as a crucial component of its immigration policy agenda and supported the attorney general's authority to detain migrants, even indefinitely.[29]

President George H. W. Bush expanded the number of immigrants allowed in each year that maintained the nation's historic commitment to family reunification.[30] But his Democratic successor, Bill Clinton, signed the Illegal Immigration Reform and Immigrant Responsibility Act (IIRIRA) and issued an executive order preventing federal contractors from working with businesses that hire undocumented workers. Clinton boasted that "For too long . . . the Immigration and Naturalization Service has lacked the resources needed for vigorous enforcement. My administration has provided the INS with the resources it needs to enforce the law."[31] By signing the law, Clinton created a large undocumented population, mostly Mexican seasonal migrant workers. Under the IIRIRA, undocumented immigrants who had been present in the United States for 6 months or more received a 3-year or 10-year bar on entrance after leaving the country. But rather than contain illegal immigration, the IIRIRA forced migrant workers to stay in the United States once they had entered. Rather than the back-and-forth migration they had long known, seasonal workers now had to stay in the United States year-round and were forced to bring their families to live in the United States with them. Legal scholars Smita Ghosh and Mary Hoopes conclude that in the early 1990s congressional leaders began asserting that asylum seekers were criminals and spreaders of infectious diseases to justify their detention. From there, the path was clear for mass detention. Ghosh and Hoopes conclude that lawmakers "may have emphasized the dangerousness of asylum seekers to resolve the dissonance between their theoretical commitments to asylum and their hesitance to welcome newcomers."[32] Then in 1996, Congress changed immigrant detention by passing the Antiterrorism and Effective Death Penalty Act of 1996 and the IIRIRA of 1996, which called for detaining not only non-citizens with criminal records but also asylum seekers. And the numbers detained grew sharply.[33]

World history is full of examples of how immigrants are classified and insulted, labeling them as "the other," different, strange, threatening, maybe even subhuman. As I have tried to show in this chapter, it has been part of

US history. The September 11, 2001, attack on the icons of American cap-
italism and the military reinforced the perception of recent immigrants as
dangerous. As Karla Cornejo Villavicencio writes, September 11 wronged
everyone, but "Because the antithesis of an American is an immigrant and
because [immigrants] could not be victims in the public eye, we became
suspects."[34] The racial prejudice, hysteria, and failed political leadership that
occurred in 1942 have happened before and since, right into the beginning
of the 21st century. The difference today is that the same mean-spirited, anti-
immigration rhetoric, actions, and reactions by the public and unwelcoming
national policies are abetted by a 24-hour television news cycle and a social
media that pushes false narratives, distorted facts, and conspiracy theories to
the deepest corners of society. Many believe the falsehoods, distortions, and
conspiracies.

In *Infamy: The Shocking Story of the Japanese American Internment in
World War II*, Richard Reeves tells of the buildup of enmity toward Japanese,
the roundups, and the transfer to internment camps, far from any contact
with Japan and its war machine. The individual stories of Japanese families
are painful. And while there was plenty of blame and shame to be assigned to
many American politicians, military leaders, and everyday citizens, Reeves
tells of the good men and women who spoke up against the internment. Some
of those who spoke up were government employees who saw the lawlessness
and cruelty of interning their neighbors and friends. Many who worked in
the camps, according to Reeves, were kind, compassionate, and helpful to the
internees.

The same, I found, can be said of US federal employees and private prison
employees in the time since 2014 who did not agree with the decision to detain infants, toddlers, children, teenagers, and mothers in family residential
centers. There are good people working for the government who must do
tasks that are distasteful. You will meet some in the next chapter.

Notes

1. Lusk & Sanchez Garcia, 2021, p. 6.
2. Seelke, 2016.
3. Illegal Immigrant Reform and Immigrant Responsibility Act, 1996.
4. Meyer & Taft-Morales, 2019; Seelke, 2016.
5. Brownfield, 2012; UN Office on Drugs and Crime, 2012.

6. UN Office on Drugs and Crime, 2007.

7. For more on the history of Central American gangs and the transnational criminal syndicates, see Bruneau et al., 2011; Dudley, 2020; Grillo, 2017; Lovato, 2021; Martinez, 2016; Wheeler, 2020.

8. Boochani, 2018, p. 74.

9. Immigrant Justice Corps, 2022.

10. Transactional Records Access Clearinghouse, Syracuse University, 2014.

11. Eagly & Shafer, 2016.

12. Transactional Records Access Clearinghouse, Syracuse University, 2017.

13. Ryo, 2019.

14. Rampell, 2015.

15. Davis & Morrison, 2015; Railton, 2013.

16. Lee, 2003.

17. Onion, 2015.

18. US Citizenship and Immigration Service, 2020.

19. Dower, 1986, p. 156.

20. See Thomas, 1952.

21. Encyclopaedia Britannica, 2021.

22. Reeves, 2015; Wakatsuki Houston & Houston, 1973.

23. Wilson, 1915.

24. Truman, 1962, p. 443.

25. Johnson, 1965.

26. Ford, 1976.

27. Select Commission on Immigration and Refugee Policy, 1981, pp. 112–113.

28. Pear, 1986.

29. Ghosh & Hoopes, 2021.

30. Bush, 1990.

31. Clinton, 1996.

32. Ghosh & Hoopes, 2021, p. 994.

33. Acer & Byrne, 2017; García Hernández, 2014.

34. Cornejo Villavicencio, 2020, p. 40.

3

I Didn't Sign Up for This

Even if families in Karnes were permitted visitors 7 days a week, neither the GEO Group (GEO) nor Immigration and Customs Enforcement (ICE) would make it easy, no matter who you were or what business you had with a mother and her kids. Karnes City is fairly remote from most cities and towns, especially for financially strapped families and friends who drove long distances. In Texas, even "nearby" is a long drive. There is no public transportation to speak of in Karnes, and the bus depot in Karnes City is about 2 miles from the detention center. Attorneys, even with cars, time, and resources, cannot just hop over to Karnes from their offices in San Antonio, Houston, or Austin. Its location was the first-order deterrent for visitors and advocates.

Once there, visitors, like me, faced a second deterrent. We would be inducted into the roles of actors in a play staged by ICE and GEO staff, a masterful piece of several acts. Back in 2014 and 2015, the first act starred GEO guards, smug with the authority they wielded in their company uniforms, indifferent to visitors' presence while finishing a conversation with their co-workers. They were well aware that our team was there on official matters. When they turned to address the visitors, the contract guards asked what our business was that day, questions viscous with skepticism and contempt. The scenes in this farce unvaryingly included hearing that there was no record that we were scheduled to see anyone that day. "Your name is not on the list" was a common line. Letters and documents the visitor produced were summarily rejected as unofficial or unverifiable, and besides neither ICE nor GEO had received copies in advance. I was not surprised that private prison staff behaved as they did, but it was particularly disappointing when ICE personnel, government employees, did the same. In the next scene, appearing annoyed that the visitor was making them work, the guard would leave the post or send someone to go find a supervisor, a cue to our group that we were entering the next act of this performance. Ten minutes later, the guard or other employee would return, ignoring the visitor, to tell the fellow guard that the supervisor was busy—the excuse was usually that the individual was on a call or in a meeting—and would come soon, which meant another 10

Through Iceboxes and Kennels. Luis H. Zayas, Oxford University Press. © Oxford University Press 2023.
DOI: 10.1093/oso/9780197668160.003.0004

minutes. Guards would resume their conversations, which only sometimes concerned official business.

The play would enter its final act when ICE supervisors appeared on stage for their part of the show. The script called for the visitor to repeat the same information given earlier to the guard. With ponderous gravitas and a studied look of seriousness, the ICE supervisor would read and reread the letter, ask a few innocuous questions, and say, "I'll be right back." "Right back" meant another 10 minutes, after which, without fanfare, the visitor was told to store any electronic devices and other belongings in a locker nearby. Sans curtain or applause, the play ended with the visitor entering the full-body scanner. Forty to 45 minutes had now passed since the visitor's arrival, with no explanations given. I never saw the same persons at the entrance and security checkpoint. Nevertheless, they knew every act and scene of the well-worn farce, a communal joke whose humor I did not share. Their mirth made me late and kept families waiting unnecessarily.

One morning in July 2015 I was scheduled to meet at 10:00 with a family at their attorney's request. Preparations had been made: letter of introduction sent; my name, driver's license, social security number furnished; and the detained family's names, alien numbers, and appointment time submitted. I wanted to be signed in without delay and given a key to the lockers in the lobby, a drill I knew well by now. But I had to act in their play, and we went through scenes and acts which by now I knew by heart. I played my part, filling in the blanks: "I should be on the list to see [family name and "A" number] at 10:00. Here's a letter from [attorney's name]. Lawyer [name] arranged my visit with ICE officer [surname]."

"Sir, the person your lawyer-friend contacted isn't here today, and she didn't leave any messages or instructions that you were coming. We don't have that letter, either. Here, let me make a copy of it."

This Saturday morning was no different except for what happened next. Owing to it being a weekend morning, there weren't many guards or visitors, and the play took less time. The ICE supervisor arrived and went through the routine of abetting my delay with barely a glance to identify me. The officer was a fit-looking White man in his late 30s, maybe 40s, in a crisp shirt and short-cropped military haircut with a stern face and a pair of sleek, tactical sunglasses with green and blue iridescent lenses propped on his head, the kind SWAT teams wear. His badge bore a Hispanic surname. He stepped around from the security desk and the metal detection machine, some feet away from the guard handling the entry. About 5 feet separated us.

"Zayas?" he asked. "Aren't you the one that wrote that report?" His English had the unmistakable accent of a Cuban American of his vintage, probably raised in south Florida. In my large extended Puerto Rican–Cuban family, it was a familiar accent.

"What report are you referring to, sir?"

"The one, 15 pages or so, that you wrote about a bunch of families and how they said they were treated here," he answered. Immediately, I knew that he was referring to the declaration that I had written for two federal class-action lawsuits, *R.I.L-R v. Johnson* and *Flores v. Johnson*.

"It wasn't a report, officer. It was a declaration that I wrote as part of a federal lawsuit," I clarified.

"Well, how did you get the information on the families? Who gave you permission to interview them? How did you get in here to talk with them?" He was deadly serious and equally as misinformed. I explained to him that the information in the declaration was gathered during a visit approved by the Department of Homeland Security (DHS) and his own outfit, ICE, a year earlier. The declaration, I underscored, contained information collected legally with the permission of the federal government and based on my area of expertise.

The officer was clearly annoyed, maybe defensive, about what I had written in the declaration. I wondered if the declaration had been a topic of conversation among ICE personnel. Despite his indignation, something—a gut sense—told me I should say more, place my sense of mission in direct juxtaposition to his. Maybe it was a macho thing that was going on between us, but it was one that could ease the tension and clear the air.

"Man," I said, striking a note of familiarity as a fellow Hispanic, "how can you do this? How can you jail mothers and kids? You look like you're a husband and father. I'm a father too. These moms and kids aren't security threats or flight risks. They haven't done anything wrong."

It was a gutsy move, using familiar language and making assumptions about him. It could have all added to my woes by delaying me even more. Worse, it could have been grounds for this officer to find other ways to bar me from entering that day and in the future. I would have to explain to the lawyers and the families why I couldn't enter Karnes anymore. But my pluck that day didn't cause a problem. Maybe pointing to us as fathers and husbands, with wives and children the same ages as those inside, struck a chord with him. The ICE officer gestured with his head to accompany him toward the front exit. I followed. We crossed the double doors into the blinding

Texas sun and oppressive heat. It took a few seconds for our eyes to adjust, even though on his head sat the sunglasses.

"I didn't sign up for this," he said, our eyes meeting. There was sincerity in his voice and face. "I joined to fight the bad guys." I understood implicitly: bad guys meaning drug lords, criminals, hitmen, cartels, and traffickers of all matter of contraband, including humans. My satisfaction that the gambit worked was quickly replaced with empathy. It felt like I had an unfair moral advantage or at least more self-righteousness. I needed to soften my approach.

"Look, I am not saying you personally. I didn't mean it that way. It is just not right to hold innocent people."

"It's not what I signed up for." No one heard us. The exchange took less than 30 seconds, during which we were entirely alone. We seemed to have reached a common understanding under the glare of a blazing sun. He was an honest career official who had enlisted for the right reasons and felt duty-bound by his pledge to the Constitution. He was one of the people Donald Trump would later call, derisively, the "deep state." The officer led me back into the cool building and allowed me into Karnes to do my job. He went on to his. We never met again.

That moment is a reminder to me of all the times immigrant mothers told of kind and gallant Customs and Border Protection and ICE agents who saved them from drowning, helped an injured child, wrapped them in warm blankets, spoke to them with civility, recognized a serious illness, and other acts of compassion and professionalism. The ICE officer · on duty that morning was, at heart, one of the good ones. Many others in the militarized border and immigration enforcement organizations were heartless. The two types were representative of society's mix of sadists and empaths.

What the ICE supervisor called a "report" was, in fact, a declaration I had written after my August 2014 tour of Karnes and fact-finding interviews with detained families. This declaration was essentially a sworn statement on a topic I knew something about and, in this case, of which I had the authenticity of having directly observed the detention center and the detainees. It is similar to an affidavit submitted under penalty of perjury, except that it does not require a notary public to certify. The declaration was used in two class-action lawsuits against President Obama's DHS secretary, Jeh Johnson, and his colleagues.

One case, *R.I.L-R v. Johnson*, was filed in December 2014 in the US District Court in Washington, DC, by the American Civil Liberties Union (ACLU), several of its affiliates, and the University of Texas at Austin's Immigration Law Clinic.[1] The case was brought on behalf of three mothers and their children from Central America who had proven that they had a "credible fear" of persecution and had been deemed as having a "significant possibility" of being granted asylum. DHS was not following its customary practice of releasing families who had passed their credible fear interviews. Instead, it was categorically denying their release on bond and keeping them detained, part of the aggressive deterrence strategy and no-release policy of the Obama administration. Asylum-seeking mothers and children, like the three mothers in this case, were being kept in detention facilities in Karnes City and Dilley, Texas, and Berks County, Pennsylvania. You might think of these as the family division of a sprawling archipelago of immigration detention facilities that are found not just in Texas but in 27 other states.[2] In February, US District Court Judge James E. Boasberg issued a ruling in which he agreed that DHS should stop its practice of keeping mothers in detention who had a significant likelihood of becoming asylees. Judge Boasberg said that the mothers had a significant likelihood of succeeding on the merits of their claim.[3] The judge didn't think that there was a sweeping ICE policy designed to deny releases, but he saw plenty of evidence that DHS was telling ICE officers to promote the deterrence of mass migration, hence raising the number of Central American mothers and children in detention.

The other lawsuit, *Flores v. Johnson*, is a case with a history going back more than two decades.[4] The case was filed on February 2, 2015, stating that, by detaining children in prison-like conditions, the government was in violation of the "Flores Settlement Agreement." Known as the *Flores Agreement* or the *Flores Settlement*, this consent decree was signed in 1997 by US Attorney General Janet Reno during the Clinton administration. The Flores Agreement set standards and regulations for the detention and treatment of minors being held in federal custody, ending years of litigation by agreeing to hold children in the least restrictive environment and ensuring their prompt release from detention. In July, US Federal District Judge Dolly M. Gee of the Southern District of California ruled that the Flores Agreement applied equally to accompanied and unaccompanied minors and that Obama administration immigration officials had violated the consent decree by refusing to release accompanied minors held in family detention facilities. Judge Gee agreed that holding parents and children for up to 20 days was within the parameters set by the Flores Settlement but emphasized that it should be without any unnecessary delays. With her decision, Judge Gee ordered the release of 1,700 families that were neither flight risks nor security threats.

To show the level of insensitivity in how detained immigrant children were treated, lawyers for the Trump administration argued that the government was *not required to let children sleep or to be given soap to wash* because it wasn't explicitly stated in the Flores Agreement. The idiocy of this argument was followed by Trump administration lawyers asking a federal appellate court to overturn Judge Gee's decision requiring the government to let kids in detention sleep and wash. The government complained in its appeal that it did not need to provide child detainees with "hygiene items such as soap and toothbrushes in order to comply with the 'safe and sanitary conditions' requirement set forth in the Flores Settlement."

It was in those two cases that my declaration was included. In the declaration, I noted that detention had serious and long-lasting impacts on the psychological health and well-being of the families. This was evident even though some of the families I interviewed had been detained at Karnes for a relatively limited period of time—2 to 3 weeks. But there were many others who had been detained for months without any release date in sight. In general, mothers and children showed elevated levels of anxiety—especially separation anxiety for the children—symptoms of depression, and feelings of despair. The declaration stated that,

> The psychological traumas experienced by these mothers and children—in their home countries, during their travel to the United States, and upon their detention in the United States—will require years of mental health services to alleviate. Moreover, the ongoing stress, despair, and uncertainty of detention—for even a relatively brief period of time—specifically compromises the children's intellectual and cognitive development and contributes to the development of chronic illness in ways that may be irreversible. Detention at Karnes puts children at risk of recurrent and distressing memories, nightmares, dissociative reactions, prolonged psychological distress, and negative alterations in cognition.

I described the families' post-migration experiences upon reaching the United States and, in most instances, their detention by US border patrol agents and other law enforcement at the border and the way US officials processed them up to their arrival and detention in Karnes. Most mothers told of elation when they were apprehended by agents, initially feeling safe in their hands. It wasn't long before mothers and adolescents were treated roughly, spoken to sternly, told to move faster, and admonished when they did not. The orders came in English, and the moms and kids simply didn't understand them.

I noted in the declaration that while some families reported initially receiving friendly and caring treatment by US officials, they also described punitive and verbally abusive treatment later on. They described GEO employees as "mean," "rude," "bullies," along with other negative descriptors. The facts, presented in the aggregate to the court, were there.

> Taking [the] scientific background into consideration and combining it with the impressions I gathered in my interviews with mothers and children in the Karnes facility, I can unequivocally state that the children in the Karnes facility are facing some of the most adverse childhood conditions of any children I have ever interviewed or evaluated. Untold harm is being inflicted on these children by the trauma of detention. . . . [Detention] is inflicting emotional and other harms on these families, particularly the children, and that some of these effects will be long lasting, and very likely permanent.

There was no way that healing could begin in detention.

Another person who had not "signed up for this" was Olivia López, a professional social worker and former GEO employee in the Karnes detention facility. I found this out on a day in the spring of 2015 when I got a call from Olivia, whom I had not met before. She introduced herself as a clinical social worker who had completed her Ph.D. at the University of Texas where I was dean of the school of social work. Her time as a student predated my arrival. Still, she knew of my work in Karnes with detained children and mothers and of my declaration.

After the social pleasantries, Olivia's voice changed slightly, enough for me to detect that she was now entering into a delicate topic. Her tone was shaky, soft, almost diffident; and as she began her story to me, I could tell that Olivia was doubting herself, not certain how to introduce the topic or whether she should be speaking to me. After a couple of minutes, it became clear that Olivia wanted to go public with the information she had about Karnes, to blow the whistle on the unethical practices she saw and was expected to participate in. I assured her that I would hold her words in confidence and that raising concerns about social work and mental health practice at Karnes would be in the best interest of the families. "If I can't help you, I will try to find someone who can," I promised.

Olivia said she had taken a job as a clinical social worker with GEO at Karnes. The salary was far better than what she earned teaching social work at nearby colleges. The money was good, yes, but Olivia assured me that her focus in this position was working with the mothers and children who had put their lives on the line to reach the safety of the United States. In the course of her work, Olivia became increasingly concerned that the medical and psychological problems of children and mothers were being downplayed or ignored. If they protested the conditions in the detention center, Olivia said, the mothers *and children* might be isolated in what she believed was an attempt to stifle their complaints. Even more disturbing than ignoring or downplaying concerns were the coercive tactics used by her supervisor to have Olivia record as little as possible in the medical records. Her notes were scrutinized, and she was given specific suggestions on how to change the wording, something that no professional with integrity would allow to happen.

"What do I do? Who can I tell? If I talk, I'm afraid they [GEO and/or ICE] will ruin my career." Olivia feared that they might do even more nefarious things against her. "Should I go public with this information?" I could not be of much help to Olivia. I had some general information about whistleblower laws and the protection they afford, but neither of us really knew how to activate them if she came forward. We talked through some possibilities that involved bringing her before attorneys we could trust and who would protect her if she disclosed publicly what she knew from inside Karnes. We agreed that I would make a few phone calls and see about getting her some legal advice. It took one well-placed call to a very understanding immigration lawyer with a rich network of contacts. I was given a name for Olivia to call; in the meantime, my contact would call ahead to the lawyer. I called Olivia back, described my conversation, and gave her the information I had. An email came a day or two later from Olivia telling me that the attorney was immensely helpful and confident that she would be protected under whistleblower laws in federal settings. We agreed to remain in touch as she went through the process, but, out of respect for the strain she was undergoing, I did not contact Olivia after that. About a week or two after our conversation, Olivia López's details hit the national news. She told her story to the *Los Angeles Times*.

"I knew I could no longer remain," the *Times* quoted.[5] She felt coerced by her supervisor and others at Karnes to do unethical things that she knew breached both the national social work code of ethics and Texas state regulations. The newspaper reported that, in some instances, GEO supervisors had told her to omit some information from the immigrants' files, including complaints about medical conditions that could be seriously debilitating or life-threatening, such as a woman with recurrent headaches who had a family history of brain aneurysms. Her handwritten notes from a staff meeting on December 22, 2014, recorded the directive from ICE: "We don't tell them anything."

Olivia told the *L.A. Times* reporter that there was no way that she could provide psychotherapy to the women whose children were not in school because there was no one to care for them during the hour-long sessions. Children had to attend the therapy sessions with mothers, thus stifling meaningful discussions of the women's histories. Instead, Olivia said, the women had to speak in generalities about rapes and assaults. Olivia learned that the sexual assaults while migrating did not stop with the mothers; young kids had experienced the same. The *Times* story recounted an experience that Olivia had of watching a 5-year-old Central American girl, who had been raped and physically abused during her journey to the United States, gradually lose weight and regress to wetting diapers again. Olivia's boss, a Hispanic male psychologist, rebuffed Olivia's concerns about the girl and issued a discharge order with a note saying the little girl was sleeping and eating better. When Olivia wrote again in response to the discharge note, reiterating that the girl had lost weight, another supervisor told Olivia that she was mistaken. Olivia replied indignantly that she could detect an increase or decrease in a child's weight. Episodes like this one were the reason that Olivia decided she needed to leave the job. "I have to be able to sleep at night," she told the *L.A. Times.* "My dad was an immigrant, and those moms and kids could be me."

Naturally, GEO administrators refuted loudly Olivia's now nationally published reports. GEO told the *L.A. Times* that the center provides "high-quality care in a safe, clean and family-friendly environment." ICE officials also pushed back, stating their commitment to timely and appropriate medical care. Neither GEO nor ICE responded to Olivia's disclosures. Later, Olivia gave me more details about what working at Karnes was like. In an email, she wrote that early in her job tenure, she could move about the prison compound to meet the women and children, get to know them, and earn trust, essential aspects of good practice by a social worker. But it wasn't long before ICE and GEO officers were commenting that mingling among the detained mothers and children was an "unusual thing to do, as no others had done so." It was a tacit order: "Stop it." During employee orientation sessions, everyone was told not to have any contact with children whatsoever, a hard ask of someone who specializes in working with children. The instruction of no physical contact with the detainees was not an unusual practice. But underlying the message was the order that she have no contact with mothers and children outside of their sessions. The trainer stressed this several times, making the message of no contact whatsoever more overt. "It was clear to me," Olivia wrote, "The trainer was [very] biased against the women and children [and] that he had a very low regard for these women and children. He stopped short of saying not to make contact because they were 'dirty and full of disease.'"

Olivia seldom saw caring encounters between guards and children, although there were guards—"good people," as Olivia described them—who understood the exceptional hardship the families had been through. One court guard was very respectful and kind to the women and children, Olivia wrote. He provided helpful information about the court processes that the women had to undergo. "The women and children [liked] and 'trusted' his word," but he was the exception to the rule. Mothers and children kept their distance from ICE officers and GEO guards who were "so damn unkind." Olivia's boss, the psychologist, seemed to be one of those persons that the children and mothers kept away from. This Dr. Cruz was "gruff" with the child and adult detainees alike. Olivia theorized that workers in Karnes had bartered their human decency away for GEO's high salaries.

Weeks later, I would have an encounter with the same Dr. Cruz. On a visit to Karnes, I made an urgent referral to the health services for a teenage boy with active suicidal ideation. First to bar the way to a psychiatric evaluation was the nurse who headed the medical section at Karnes. She downplayed my request, saying that they would look into it. I wasn't having it and insisted, all in the presence of my legal and social work colleagues in the visiting area at Karnes, on making a direct referral to the mental health provider on site. Perhaps because of my insistence, maybe aided by the snit I was having with a watchful audience, the nurse conceded and went to look for the psychologist. Twenty minutes later, the imperious Dr. Cruz entered the visiting area and asked, to no one in particular, who had made the referral. I identified myself as the referrer, still standing in the visiting area with others who shared my concern for the boy. Dr. Cruz didn't ask to confer privately with me to discuss the case, something I would have expected of a fellow clinician. Instead, his opening line, asked in front of my colleagues—and leaving us all aghast—was "Do you have a Ph.D.?" That's it. That's all. He made no effort to ask me anything else and simply escorted the teenager out with him. I never knew what became of the suicidal boy, even when I asked on a subsequent visit to Karnes. I understood on this visit how astute the mothers and children were about the house psychologist.

Olivia earned the trust of mothers, but the breakthrough with them was her growing relationship with the children. The mothers at Karnes were initially and understandably reserved, mistrustful of Olivia after their experience in detention and before that in *hieleras*. But their children liked and trusted Olivia, and the mothers saw the warm, playful, caring interactions with Olivia. Mothers then began to feel relieved to be able to speak to a kind female in their own language about their issues and concerns. It was the kids, Olivia wrote, who eased mothers' fears and made them more comfortable with her. Through the use of a Hispanic interactional style often referred to as *personalismo* (in which a respectful but informal interpersonal manner is used), Olivia tried to create as much of a sense of normality with the women as she could, "treating women with the same respect as I treated my colleagues."

Cells, the prison rooms that the women co-occupied with strangers, were often a source of conversations—seen with all the oppression of prison but also all the good that comes from being part of a community. To room with others, they did not know generated in most women a preference to keep to themselves, anonymous, unengaged. But in time, the women sharing cells became surrogate families to one another, which eased prison time, not in all cases but in many. These were relationships forged in fire.

"Without question, the women and children were strong," Olivia wrote.

> Faith fortified them, without question. But there is more to these women than that. At their core, they are survivors and warriors. They are risk-takers [when it comes to] the future and betterment of their families. They have ingenuity, integrity, and a fierce courage. . . . They represent what is good and demonstrate what love of family truly means. In the face of all they suffered on their journey to the U.S. and in family detention, they kept their heads high and kept their children shielded from malice and unkindness.

Weeks after our initial telephone conversation, I met Olivia López in person. It was on July 28, 2015, just days after Judge Gee's ruling against the

Obama administration's practice of holding migrant children in detention in violation of the Flores Agreement. We met in a hearing room in Congress at the invitation of Representative Zoe Lofgren of California, the Congressional Progressive Caucus, and House Judiciary Democrats. Sitting with us at the table facing the lawmakers was Sonia, a formerly detained mother. At the table also sat Barbara Hines, a University of Texas law professor and legend in immigration circles as the litigator who forced the closing of the T. Don Hutto Residential Center in Taylor, Texas, in 2009. Opened in 2006 by ICE, the Hutto residential center was a detention facility where immigrant fathers, mothers, *and children* wore prison uniforms; where a 3-month-old Iraqi baby wore prison scrubs; and where a mother asked a student lawyer to take her 6-month-old baby, an infant who had known only prison garb her entire life, outside for some sunlight.[6]

Congresswoman Lofgren greeted everyone and made an opening statement in which she said that "One of the things that keeps me awake at night is the memory of the faces of the women in those jails. I remember, as we were at Karnes, a hundred woman running up to me holding their little children in their arms crying."[7] Olivia was the first to speak to the representatives and press covering the briefing, affirming that what she saw in Karnes was tantamount to abuse and neglect. Then, the formerly detained mother told the congressional panel that she cannot erase the memory of the detention from her son's mind.

"My 3-year-old son always says to me, 'Mommy, I'm here,'" she said. "He won't leave my sight. He asks me, 'Are we going back to Room 108?'"

When the briefing ended, Olivia told me she had no regrets about coming forward and was grateful for the help everyone had provided. As we parted, I shook the hand of a very brave and ethical woman. The day after the congressional briefing, I received an email from Olivia.

> While Sonia was sharing her story at a late meeting yesterday, I took her [3-year-old son] to the restroom. I went into the restroom to show him where the stall was and asked if he [knew how to] use the restroom by himself. "Of course," he said. He turned to me and, in Spanish, [in a] little, tiny, cutie voice, asked if I was going to jail him in the bathroom stall. It just broke my heart.

In the congressional briefing, Olivia testified that some mothers at Karnes, leaders of a group who went on a hunger strike that spring, had been placed in isolation in the medical unit *with their children.* The same story had been reported in the press. Olivia recalled that her supervisor announced that the warden wanted the "ringleaders" placed in medical observation rooms to isolate them and their children from other mothers, punish them, and use them as an example of what would happen to others if they dared to challenge their authority through a hunger strike or any such protest.[8] GEO and ICE denied loudly that any such action had been taken, and certainly not as isolation or solitary confinement. They insisted that nothing of the kind had ever happened.

But I knew it was true that mothers and their children had been placed in isolation. I had proof. My evidence came from an evaluation I did in April, precisely of one of the mothers known to Olivia. The referral came from a case manager with a non-profit organization and the pro bono attorney representing the woman and her son. The lawyer had contacted me in March, but due to our hectic schedules, we just could not connect. On April 18, I received an early morning email forwarded to me from the lawyer. The message was from the case manager.

> I visited Valentina yesterday and saw Fernando for 5 minutes. Valentina reported that Fernando is bedwetting, hides under the sheet and won't get out of bed, won't bathe unless coerced into doing so, and I saw white splotches on his face. He hadn't eaten lunch yesterday, said it was horrible. Are you going to be able to get in to see him soon, Dr. Zayas? He is really needing to get out of there.

Unknown to the case manager, I was scheduled to be there that same morning at 10:00. That's the day I would get corroboration that medical treatment and observation rooms were being used as isolation rooms to punish and warn. It was also the day I would learn of the gruff Dr. Cruz, foreshadowing my own encounter with him weeks later.

The usual farcical dialogue took place at the Karnes security desk, and I was delayed in seeing Valentina and Fernando. The act was less irritating that morning—my thoughts were on the child—but no less exasperating. I had set aside 2 hours for this family, with a large cushion of time if I had to come back after lunch. With the urgent need for an evaluation, I had scheduled only them and no other families that day. There were unique circumstances to this family that I needed to attend to. My plan was fairly typical: collect as full a developmental and medical history as I could from his mother, ask

Fernando to complete some tests, and conduct clinical interviews with them together and separately.

Fernando was a well-developed boy at almost 12 years old, dressed appropriately in pants, T-shirt, and running shoes. Around his neck hung a rosary and a religious medallion. Fernando seemed amazingly comfortable coming to see me. His friendly demeanor belied a sadness underneath. When I asked how he was feeling, he said, "I'm not well." He volunteered that he had been in Karnes for so long and that he didn't understand why and wanted to leave. In Honduras, his father had abandoned Valentina when she told him she was pregnant. The father had not factored in Fernando's life in any way. Even at his tender age, "bad people" came, according to Valentina, "to force him to be a gang member and sell contraband, guns, and take drugs."

Over the last 7 years, Valentina had ferried back and forth from Honduras to the United States. She left Honduras in 2007, leaving Fernando in the care of her parents. In California, she gave birth to a son, now 6 years old. She then returned to Honduras with the new son—the first meeting of half-brothers. The plan was to send the US citizen-child to Los Angeles in August 2014 to live with his father. Then, Valentina and Fernando would set off to get to the United States. The plan was put into effect, and the two were apprehended in early September and transferred to Karnes.

After about 3 months in detention, according to Valentina, Fernando began to complain of headaches. He didn't want to get up in the morning and didn't want to go to breakfast. Fernando was then seen by the gruff Dr. Cruz, the staff psychologist at Karnes Olivia had mentioned in her note to me. However, Fernando stated that he stopped going to Dr. Cruz because "all he ever did was ask me to tell him again all the things that happened to me in Honduras." Valentina said that Fernando had wet his bed several consecutive nights in the past week, a sign of *secondary nocturnal enuresis*, a resumption of bedwetting after a child has maintained proper bladder control at night. This was the first time the bedwetting had occurred since Fernando was a toddler.

In the margins of my notes, I jotted "*N.B.*: Onset of nocturnal enuresis after meetings with Dr. Cruz?" Naturally, I wondered if there was a relationship between the meetings and the bedwetting. If Fernando's comment that the psychologist wanted to talk about what happened to him in Honduras was accurate, what were the clinical indications for dredging up traumatic material while in detention? What purpose would it serve? I could not determine causality, but I was left with the question of whether it was the result of the sessions or merely a coincidence. All I knew is that detention was not the place to be digging up traumatic material from the mind of a young boy whose stay would probably not be enough time to do long-term therapy, and certainly not while he and his mother were jailed and mistreated.

For the evaluation, I met with each of them individually. Valentina went first. She told me that she had, in fact, been part of the hunger strike but implied that she was a follower and not a leader. For her part in the hunger strike, Valentina said, in the afternoon of "Monday after Palm Sunday" around 2:00 or 3:00 p.m., she was placed in a room. It seemed to be a medical room where "doctors do exams," she explained. About an hour later, Fernando was brought into the room with her. They were not given an explanation about why they were being segregated in a medical observation room when neither of them was ill. Valentina said that the guards accused her of being a principal player in the hunger strike. Mother and son spent the night together, away from their cell and cellmates, who wondered where the pair was. The next morning Fernando was taken out at 10:00 a.m. and sent to school. An hour later, Valentina was released.

I asked Valentina to describe the room and to help me draw a picture of it. Valentina described the room, and I drew it, with Valentina making corrections to my depiction. We mapped the room and the location of the furniture. The room had a bed, a crib, a small television, a toilet separated by a half-wall, a shower, and a camera in the corner of the ceiling. She assumed it was a surveillance camera. Together, we produced a floor plan of the room. Throughout our meeting, Valentina said she felt pressure to return to the lunchroom or they would not eat until dinner.

I then met with Fernando. He explained that three times a day he had to show his ID card as part of the census count. He said that guards were not nice and always "threaten to report me." The morning of my visit, he had not gotten up early enough to produce his ID card; and when he later requested toilet paper, he was told by a guard that he would not get any paper until he was counted in the census. It was not the first time he was punished this way. Another time he was refused shampoo, and the officer insisted that his mother come get the shampoo because he was too young to be given it.

Fernando said he cried a lot and that when he woke up, he didn't feel like doing anything. "I go out and then when I'm with others I get more into it. Mostly, I want to be out and be with my brother. I have faith that we will get out. But we can't go back to Honduras because of *las maras*. I never thought I would be here this long. I thought, 'I'm a kid. They won't keep me here,' but now I'm here 8 months. *Estoy desesperado* [I am desperate]." When asked to explain this mature emotion, Fernando said that he just wants to get out. What I saw and what the tests told me aligned. Fernando was suffering from a clinically meaningful level of depression and high anxiety. He used fantasy as a means of dissociating from the reality he was living. Interestingly, even though he tried to respond in ways that wouldn't necessarily show the many traumas and stresses he had suffered, his results were well within the clinically significant level.

Our conversation meandered back to the nearly 24 hours he spent in the medical observation room with his mother. I asked Fernando about the room, and he offered to draw it. Carefully, and with some erasures to make sure he got it right, Fernando drew the same floor plan that his mother had guided me to draw. He identified every furnishing including the surveillance camera.

Well into the time we were chatting, Valentina knocked loudly on the door and opened it before I could react. Her eyes were open wide; in them was panic and fear, a look of removal from the present.

"I heard them say it. I heard on the guard's 'walkie-talkie' or the PA, something about toilet paper. I think they are listening to you because I know about the toilet paper." Needing to clarify for me what she meant about the toilet paper, she said, "They punish Fernando by not giving him toilet paper. They hear you talking in here." The next 3 or 4 minutes were a full display of Valentina's mental health crumbling under the pressure of detention and the time in isolation. She was anxious, in an agitated physical state, standing and pacing and quickly sitting. She suspected that we were being bugged. She sat for a moment, scanning the small office. The guards, she said, had microphones and cameras in the room where I was interviewing them. Valentina jumped from her chair, looking up at the ceiling, walls, the corners of the floor, and ceiling lines. On her hands and knees, she studied the electrical outlets. She found nothing, just as Fernando and I saw nothing. She sat down, still agitated, her feet a study in hyperactivity, as if driven by an unseen engine. Just as quickly as she sat down, Valentina began to feel under the table we were huddled over, checking for bugging devices. She did the same with each of the four chairs, two of them occupied by Fernando and me. Valentina rose at least one more time and walked around the room briefly to look for any indication that our conversation was being recorded or heard by the authorities.

When I calmed her enough to sit down, I turned to look at Fernando and saw his terrified eyes trained on his mother, tears beginning to collect and roll down his cheek. It was the look of a child seeing his mother deteriorate mentally and realizing that she is all he has and that he is all she has. We sat in silence while Valentina composed herself, her eyes calming as she regained her senses, her equanimity, once again in control. After several minutes, as Valentina seemed composed, I asked Fernando to wait outside. Swiftly, I ran through a mental status exam, asking Valentina her name, the date, the place she was in, who I was, and who the boy was who had just left the room. I continued with some other questions until it was clear that Valentina had returned from the paranoid place she had been sent spiraling to. After Valentina assured me, abundantly and embarrassed, she left the room. Fernando declined politely to sit with me again, preferring to stay with his mother and return to their cell, together.

It was never made clear by anyone at Karnes why mother and son had been quarantined or segregated in that room for nearly a day. When I pushed at a subsequent meeting with ICE and GEO staff and could not get an answer, I remarked that they had placed them in isolation, in solitary confinement. A GEO official said, "The door was never locked. They could have left at any time and returned to their cell."

Two months later, an email popped on my computer screen with the subject line *Libre!!!!* There was no text, just a picture of Valentina and Fernando freed from detention. Sitting in the front passenger seat of their attorney's car, Valentina's face showed a hint of joy, more relaxed than the day I saw her but still with expressions of fear, bewilderment, and sadness. In the back seat, Fernando, handsome as ever, bore a broad smile, his eyes joyful but holding apprehension like his mother. It would take a long time before either of them breathed freely.

Notes

1. The group of co-counsels was led by the ACLU's Immigrants' Rights Project, the ACLU of the Nation's Capital, the ACLU of Pennsylvania, the ACLU of Texas, the Immigration Clinic at the University of Texas School of Law at Austin, and Covington & Burling LLP.
2. The ICE web page lists the other 27 states are Arizona, California, Colorado, Florida, Georgia, Illinois, Indiana, Kentucky, Louisiana, Maryland, Massachusetts, Michigan,

Minnesota, Mississippi, Nebraska, Nevada, New Hampshire, New Jersey, New Mexico, New York, Ohio, Oklahoma, Tennessee, Utah, Virginia, Washington, and Wisconsin. See US Department of Homeland Security, 2022a.

3. For more details, see *R.I.L-R v. Johnson*, 2015.
4. *Flores v. Johnson*, 2015.
5. Hennessy-Fiske, 2015
6. Confirmed by Barbara Hines via email, May 25, 2021. For more information, see La Sonrisa Productions, 2009.
7. Ordoñez, 2015b.
8. Gonzalez, 2015; Hilton, 2015; Ordoñez, 2015b.

4

Detention as Licensed Child Care—Texas-Style

The "breaking news" banner that popped up on my mobile phone read, "Abbott Orders Texas Child Care Regulators to Discontinue Licenses of Facilities Housing Immigrant Children." It was June 2, 2021. A stream of other pop-ups followed from the various news sources I was plugged into.

"Texas Will Revoke Licenses for Child Care Facilities That House Refugee Children."

"Texas Governor Bars Facilities from Housing Children in the Country Illegally."

All told the story in various ways, but the message was the same: Texas Governor Greg Abbott, a Trump Republican, had threatened to revoke the licenses of shelters housing unaccompanied minors. In a proclamation, Abbott directed the state's Health and Human Services Commission (HHSC) to look into revoking the state-issued child care licenses of nonprofit organizations that were housing unaccompanied minors on behalf of the Office of Refugee Resettlement (ORR).[1] Using a disaster declaration typically employed in floods, hurricanes, and health crises, Abbott gave the organizations until August 30 to end their care of unaccompanied minors. If not, shelters providing care to "individuals who are not lawfully present in the United States" under a contract with the federal government would have their licenses taken from them by HHSC, deauthorizing them from operating as shelters in Texas.

A week later, the *El Paso Times* reported that DHHS was threatening to sue Abbott on the revocation order. The text of the letter was polite—"Although we prefer to resolve this matter amicably"—but it was clear that the feds weren't taking this lying down. Invoking the Supremacy Clause in Article VI of the US Constitution which says that federal laws and the federal government take precedence over state laws and constitutions, the Biden administration was asserting that it was free from regulations like the one that Abbott was mandating. The Biden administration gave Abbott until June 11 to halt

Through Iceboxes and Kennels. Luis H. Zayas, Oxford University Press. © Oxford University Press 2023.
DOI: 10.1093/oso/9780197668160.003.0005

his rescission order or face "whatever appropriate legal action is necessary to ensure the safety and well-being of the vulnerable youth that Congress entrusted to ORR."[2] The lines were drawn between the Texas state government and the Biden administration. On August 30, Abbott's order went into effect and continues to disenfranchise legitimate residential child care providers working with vulnerable children.

Abbott's theatrics to reverse, very selectively, the licensing of a legitimate set of actors—non-profits with decades-long experience in providing residential care for children—were nothing more than a ploy to stick it to the new president, Joe Biden. They were also representative of Abbott's extreme antipathy toward immigrants. Texas had long had immigration prisons for children and parents operated by private prison companies under the authority of Immigration and Customs Enforcement (ICE).[3] The T. Don Hutto Detention Facility in Taylor opened in 2006 operated by Corrections Corporation of America (later renamed CoreCivic) to hold immigrant fathers, mothers, and children. Hutto was encircled by two sets of fences with coils of razor wire at the top. Children and families from around the world were detained there. Fathers were separated from their wives and children, and older children waited in other cells. Everyone lived in cells with twin beds or bunk beds, a thin mattress, a small metal or porcelain sink, and an exposed toilet, like every prison cell you've ever seen in movies. Lights in the cell were on constantly, and guards woke families up at 5:30 in the morning. Families were given 15 minutes to eat their meals. Parents had to bring their children to meetings with their lawyers, exposing children to graphic conversations about the violence and persecution parents had faced in their home countries. Prison guards wore uniforms, did seven head counts a day, each lasting about an hour, and acted like guards in a maximum-security prison filled with career criminals and murderers. If these conditions weren't degrading enough, detainees wore prison-issue scrubs in green or blue. Fathers, mothers, teenagers, children, and, yes, even infants donned prison garb and prison-issued underwear. Everyone. Even newborns wore prison onesies. A doctor visited the facility once a week to care for all the families incarcerated there. The Hutto facility was closed within 3 years after a legal battle led by Barbara Hines, the University of Texas law professor with whom I testified at the congressional briefing in 2015. It is important to note that this facility was then promptly reopened as a female-only detention center, housing primarily women seeking asylum, a majority of whom were mothers separated from their children.

The irony of Abbott's proclamation was stunningly transparent because Texas was already licensing detention centers as child care centers. Now he wanted to revoke the licenses of legitimate child care facilities only because they had contracts with the ORR to aid unaccompanied children. Abbott seemed to have forgotten that in the year he was sworn in as governor, the state government was actively finding ways to award child care licenses to two other family detention centers, Karnes and Dilley. It was in 2015 when Texas allied itself with the two detention centers to permit them to be licensed, bending over backward while breaking its own state regulations to please the private prison companies. How Texas arrived at the distinction of being a place where a child's daycare center and prisons with detained mothers and children from newborns through age 17 were considered nearly equal is a story that must be told in the context of how most states protect children's and families' well-being.

Child protection is a duty of the state, and children's and family's well-being is often protected by a quasi-police entity with considerable legal authority, child protective services (CPS). CPS has the authority to remove children, weigh in on custody matters, and require parents to undergo treatment and other interventions before a child can be returned to its family. The structure and function of child welfare bureaus vary from state to state. But it is typically a state's designated child welfare authority that also protects children and families by imposing standards that child-serving organizations must follow if they want to stay in business—they may be licensed, monitored, audited, sanctioned, or sued by the state. One of the functions of child welfare departments is to regulate the licensing of child care facilities to provide residential care. Narrow definitions of child care and equally narrow procedures set by the state child welfare division are guided by the universal principle of the "best interest of the child." In Texas, it is the Department of Family and Protective Services (DFPS), part of the Texas HHSC.

In 2015, under pressure from ICE and legislators whose campaigns received support from the private prison industry, DFPS agreed to cooperate in accommodating the applications by CoreCivic and the GEO Group (GEO) for licenses as residential child care facilities. But the prison companies did not want to comply with all of the state's regulations, and Texas was all too willing to waive key provisions of the state's child care licensing regulations that related to general residential operations for children and families. In September, DFPS adopted a rule (§748.7) on an emergency basis to allow the prisons to circumvent the usual regulations for child care settings that housed children. Traditional state regulations establish certain minimum standards for child care settings, rules that range from the qualifications of the child care administrator to requirements for proper food storage to restrictions on the use of emergency behavioral interventions. The private prison companies, with the emergency adoption of §748.7 by DFPS, would not be required to comply with all of the requirements set up by the state, all in the name of better protecting children in their jails. In their sanctimonious self-interest, the prison companies argued that it was better that they be granted a license than to operate without one. In effect, the companies argued that it was a superior arrangement to have children and mothers in licensed facilities that were prisons than to have children under no care or unlicensed care. Twisting this argument to their advantage, the prisons knew that DFPS does not oversee requirements that pertain to facilities classified as secure, like jails and prisons.

If using self-righteousness as a reason for them to be awarded licenses was not repugnant enough, the prisons wanted four exemptions that would apply solely to them and no other settings that housed children. The first was to be released from restrictions governing the maximum number of children that could occupy a dormitory room. State regulations ruled that no more than four children may occupy a room at one time in a congregate-care facility. This exemption for the prison companies would allow the detention centers to house more than four children, as well as adults, in their cells. The reasoning presented by the detention centers was that since children roomed with parents or family members and they were mostly in family units of two or more children per family, the waiver was needed to keep the companies profitable.

The second exemption was from the state regulation that required facilities to allot a minimum of 60 square feet per child. The third exemption that prison companies requested was to allow children to sleep in the same room with unrelated adults. All other child welfare agencies have to follow the rules but not CoreCivic and GEO. With the configuration of cells in Karnes, children were already sharing rooms with adult women who were not members of their families. The waiver was provided based on a narrow reading of the regulation prohibiting adults from sleeping in the same room as children. To justify the prisons' request, DFPS stated that the rule was related to adults who were employees of the facility, unlike the detained mothers, who were not employees. Regardless, children were permitted to sleep in the same quarters with adult women who were not members of their families. DFPS further washed its hands of responsibility by making it clear that the criteria be applied flexibly, at the discretion of the detention center.

The fourth exemption from critical DFPS rules was provided under the guise of "the preservation of family units." In this exemption, children of opposite genders and who were unrelated were permitted to sleep in the same room, something not permitted by other licensees. Normally, permission was given to allow children of the opposite gender to share a room only if they were siblings or under the age of 6. But there were often three to four families per cell, and therefore children of the opposite sex but not siblings would occupy the same cell. In the fine print, DFPS emphasized that the facilities "would not be required to comply with *all* of the provisions in the standards," making it clear that the detention centers could potentially be required to comply with portions of the standards in question.

The state observed the obligatory period for public comments. Hundreds of letters and emails from law schools, legal scholars, professional associations, religious groups, pro bono projects, pediatricians, mental health professionals, secular immigration organizations, private citizens, and Texas state senators and representatives came in—all in opposition to the emergency rule that would permit the prison companies to be exempt from essential requirements. The comments reflected concerns in an array of areas. Licensing the Karnes County and Dilley centers with exemptions was nothing more than a rubber stamp of what the prison companies wanted without full consideration of whether they had the staffing, operations, and experience to provide adequate child care. No matter the rules or the exemptions and the licensing, nothing about the centers would change: They would continue to be prisons for parents and children. Licenses would change nothing about the overall substandard environment of the Karnes County and Dilley centers, not to mention their inherent purpose, to jail families. The exceptions given to the prisons were silent on the potential for child abuse and neglect. Moreover, the exemption from rules would actually increase the risk for sexual and physical abuse by having unrelated adults and different genders living in such close quarters. There had been allegations of assault and sexual abuse because of the lack of age and gender restrictions. The exemptions further weakened a parent's ability to lodge a complaint about improper or poor care, such as their living conditions or abuse by other adults, staff members, or older children. At Karnes, one guard was known to have had a sexual relationship with a detained mother while his wife and sister worked in the facility.

Detention centers, most reasonable persons agreed, were not child care centers. They weren't places where anyone would want to voluntarily enroll their children. The mindset of the operators was a penal one: to hold people who had committed crimes to serve out their terms. This is not why families were in detention. Karnes, as I mentioned in the opening chapter of this book, was previously a county prison with high walls, guards, and barbed wire to prevent escape, even though mothers and children were not flight risks. These so-called child care centers held hundreds of mothers and children in a prison setting with no specific staff–child ratios to adhere to. Instead, there were headcounts a few times a day, and passage to any place within Karnes involved electronically locked doors for access to even the most basic of needs. The families had limited access to telephones and computers, and the cost of phone calls and commissary items was prohibitive. Pepper spray was said by a commenter during the public input period to have been used when children or mothers "misbehaved," which could have simply been when parents exercised their rights or questioned staff decisions. Guards threatened to remove children from their mothers for failure to follow rules. Supervisors, in particular, were persons with law enforcement backgrounds, not child care backgrounds. Besides the deprivation and threat that children experienced in detention that added to their traumatized lives, there was the fact that parental authority was taken from the mothers. To upend the dynamics of the role of parents to monitor, discipline, guide, teach, and nurture their children in the manner that they knew and was supported by their cultures was to disturb important parenting roles and families' homeostasis.

The state of Texas through DFPS acted as a contortionist, bending rules to justify its decisions. In response to concerns about invalidating mothers' roles as parents, DFPS said, "Precisely because it appears that the mothers in the [family residential centers] are divested of some or even all of their parental authority (when separated from their children, for example), DFPS has concluded that the [centers] and their staff are providing child care."

Even statements in the public comments that cited well-regarded scientific evidence were dismissed or rationalized away. People from Texas and throughout the United States wrote in, reminding DFPS that these parents and children were escaping persecution, abuse, and frequent trauma in their homelands and that incarcerated children are especially at risk of developing short- and long-term mental health issues. The science that was cited by opponents of the licensing and the exemptions included the damage of incarceration on children's brain development and social functioning, maladaptive social and emotional development, academic failure, and later criminal involvement. Women and children in the centers were exhibiting symptoms of post-traumatic stress disorder, anxiety, depression, and other mental illnesses, yet they were not receiving adequate treatment for these issues. The resounding chorus was that prison companies were not the right organizations to provide care for the complex mental health issues that were evident in mothers and children. Many public comments argued that the prison-like detention center operated by GEO and CoreCivic violated the Flores Agreement. Licensing the centers with various exceptions would not remedy the violation of Flores. In a prescient note, one commenter raised concerns that licensing the two detention centers in Texas would permit ICE and its private partners to claim that they were following Judge Gee's orders.

One letter opposing the emergency exemptions was addressed to DFPS commissioner Judge John J. Specia, Jr., and his general counsel. That letter came from Satsuki Ina, a professor emeritus from California State University, Sacramento. Interned as a child during World War II for being Japanese American, Satsuki's letter was dated December 7, 2015, precisely 74 years after the Japanese attack on Pearl Harbor. It was a powerful statement from someone with deep insight into what had happened and could happen again:

Dear Judge Specia, Mr. Woodruff, and Ms. Carmical,

Over 70 years ago, I was incarcerated with my parents in a federal "family detention facility" in Crystal City, Texas. We had not committed a crime, and our right to due process of the law was exempted and bypassed as hate and fear gripped the country in 1941. We were held for 4 years and 3 months for what was later determined the result of "hysteria, racism, and the failure of political leadership." As a Japanese American and former victim of the trauma of unjust and indeterminate detention, I am appalled by the possibility that the state of Texas would consider exempting the two facilities that currently house thousands of children, from basic regulations deemed essential for the care and welfare of children.

"Bending the rules" to justify the incarceration of children in a prison-like environment is no less than putting lipstick on a pig. In April and in May of this year, I visited children and their mothers in what is euphemistically called, the "South Texas Family Residential Center" in Dilley, Texas. Not unlike the prisons where my family and hundreds of other Japanese American children were held, our prisons were named "relocation centers and family camps" in order to mask the truth of our circumstances. As a child therapist specializing in the treatment of trauma, I was deeply disturbed by what I witnessed and heard from the children and their mothers during my visits.

Stern, unfriendly guards led me and my fellow visitors, through locked doors to the visitation room after requiring us to leave all of our belongings, including art supplies and writing materials in lockers outside. During my visit, I met with six families who had been held for varying lengths of time. Aside from the intense anxiety, depressed mood, and grief expressed by the mothers, I noted significant signs of what I would consider "captivity trauma" of the children. Hyper-vigilant checking of the guards, fearful clinging to the mothers, sad and guarded demeanor, signaled the child's consciousness of being under guard. No doubt these children had previously been traumatized in their home country, and then during the uncertain journey to the US border, and now their incarceration living with strangers who arrive and depart with no regularity, while under the constant, watchful eye of prison guards. When visitation time was up, the children, clearly rule-bound and fearful, would immediately stand and leave the room like little automatons.

Confining innocent children and their parents in prison settings is the cause of long-term consequences leading to mental health problems. For the past 30 years I have served as a therapist to many Japanese Americans who were, like myself, children while incarcerated during WWII. Decades later, having lived in a state of long-term anxiety, separated from familiar surroundings, sharing intimate space with total strangers, being held in the arms of anxious mothers, not only set an emotional baseline of fear and mistrust, we know now from research in neuroscience that the constant release of stress hormones under such circumstances has a negative effect on the developing child's brain.

More than 40 years after the war, the United States government apologized for the dehumanizing incarceration of thousands of families. For many, the apology and redress was [sic] too late in repairing the long-term damage.

I hope that you will consider the parallels of what is happening in our country today with what was happening back then and take strong steps to declare that the human rights of these children must be upheld to the highest standards of care. Do not allow these private prison facilities to masquerade as "child care centers"!

The very nature and design of these detention facilities cause harm to the children held there. These facilities simply cannot be made humane, particularly through a licensing process that exempts the facilities from basic child welfare standards and ensures that the detention centers will continue to operate essentially as they do now.

Let us learn from our past. Do not waiver [*sic*] in the face of the current climate of fear that is gripping our country today.

Satsuki Ina

DFPS's responses were dismissive:

So long as children are housed there, and so long as mothers are not permitted to fully exercise their parental responsibility, DFPS considers that the [family residential centers were] providing child care, effectively disempowering the mothers. It is more protective of the children in the [centers] for DFPS to exercise its oversight than to abdicate its responsibility based on the notion that the centers are harmful. While DFPS is sympathetic to the concerns raised, the agency has no role in whether a person is placed or detained in one of the [detention centers].

The only ones who submitted comments that supported the emergency rule were a state representative and a representative of the Karnes County Residential Center.

Hearings held in the state legislature brought many of the individuals and organizations opposed to licensing out of the woodwork together. The establishment powers—the government, the legislature, and the judiciary—were formidable foes.

In September 2015, DFPS adopted the emergency regulation to allow the state to issue child care licenses to the detention centers. Ironically, DFPS had historically denied that it had the authority to license family residential centers of any kind. Still, DFPS went ahead with applying §748.7. Grassroots Leadership, Inc., a non-profit organization in Austin that opposes profiteering by private prison companies, and the criminalization and deportation of immigrants, filed a lawsuit in state court with 22 detainees (11 mothers and 11 children) and a licensed child care service provider.[4] Litigated by attorneys from the Texas-Rio Grande Legal Aid, the class-action filing was heard in the 353rd Judicial District Court of Travis County and was intended to prevent the licensing of the two detention centers that were under ICE control. Grassroots Leadership argued that the length of the detention of children could lead to even longer periods of detention under lower standards of care. Grassroots Leadership wanted the court to order that providing state licenses as child care centers went against Texas law.

The case rested on the 1997 Flores Settlement, which called for the US government to house detained immigrant minors in non-secure, licensed settings that offered the least restrictive environment. US District Judge Dolly Gee had ruled that the Flores Settlement applied to minors who were apprehended with or without their parents. Dilley and Karnes fell under Judge Gee's order. The lawyers for Grassroots Leadership argued that the bid to license the detention centers was an effort to exploit a loophole in the Flores Agreement that allowed for longer—and possibly indefinite—detention of immigrant parents and their children (something that the Trump administration later threatened after the family separation policy was rejected by the American public). When CoreCivic and GEO intervened in the case, they were added as defendants. In October, perhaps to find a more sympathetic venue, Texas tried to move the case from the state court to a federal court in the western district of Texas, which was based in San Antonio but had a presence in Austin. A judge in the federal court rejected the attempt to move the case to federal court since there was no federal jurisdiction; the lawsuit had arisen under state as opposed to federal law.

Another point that Grassroots Leadership made in state court was that regulation §748.7 was improper on procedural grounds because there was no true emergency occurring. In mid-November 2015, Texas trial court Judge Karin Crump agreed and temporarily enjoined the regulation. Judge Crump ruled that there was "no imminent peril to public health" as called for by the Texas code and that no federal or state law required Texas to use the emergency procedure. Judge Crump issued a temporary injunction halting the emergency-rule adoption. She scheduled the next hearing for May 2016.

On December 9, 2015, there was an in-person public hearing at DFPS that was attended by hundreds of concerned citizens. It was a remarkable event as it provided structure and relationship-building among advocates that served future advocacy efforts at the Texas legislature. The testimony given was wholly in opposition to the rule. Empty chairs with posters made by children lined the room. Press conferences and rounds and rounds of oral and written testimony were presented in the spring of 2016.[5]

In response to the ruling, DFPS reissued the regulation but this time used the ordinary, non-emergency procedure. DFPS opened it up for public comment, after which the regulation went into effect in March 2016. A few days later, Karnes was licensed. Subsequently, Judge Crump issued another injunction preventing DFPS from licensing Dilley as child care. Advocates did not let up. In October 2016, a group testified before the United Nations High Commission for Refugees' Working Group on Arbitrary Detention, specifically speaking on family detention. The family detention issue in Texas was receiving international attention. Judge Crump's final order came in December 2016 when she held that the emergency rule violated Texas statutory standards for licensing residential child care facilities.

During the 2017 legislative session, bills in the House and Senate were considered in public hearings, and again testimony was overwhelmingly against attempts to license prisons as child care facilities. At one of those hearings, Refugee and Immigration Center for Education and Legal Services staff had gathered testimony directly from women inside Karnes; and volunteers read these accounts aloud during the hearing, getting the first-hand experience into the record.[6] DFPS and the private prison companies filed an appeal shortly after Judge Crump's ruling, and the Texas Court of Appeals transferred the case from the district court in Austin to one in El Paso.[7] The Texas Supreme Court transferred the case back to the district court in Austin, which heard the case in September 2018.

Sadly, in November, a three-judge appeals court panel reversed Judge Crump's order, dismissing it since there was no "live controversy" at the time the trial judge ruled. The appellate court said that Grassroots Leadership did not have standing to bring a lawsuit because it could not show it was personally injured by the emergency rule. Additionally, the appellate court argued that the private child care provider that was among the plaintiffs would not be directly affected financially since it would not be in direct competition with Karnes and Dilley. The appeals court also stated that detainees did not have any standing in Texas to challenge the licensing rule because they could not show that undocumented immigrants would be held for longer periods of time in a licensed facility or would be held under dangerous conditions. The length of detention is determined by federal policy, the court reasoned and had nothing to do with whether a facility is licensed by the state. Moreover, the immigrants were no longer detained in the facilities and had not claimed specific ways that the licensure would place them in harm's way. Two appeals by Grassroots Leadership and its co-plaintiffs were denied by the appeals court subsequently. Immigration detention at Karnes was licensed as adequate to be considered child care despite the waiver of key regulations that the state imposed on all legitimate providers.

Notes

1. Gomez Licon & Coronado, 2021.
2. Villagran, 2021.
3. Schrag, 2020. The documentary is titled *The Least of These*, by La Sonrisa Productions, 2009.
4. *Grassroots Leadership, Inc., et al., v. Texas Department of Family and Protective Services*, 2015.
5. Laurie Cook Heffron, February 5, 2022, email communication.
6. Laurie Cook Heffron, February 5, 2022, email communication.
7. After Judge Crump's ruling and before the case went to the Texas appellate court (May 2017), the Texas State Senate passed a bill that would have overridden the judge's decision. The bill was intended to permit DFPS to license both Dilley and Karnes detention centers as child care facilities. The GEO Group and CoreCivic lobbied senators and representatives for the bill. But they could not persuade the Texas State House, and the bill was defeated.

5

Take the Children. Age Doesn't Matter

An editorial in the *Washington Post* about detention read, "The outright deprivation of civil rights which we have visited upon these helpless and for the most part, no doubt, innocent people may leave an ugly blot upon the pages of our history."[1] While you may naturally attribute that editorial to modern US immigration because of the topic of this book, it was actually published in 1943 and decried the continued detainment of Japanese Americans. It was as apt then as it was in the summer of 2014 when the Obama administration began detaining immigrant mothers and children—families—who had come to the US border with Mexico, the beginning of another ugly blot on the pages of US history.

Immigration advocates, legal teams, activists, politicians, religious leaders, and everyday Americans raised their voices to oppose the detention of families as a means of deterrence. Tireless battles were fought, some won, some lost, but never leaving advocates and activists deterred. Parents traveling with children were "family units" and were detained together, but fathers alone with children were placed in different detention centers. It was revealed years later that whispers were heard in the Obama administration about separating children from parents to keep migrants from making the journey. The idea had a short lifespan; it was too repulsive to Obama's appointees and career officials.

In 2018, the idea of separating families was reintroduced in the Trump administration, this time not in whispers but openly, no longer a murmur. Donald Trump's zero tolerance policy took the idea of detention and deterrence that was shelved by his predecessor and created a grim scenario: ripping children from their parents' arms at the southern border, a deterrence policy more draconian than anything considered previously.[2] The Department of Justice, led by Attorney General Jefferson (Jeff) Beauregard Sessions III, announced the zero tolerance policy on April 6, 2018. The policy was to be implemented through a memorandum issued by Sessions to federal prosecutors along the US–Mexican border. The federal attorneys were instructed to prosecute all referrals for unlawful entry by the Department of

Through Iceboxes and Kennels. Luis H. Zayas, Oxford University Press. © Oxford University Press 2023.
DOI: 10.1093/oso/9780197668160.003.0006

Homeland Security (DHS) to the extent practicable. The policy was expanded on May 7, 2018. In a meeting between Sessions and federal prosecutors from the southwestern border states on May 11, the memorandum on family separation came up.

"We need to take away children," Sessions told the group, because the president was putting "very intense, very focused" pressure on him about the immigration situation.[3] A note taken by someone at the meeting read: "INTENSE: prosecute everyone." The *New York Times* reported that the five US attorneys representing states along the border with Mexico "recoiled" when they were told that May to prosecute all undocumented immigrants even if it meant separating children from their parents.[4] The group of US attorneys told top Justice Department officials they were "deeply concerned" about the children's welfare. Despite the federal attorneys' profound worry, Deputy Attorney General Rod J. Rosenstein added, "Age of child doesn't matter."

This meeting was a prescription for inflicting far-reaching psychological, physical, and emotional pain to children of all ages, parents, grandparents, and others. We could only watch for months as family units that arrived at the border were separated, creating a large group of "unaccompanied alien children." These children were transferred to the Department of Health and Human Services' (DHHS's) Office of Refugee Resettlement (ORR) and locked up in "government-run facilities, for weeks or months while agency officials [searched] for relatives or sponsors to care for the child while their immigration case [was] pending."[5] Parents were sent to detention centers with other adults, sometimes separated from their children by thousands of miles: One Congolese mother was detained in San Diego while her 6-year-old daughter was moved to Chicago.[6] If I had been concerned with the damage to children and parents being held together in detention, I was now exasperated and outraged at how the government was harming children by removing them from their parents' side, a rupture of the universally understood parent–child emotional bond. Everyone knew, except, apparently, the people in the administration, that this would not go well. If detention was hurtful, family separation extended emotional torture for both parents and kids. It was an enlargement of one of those shameful moments, a time in US history that would take decades to undo, understand, and repair.

A timeline of major news reports reveals the government's poor handling of family separation and obfuscation of the facts.[7] In March 2018, Reuters reported that, even before the signing of the memorandum and the meeting with federal prosecutors on the southern border, asylum officers were told in February, a month before the report, that "Women and children crossing together illegally into the United States could be separated by U.S. authorities under a proposal being considered by the Department of Homeland Security, according to three government officials."[8] Well before any official executive order or other policy announcements, the plans were in the works for the family separation policy that shook the summer of 2018. Two unnamed officials at a February 2 town hall for asylum officers reported that the asylum chief of the US Citizenship and Immigration Services, John Lafferty, had made the announcement. A third official, linked in the Reuters story to DHS, said that the proposal was to separate children from their mothers at the border as a deterrent to other migrants. As part of the proposed plan, parents would be held in detention until their asylum hearings or if they contested their deportation.

While the decision to separate families appeared on the national news in 2018, the reality was that 8 months earlier, on November 25, 2017, the *Houston Chronicle* had reported that the Trump administration had been separating children from their parents at the border since June 2017.[9] Twenty-two cases of separation of children and parents had taken place by the time the *Chronicle* reported the story, noting that the removal of children from parents violated due process. While it was not until mid-June 2018 that national revelations and stories detailing the family separation policy emerged, the fact of the matter was that DHS had separated nearly 2,000 children from their parents or legal guardians between April 19 and May 31, 2018.[10] Still, Secretary of Homeland Security Kirstjen Nielsen issued a statement through her spokesperson on April 26 that "DHS does not have a policy of separating families at the border for deterrence purposes."[11] It was a statement that she would repeat several times. It was later reported by the *Washington Post* that a Honduran man had died by suicide in a Texas jail on May 18 after a "nervous breakdown" when he was separated from his wife and child at the border. The death had been kept secret until the *Post*'s report.[12] On June 14, Ed Lavandera and other CNN reporters wrote that federal officials had taken the daughter of a woman from Honduras as she breastfed the child in a detention center in McAllen, Texas.[13] While the story did not identify the affiliation of the federal officials, it would appear that they were Immigration and Customs Enforcement (ICE) employees because of the location of the merciless act. The mother reacted as any parent would and resisted the taking of her child from her embrace. She was restrained with handcuffs immediately.

On June 17, a group of journalists and human rights advocates toured a warehouse on Ursula Street in McAllen, Texas, which was holding several hundred children in cages of metal fencing. Television news correspondents reported from outside the warehouse as crews were not allowed to film inside.[14] Reporters and advocates told of disarray, vicious disregard and insensitivity to children's needs, and lack of common human decency in the care of children. One guard scolded a 5-year-old for doing what preschoolers do, being rambunctious. Their reports revealed the effects of traumatic separation, loss, and detention on children.

Even with such a brief report, I could deduce the damaging effects occurring now and in the future of these children. The caged children endured lights on 24 hours a day, slept under large Mylar foil blankets, and had no books or toys. One boy was seen in a cage but not playing with others. Instead, he sat quietly "clutching a piece of paper that was a photocopy of his mother's ID card." A 16-year-old girl was responsible for changing a toddlers' diapers because the child's aunt was somewhere else in the facility. First thought to be 2 years old, the child was 4, but it took days for someone to find the aunt to discover that the girl spoke K'iche, a language indigenous to Guatemala. The toddler was so traumatized that an advocate told the Associated Press that she "wasn't talking. She was just curled up in a little ball."

The same day as the journalists and advocates toured the south Texas warehouse, DHS Secretary Nielsen, took to Twitter: "We do not have a policy of separating families at the border. Period."[15] The tweet was deemed a flat-out lie by those who knew precisely what was being done. Everyone inside the administration knew that Nielsen had quietly signed off on the policy on May 5.[16] The day after Nielsen's tweet, perfectly timed to reveal Nielson's lie, ProPublica published a story that included a short audio recording in which Central American children separated from their parents are heard crying, sobbing, calling for "Mami" and "Papá." In response to the cries of many of the children in raw despair after losing their parents, a border patrol agent is heard saying, "Well, we have an orchestra here. What's missing is a conductor." The recording was of children between 4 and 10 years of age.[17] No amount of comforting with snacks, toys, and other enticements could distract inconsolable children from their horrific losses.

In June 2018, Sessions said on a Christian network, "We never really intended to do that,"[18] "that" being separating children from families. In 2021, a *Washington Post* editorial said bluntly, "That was a lie." In fact,

The administration's cruel treatment of migrants has been intentional, calculated and surgically effective in dispensing pain and suffering. [Sessions's] leading role in carrying out that infamous policy will stand as an enduring disgrace, but no one who joined in is untarnished. The administration's indifference to the misery of toddlers, tweens, and teens was as callous as it was premeditated.[19]

As the headlines mounted and Americans decried the practice of separating children from parents, Donald Trump began to feel pressured. On June 20, 2018, Trump signed an executive order instructing DHS to cease the separation of families at the border except for circumstances in which the parent was deemed a risk to the child.[20] On the same day, the *Detroit Free Press* published a story under the headline, "Torn from Immigrant Parents, 8-Month-Old Baby Lands in Michigan." There was also an 11-month-old baby who arrived in Michigan in the middle of the night, somewhere between 11:00 p.m. and 5:00 a.m.[21] The many displaced children, some of whom had been separated from their parents without contact for more than a month, screamed for their parents. One boy, age 7, was heard on a telephone call asking his mother, somewhere unknown, "Are you OK? Are you hurt? Is someone hurting you?" Yet days earlier, on June 18, Kirstjen Nielsen had said at a White House briefing that "We are a country of compassion. We are a country of heart. . . . We must fix the system so that those who truly need asylum can in fact receive it." Her words did not align with all the news that was appearing. CBS News reported on the same day that 2,342 children had been separated from 2,200 parents at the border between May 5 and June 9, 2018. The CBS report stated that, on Twitter, Nielsen had accused the media of "misreporting," placing the blame on Barack Obama.[22] There is no indication that the Obama administration forcibly removed children from their parents' arms. Not only did Obama-blaming continue but Trump falsely asserted that it was also the fault of Congress and the courts.

The disclosures of the family separation policy moved many American hearts but not Trump's or his wife Melania's, who made her position very clear on June 21 from the words printed on a coat she wore.[23]

Federal courts, in response to lawsuits filed by immigration advocates, began to rule in favor of reunifying families. A week after the executive order was signed, on June 26, a federal district judge in San Diego issued a preliminary injunction that required immigration authorities to reunite most separated families within 30 days and to reunite children younger than 5 within 2 weeks. US District Judge Dana Sabraw also forbade any further separations unless parents posed a danger to the child or had a criminal history or communicable disease. A *Politico* report quoted Judge Sabraw as writing that it was "a chaotic circumstance of the Government's own making." The report quoted Judge Sabraw's ruling.

> The government readily keeps track of personal property of detainees in criminal and immigration proceedings. . . . Money, important documents, and automobiles, to name a few, are routinely catalogued, stored, tracked and produced upon a detainee's release, at all levels—state and federal, citizen and alien. Yet, the government has no system in place to keep track of, provide effective communication with, and promptly produce alien children. The unfortunate reality is that under the present system migrant children are not accounted for with the same efficiency and accuracy as *property*. Certainly, that cannot satisfy the requirements of due process.[24]

It surprised few of us in the immigration field when NBC News published a report on July 3 that the Trump administration sidestepped the injunction by forcing immigrant parents to decide between leaving the United States with and leaving without their children. Parents were read a statement by ICE agents and told to sign one of two lines on a form. The choices were "I am requesting to reunite with my child(ren) for the purpose of repatriation to my country of citizenship."[25] It was a binary decision: one or the other.[26] The government ran a hustle on parents as good as any by a con artist.

Nearly every day in June and July of 2018, revelations came out in the press about the deliberate and intentional wickedness being brought on infants, toddlers, young children, teenagers, and parents by the president's men and women. There was no sign of compassion or heart, the very words often uttered by Nielsen to describe the United States's handling of immigrants. Even with federal courts ordering a stop to harmful policies and practices, the government continued its ruthlessness. On July 13, for example, NBC News said that 2,551 children ranging in age from 5 to 17 were still separated from their parents despite Judge Sabraw's injunction, a month after Trump had revoked his family separation policy.[27] Nearly 2 weeks later, the *New York Times* and CNN followed with a story that over 900 parents were still to be reunified with their kids as required by Sabraw's order. Adding to the tragedy of the still-fractured families was that 463 parents—more than half of those whose children were removed—had been deported without their kids. The fate of many families would be to never be reunified, ever.[28]

In July 2018, about 37 kids, some as young as 5, were taken by van to the Port Isabel Detention Center in Los Fresno, Texas, to be reunited with their parents. Once there, as Julie Hirschfeld Davis and Michael Shear reported, DHS officials told the children, bus drivers, and children's supervisors that the parents were not ready to be released.

> For weeks, there had been twice-a-day conference calls between [D]HHS and DHS officials to coordinate the handoff. But somehow, the officials at Port Isabel had not completed the paperwork that needed to be done to release the parents. Worse still, the station didn't have anywhere the children could wait.... Unsure of what else to do, the adults who were accompanying the children on the bus drove to a nearby Walmart and bought blankets, pillows, snacks, and other supplies for the children. As the final phase of their harrowing ordeal, these kids would have an impromptu sleepover inside a DHS bus in a barren parking lot on the border.[29]

The more than three dozen children waited in the van for as long as 39 hours to be reunited with their parents.[30]

Later that month, the Associated Press disclosed horrific news that a facility in Clint, Texas, near El Paso, held about 250 migrant children and teenagers, some taken from their parents at the border. They had been locked up for 27 days in "appalling" conditions—unable to shower for days, even weeks, and served inadequate food. Neither soap nor toothpaste was available to the children. Fifteen or more of the kids suffered from the flu. When they were seen by the public, the children wore dirty clothes covered in mucus and urine.[31] On the heels of the Clint discovery and the removal of children to better facilities, in July, the House of Representatives Committee on Oversight and Reform heard testimony from witnesses who described the trauma inflicted by the Trump administration's family separation policy. Witnesses addressing the congressional committee said that the government had not been transparent about the purpose of the still-ongoing separations.[32]

The summer led into the fall, and children were still being separated, after a court order, a national outcry, and a president's executive order. Through a report by Amnesty International, we learned that Customs and Border Protection (CBP) had separated 6,022 family units between April 19 and

August 15, 2018, showing again that the government had lied about the true number of separations and had not stopped the practice as ordered by a federal court. On October 15, the government reported that 2,654 children had been separated and that the vast majority, 2,363, had been discharged from ORR. Still, 125 kids chose to seek asylum in the United States without their parents, a decision probably urged by parents to ensure their children's safety. Another 120 children were in ORR custody, waiting to be reunified after waiving asylum.[33] On October 8, a 2-year-old Honduran girl appeared in a federal immigration courtroom. The girl, originally from Tegucigalpa, had been separated in July from her grandmother at the border and was now appearing in court alone, without any family present, only a caseworker. According to the *New York Times*, she was emblematic of the kids

stranded at the junction of several forces: the Trump Administration's determination to discourage immigrants from trying to cross the border; the continuing flow of children journeying by themselves from Central America; the lingering effects of last summer's family separation crisis at the border; and a new government policy that has made it much more difficult for relatives to claim children from federal custody.[34]

It was followed by a story in the *New Yorker* of a 5-year-old, barely able to write, persuaded to sign away her rights after being separated from her grandmother.[35]

In mid-November 2018 ProPublica reported that separations were still happening, with CBP officers saying that they suspected gang activity as the reason for separating families.[36] Just before Christmas, Nielsen once again claimed falsely that there was no family separation policy. "I'm not a liar, we've never had a policy for family separation," Nielsen was quoted as saying.[37] Her gaslighting went on, that if such a policy existed, then it "would mean that any family that I found at a port of entry I would separate, it would mean that every single family that I found illegally crossing, we would separate. We did none of those."

In the months between 2017 and the summer of 2018, at least 5,556 children were separated from their parents under the misguided belief that such a cruel action would deter migrants from risking their lives and their children's lives. But, later, an inspector general, this one from DHHS, reported in mid-January of 2019 that more children than previously known may have been separated from their parents since 2017. The number that had been reported, 2,737, did not represent the full scope of family separations. Thousands of children may have been separated during an influx that began in 2017, before the accounting required by the court. In addition, as of early November 2018, HHS had received at least 118 separated children since the court order.[38]

By March 2019, the government could not dodge the reality of its quandary: It had to admit to Judge Sabraw that it had separated 245 children from their parents and other relatives well after the family separation policy had been rescinded.[39] A month later, the government reported in court that the estimates showed that it could take 2 years to identify thousands of children who had been separated.[40] The shoddy record-keeping was catching up with the government. It was now issuing report after damning report of the catastrophe it had created for itself and the innocent children and families. The *Los Angeles Times* reported that the government had acknowledged that it had separated 389 families since June 2018, although immigration advocates asserted that the number was far higher. It noted that at least 40 separations were occurring daily on the California border and that other separations were continuing in Texas, New Mexico, and Arizona.[41] Moreover, the government had separated another 1,712 children before the zero tolerance policy went into effect in May 2018.[42]

Days before Thanksgiving 2019, the DHS inspector general issued a report, bluntly titled "DHS Lacked Technology Needed to Successfully Account for Separated Migrant Families." DHS admitted it had kept "poor data entry, data tracking, information sharing and IT systems capabilities" to track and reunify families during the entire family separation crisis of 2018.[43] The government's own data showed that the numbers of separations were far higher than the 1,110 reported because of wildly inconsistent record-keeping.[44] To Trump, causing suffering and damage to children by separating them didn't matter. He ramped it up.[45] It was not going well for anyone: the Trump administration, migrant parents, their children, or the courts. Separations were still happening, and federal court rulings were being defied, scorned, and trampled. And the Trump administration was not getting any positive press on its policy.

Even the count that over 5,000 children were separated is questionable; there were probably hundreds more. The undercount is believed to be the result of careless record-keeping and very little effort by the DHS, CBP, and ICE to ensure that children's identities were linked to their parents' identities. In 2020, the Government Accountability Office (GAO) reported that from October 2019 to mid-March 2020, DHS and Department of Justice (DOJ) processed about 5,290 individuals, most ending in negative fear determinations from asylum officers. Yet, the Executive Office for Immigration Review, part of the DOJ, could not account for the status of about 630 individuals who had received positive determinations. DHS had failed to file essential documents for those individuals.[46]

It is simply inexplicable how a system could not keep records of which children belonged with which parents. Procedures have long been in place to process asylees. Upon entering the United States, every person is issued an "alien registration number," an identification number for non-citizens that helps the government keep track of anyone who enters the country as a refugee or asylum seeker. It is a number that the individual keeps for life, much like a person's social security number. The *A number* is between seven and nine digits long, and parents' and children's A numbers can be connected when they have entered the United States together. Like Judge Sabraw said in his ruling, the government can track detainees' personal property, money, and important documents that are kept and then returned to detainees upon release—and it happens at all levels whether state or federal, citizen or immigrant.[47] The problem of keeping track of children and parents, among all the other misadventures in tracking children and parents, was that the DHHS computer system used to track the children in the department's care, called the *ORR Portal*, contained almost no information about a child's parents.

> Each child was given a unique identifier. But the Family Unit Number, which DHS assigns to families that cross the border illegally, was not consistently provided when children were separated from their parents and reclassified as Unaccompanied Alien Children. Occasionally, a caseworker or a Border Patrol agent might have made a notation that the child came with a parent. But beyond that, there was no way of knowing for sure how many they were looking for. It was infuriating. Customs and Border Protection gave the HHS team one number; Immigration and Customs Enforcement gave another; DHS headquarters offered a third. 1,000. No, 1,500. No, 2,100.[48]

The cruelty continued into 2019. In one incident reported by National Public Radio, border patrol agents were presented with a 3-year-old Honduran girl who suffered from a heart condition. A doctor told the agents that the child should stay in the United States, whereupon the agent told the family that only one parent could stay with the child and the other had to return to Mexico. In the most malevolent act I had ever heard of or read, the agent asked the toddler to choose which parent would stay and which would leave. Fortunately, the insistent doctor asked another agent to intervene, and the family was kept together in the United States.[49] Such a wicked action framed for many people how a presidential policy allowed for heartless people to unleash their most sadistic impulses. And this would not be the only time US agents and staff at the detention centers were found to have mistreated children. A *New York Times* report 4 months earlier found that more than 4,500 complaints about the sexual abuse of immigrant children held in detention had been filed from October 2014 to July 2018. Of these, 1,303 were deemed to be grave incidents, and 178 included accusations of sexual assault (rape, fondling, kissing, and watching children shower) by adult staff members.[50]

The news in 2020 changed little or not at all. The Trump administration was again sued, this time for deliberately cruel actions that harmed families.[51] Judge Sabraw refused to issue new guidelines to further limit the government's ability to separate migrant families, allowing immigration officials to use their "discretion."[52] Attorneys said that they were having enormous difficulty reaching hundreds of parents of separated children. The GAO reported that arrests of parents with children under 18 had grown from 22% of the total southwest border apprehensions in 2016 to about 51% of such apprehensions in 2019.[53] The DHHS inspector general revealed that CBP had separated more asylum-seeking families at ports of entry than previously reported: It wasn't only seven families between May 6 and July 9, 2018; it was at least 60 families.[54] The year of the pandemic was no better for the Trump administration than the year prior.

Since 2014, the United States had been detaining mothers and children as well as fathers and children. Four years later, under a new president, it took to separating families with many tragic outcomes, from psychological disorders to sexual and psychological abuse of children to suicides. At every step, the administrations stalled, delayed, skated around, and appealed federal injunctions. Federal courts were not having any of it; they would not be accomplices to a national crime that kept parents and children in family prisons. Judges sided with lawsuits that challenged the government based on civil rights, habeas corpus, and other violations of the Constitution's safeguards. Detention and separation continued.

With pressure in the courts and public opinion mounting on the detention and separation of families, the Trump administration decided on another approach to circumvent the courts. In August of 2019, the administration proposed to end the Flores Settlement while using it for purposes for which it was never intended. Arguing that because it is required to treat accompanied and unaccompanied children in its custody with "dignity, respect, and special concern for their particular vulnerability," the government would "maintain family units" by imposing another harsh standard: detaining migrant families *indefinitely*. It was now using the very settlement it wanted to abolish for its own purpose: to hold "families with children in licensed facilities or facilities that meet ICE's family residential standards" for as long as needed.[55] Families would "do time" without a conviction or sentencing. Criminals, after a trial, are convicted and sentenced to lengths of time, usually following sentencing guidelines, that are clear and specific, including the amount of time to be served. Not so for innocent families. The idea was just to keep them in detention until, well, whenever. No release dates. No early parole for good behavior. In Los Angeles, Judge Dolly M. Gee of the US District Court for the Central District of California rejected the administration's plan to end the Flores Settlement. Legal representatives argued that terminating Flores was "cruel beyond imagination," citing the death of seven children in detention.[56]

In the case of *Ms. L. v. ICE* in 2019, Judge Sabraw of the US District Court in San Diego admonished the Trump administration, ordering the government to reunite 11 children with parents who had been deported under its family separation policy. His ruling also ordered the government to halt the zero tolerance policy and placed specific restrictions on future separations.[57] Judge Sabraw found that some migrants were pressured to consent to deportation during the very time they were separated from their children. The judge determined that migrants should be allowed to return to the United States for a chance at asylum.[58] As a result of the judge's ruling, about 2,000 children were reunited with their parents in the United States. The court added parents and children who had entered the United States on or after July 1, 2017, and had been separated, even if the children were no longer in ORR custody in the summer of 2018.

Judge Sabraw further instructed the plaintiffs in the *Ms. L* case to create a steering committee that would focus on locating parents that had been separated and deported without their children. The task of the steering committee was to contact parents who had been removed to determine if they wanted their children returned to them in their home country or released from the custody of ORR to live with a sponsor in the United States. Reunifications occurred in the family's home countries when they took place, but very few parents were given the opportunity to return to the United States for reunification.

Back at the US District Court for the Southern District of California in Los Angeles, another judge ordered the government to initiate mental health screenings and treatments for parents who had been separated because of the abundant evidence of trauma due to the Trump administration's policy.[59] The case was known as *Ms. J. P. v. William P. Barr fka Jefferson B. Sessions.*[60] Ms. J. P. was a Guatemalan woman who spoke a Mayan language, not Spanish. She had been separated from her teenage daughter at the border on May 21, 2018. For over a month, J. P. did not know where her daughter was being held. It took 40 days before J. P. and her daughter spoke, and it was a chance occurrence in which an immigration attorney met J. P. by happenstance during a visit to the detention center in Irvine, California, where she was being held. Her 16-year-old daughter was in a shelter in Phoenix, Arizona. For more than a month, J. P. suffered, without an explanation of where her daughter was or what had happened to her. Lawyers for Ms. J. P. and similarly situated families alleged that they had suffered "life-altering" trauma that could continue to affect their mental and emotional well-being for years to come as a result of the separation from their children at the Mexican border.

On November 5, 2019, the judge in *J. P.*, Judge John A. Kronstadt, certified that there was a class of separated migrant parents that could bring action (and was the best option to manage an equitable remedy for the hundreds of potential claims). Judge Kronstadt issued a preliminary injunction requiring the Trump administration to "work collaboratively and promptly to establish a process to provide members of both the Custody and Release Subclasses with notice of the available mental health screenings and treatment." Furthermore, the judge ruled that the government deliver "medically appropriate" mental health assessments and treatment to the members of both subclasses and that the assessments and treatment be offered at locations "reasonably convenient to [class members] given their current locations and restrictions on travel under respective terms and conditions of release."[61]

Judge Kronstadt's decision was a rare ruling in which the government was being held accountable for inflicting psychological trauma on migrant children and parents because of its policies. The court recognized that, when a government not only creates but inflicts trauma, it is responsible for providing treatment and other services to those it harmed. The ruling was described by experts as "truly groundbreaking," "pathbreaking," something few had seen a court do previously.[62] Kronstadt drew on previous federal cases in which governments had been found liable for damages to people because they had placed them in dangerous situations with "deliberate indifference." The judge also drew on the "state-created danger" doctrine that had often been applied to public employees who had failed to act to protect others. In this situation, the judge concluded that the government had taken "affirmative steps to implement the zero-tolerance policy." When implemented the policy did nothing less than cause "severe mental trauma to parents and their children." In other words, the Trump administration was responsible for mental health harm caused by forcibly removing children from their parents without any indication of when they would be reunited or even how that would occur. Not only was it inhumane to separate children from their families with uncertainty but it violated the families' constitutional rights.

As in many of the government's responses to federal court injunctions, lawyers argued that the government could not be held liable for the mental health problems that could occur in the future. Moreover, the lawyers argued that there was no proof of irreparable harm to any of the children or parents; and, besides, they said, any harm that might have come to the families was repaired when they were reunified. Judge Kronstadt's preliminary injunction may have required the federal government to make available mental health screenings and treatment, and possibly other services, such as case management, for years to come. But it would not be easy. Finding the parents and children who had been separated given the poor record-keeping would take time. After all, there had been no comprehensive process in place connecting the many federal agencies involved in apprehending, separating, and housing children and their parents. How would they track parents separated from their minor and tender-age children or even ensure that families were reunited as expeditiously as possible? The process would certainly be unwieldy, cumbersome, slow, and very expensive. The thousands of parents and children would be spread throughout the continental United States and in varying stages of the immigration process. Some parents had been deported or duped into returning to their countries. Mental health care for those outside the United States would prove especially difficult unless they were returned to the United States.

Little was heard publicly about the mental health services being offered, until February 2, 2021, when President Biden signed Executive Order 14011,

"Establishment of Interagency Task Force on the Reunification of Families," which mandated the location and reunification of all separated families. The executive order also called for the provision of additional services and support to the children and their families, including trauma and mental health services. The task force was to be headed by the DHS secretary, with the US attorney general and the secretaries of state and DHHS as vice chairs. In fulfilling its mandate, the task force had to establish a mechanism for processing the return of eligible parents and family members and reunifying hundreds of parents who remained separated from their children.

Donald Trump was not only facing a national backlash about the family separation policy. He had to confront also that his border wall, the embodiment of his deterrence strategy, was not coming together as planned. Despite a promise made during his presidential campaign that he would build a concrete wall on the entire 2,000 miles of the US–Mexican border, Trump had to admit that it would only span a thousand miles, still asserting that it would not cost the United States a dime since he, with his prowess in the art of negotiation, would get Mexico to pay for it.[63] By October 2018 there was no newly constructed border wall because there was no money (and Mexico had no intention of paying). In his 2018 State of the Union address, Trump had to walk back his bravado some more: His grandiose pledge was reduced to a wall that was "substantially more than 500 miles" by January 2021. Contracts had been issued for parts of a new wall in Texas. Spending bills for 2017 and 2018 were intended primarily to replace old barriers, not quite the new thousand-mile-long wall of concrete Trump had boasted would rise in the American Southwest. In San Diego, a 14-mile stretch of construction that was actually replacement construction and not a new wall was begun in June and would take a year to finish. In El Paso, a 4-mile replacement project was to be started in late September and was expected to be completed by late April of 2019. In the Yuma and Tucson sectors of Arizona, a 32-mile replacement project was slated to begin in April 2019. It was slow going for the president. With little progress and not much to celebrate, Kirstjen Nielsen, the DHS secretary, was in Calexico, California, in late October 2018 to inspect the completion of the "first section" of Mr. Trump's border wall—a mere 2.2-mile *renovation* project in Calexico in the El Centro sector.[64] The only thing left that Donald Trump could brag about was a project in the El Paso sector of the border that had merely converted 20 miles of automobile barriers into pedestrian barriers. Moreover, the wall project did not reduce in any meaningful way the border crossings that the president was trying to end. In El Centro and El Paso, the monthly border apprehensions increased in the 12 months spanning November 2017 and November 2018.[65]

Despite it all, desperate people kept coming. The press of families and unaccompanied children entering the United States, even with Trump's efforts to stop them, left CBP and ICE unable to process and detain them all in the large facilities, already at or beyond capacity. CBP and ICE were overwhelmed by parents, mothers mainly, and children; the detention centers were full. It became the practice for CBP and ICE to process families quickly and send them into the interior United States to be with their families and friends, although this was not publicized widely in 2019. There were no beds, no detention centers able to house the deluge. Many parents and children spent only several days in holding centers, mostly *hieleras*. From there, asylum-seeking families communicated with relatives across the country, who then wired funds, bus tickets, or airline tickets to help the newly arrived migrants travel to their towns and cities. Despite Trump's belittlement of Sessions, Nielsen, and anybody else in his crosshairs, as well as his executive orders, rhetoric, threats of prolonged detention, and enlarged border force, Trump was not able to stem the flow of immigrants as easily as he imagined. His big, beautiful wall was still in progress, without a penny from Mexico, while costing the United States millions upon millions; and determined parents were not going to be deterred from finding safety and security for themselves and their children.

People kept coming. The wall was floundering. And mothers continued to be detained and separated from their children. The pain and sorrow suffered by mothers were captured in letters to their children, part of a project conceived in late June 2018 by Grassroots Leadership, Inc., the Austin-based advocacy group that played a lead role in the Texas child care licensing of detention centers. Mothers were offered a chance to write letters of their experiences of detention and separation that would be made public.[66] The contents of the letters are profoundly touching, and the images of the letters—formed with basic Spanish, misspellings, punctuation errors, and the scratchy writing of a human hand—capture the universal pathos of parents who lose their children.[67]

The letters show a pattern of separation of mothers from their children shortly after apprehension at the border. Commonalities are *hieleras,* trickery, lies, verbal abuse by detention guards, uncertainty, desperation, shackles, and, in one case, the mismanagement of life-saving medications. A letter from Claudia is typical of the lies.

My story began when I crossed the river on May 21, 2018. Immigration took me that day. I was coming with my son Kevin. They took down our information and took us to the ice box where we spent 3 hours. Then they transferred us to another place that they call the kennel. My son and I were there. He was very worried and would tell me that he did not want that food, that we are prisoners and on the 23rd of that same month, they separated me from him with lies and that hurt me a lot because I was not able to say goodbye to my son. I only told him they were taking me for some medical exams, but in reality, I was headed to criminal court. Supposedly, on the way back from court we would be reunited with them but it was not so. I cried so much. I felt that I was going insane, and something was missing in my life. I was not complete. They transferred me to Laredo [for 12 days and another 24 days in another facility].

An anonymous letter written by an anonymous Guatemalan mother a month after her apprehension added to examples of women lied to and shackled as they were taken to court. She wrote,

They took my son from me on May 31, and they put him in an icebox and put me in another one. After that night I no longer knew about him, until 20 days later they gave me a call and on Tuesday I received another call. They took us to court with a judge and they chained us by the feet and the hands and they told us when we returned they would let us see our children, and it was all a lie because when we returned, our children were no longer there.

A mother named Toni wrote that her son was taken from her a month earlier while she was held in a *hielera*. When she asked to see her son, she was told they would be reunited on the day of her court hearing. "But that wasn't true," Toni wrote. "I want them to bring him back to me in the same state as they took him from me."

Another mother wrote in her letter that she was HIV-positive. Her dire medical condition was made worse by being chained, separated from her son, and missing her medication due to the incompetent, careless, and thoughtless handling of her medicines. She and her son were held in separate *hieleras*. At one point, mother and son passed each other in a hallway as they were being led by guards. She asked to see him, and the guard conceded. "[My son] hugs me crying and tells me that he wants to stay with me. [They tell the guard that they want to stay together but] official responds that he can't, you already knew that this was going to happen, that you would be separated from your children." The guard tried to calm them by saying that the son was going to go to a shelter and that they would be together after the mother's hearing in immigration court. "All of this was a lie," she wrote. Early in the apprehension, their belongings were rummaged by border agents.

> [An] official asks me about a medicine that I had in my things. I answered her, fearfully, that I am HIV positive. She threw out everything except for my medicine but I hide 3 doses because she told me that if she found anything she would throw it out. Very fearfully, I hid these doses because I knew that this is part of my life. . . . I was very worried, 8 days without showering, without my medicine, I thought that I would get sick. Later they take us to the court and they chained us by the feet and hands as if we were criminals, for about 8 hours without eating breakfast or lunch. It is not just how they treat us as if we were animals. From there on we only went out while chained but because they did not give me my medicine my CD4 [T-cell] count got low and they sent me to get my exams and I went out a little unwell. The doctor asked me if I had stopped taking some doses. Only in the dog kennel when they didn't give them to me. Now it's going to be two months and I still haven't seen my son.

A letter by Yasmin continues to corroborate the letters of others. She writes,

> The day I entered this country on May 22, I was separated from my 13-year-old daughter, and on May 23, from my 12-year-old daughter. They took them from me at the [*hielera*] and said it would just be for a short period, that afterwards they would reunite them with me, but it wasn't true. I was then transferred to McAllen, the dog pound, as they call it. I was there for 7 days without showering or brushing my teeth. I ate bread with cold-cut processed meat and a juice for every meal. I was surrounded by a lot of mothers crying for their children. . . . For 7 days, I had no information about my children because they were not giving information to any

mother. I finally got some information when I was transferred to the detention center in Laredo and I was able to communicate with my husband. He informed me that he was going to be reunited with the girls, that he knew where they were. . . . After 14 days of being separated from my girls, I was able to speak to them when they were with their father.

Sandra began her letter with a plea:

The reason for this humble letter is to ask you for help regarding the case of my son whose name is Juan. He is 12 years old. An official told me that our separation was going to be a matter of hours, but it was all a lie. Later, they sent me to the Dog Pound, telling me that they were going to bring my child in an hour and a half, to reunite us. But to this day, they have not given me any effective answer about what is going to happen to him or if they are going to give him back to me.

Another unnamed mother who was tricked to be separated wrote,

They took my two children, a 7-year-old girl and a 10-year-old boy on June 3, 2018. They told me I would get them back in 2 days, so I agreed, but they tricked me because I am still locked up and I don't know what is going to happen to them and to me. . . . I am one of the mothers that is running away from their own country because they threatened to kill me and my children, and that is why we ran away, but *here they killed us alive by taking away our children.* (emphasis added)

Miriam fled with her 10-year-old son from El Salvador,

in fear of threats and sexual assault from the gangs. This group, Mara 18, [cornered me] at a dead-end street and for fear of them I had to emigrate here to this country with the faith and hope that here I would find protection.

She went on,

I'm a mother and father for my son and I couldn't find another way out. I did not know about the new law that would separate children from their mothers and as a mother I can tell you this is the hardest and most cruel thing a mother can feel.

Her son was taken from her side on June 1 and when she wrote the letter, on June 28, she had still not seen him. "After 14 days they let me talk to him. That day I talked to him he was sick with a fever and a sore throat." It would be another 2 weeks before they would talk again. "Fourteen days of anguish of knowing nothing about how my son was doing. It has been almost a month that I have not seen him."

Fabiola was separated from her son on May 19. "The day we were separated they told me, 'You will be separated from him.' It was a very distressing moment. He screamed, begging them to please not separate us." Still, they were kept apart for many days, and she returned to the *hielera*. When she was transferred, she went to a *perrera* where she saw her boy. "He came close to me and gave me so many kisses. He was locked up behind some bars, and between them he was able to kiss me but the officer made him go sit down. I'm afraid of losing my son."

Delia migrated with a 15-year-old son, was separated, and faced the cruel threats of officers. Transferred from one *hielera* to another over several days, she didn't know where her son was.

> I asked for my son and they told me, "Lady, your son isn't here. He's very far away. You are getting deported back to your country," and I started to cry and I begged them to give me my son and the guard told me, "Don't make me give you an electric shock."

Those around her told Delia that she had passed out. She had gone for 23 days without hearing from or about her son.

Most letters were intended to be read by the world, to show what was happening to them. Carolina, however, took a different tack and wrote a letter to her son whose age is unknown. It is endearing and encouraging, shown here as written and punctuated.

> Hello my love my handsome son, I want you to know that I love you very much my prince and that we will be together soon. God willing very soon my son and we will never again be separated I am going to care for you and protect you always my love I send you many kisses and hugs I love you. And when we are together I am going to spoil you as always. I am going to make

you your meals and we'll go out walking. I'll lay [on your bed] until you fall asleep. I love you my prince. May god care for you and bless you always. Soon, soon my son we are going to be together and we will never again be separated. I love you baby. Sending you kisses.

Notes

1. Reeves, 2015, p. 161.
2. For a particularly graphic description of the inner workings of the White House, Departments of Homeland Security and Justice, see Hirschfeld Davis & Shear, 2019.
3. Shear, 2021; Shear et al., 2020.
4. Shear et al., 2020.
5. Holpuch & Gambino, 2018.
6. Huppke, 2018.
7. National Immigration Justice Center, 2021.
8. Ainsley, 2017.
9. Kriel, 2017.
10. Kopan, 2018.
11. Hirschfeld Davis & Shear, 2019.
12. Miroff, 2018.
13. Lavandera et al., 2018.
14. Merchant, 2018.
15. Nielsen, 2018.
16. Soboroff, 2020, p. 174.
17. Thompson, 2018a.
18. CBN News, 2018.
19. "Trump Administration's Cruel Treatment," 2021.
20. Exec. Order No. 13841, 2018.
21. Baldas, 2018.
22. Kates, 2018.
23. On a visit to a south Texas facility that housed children taken from their parents at the border: "I really don't care. Do U?" Melania later said the message was about the politics her husband was encountering. But the damage was done.
24. Gerstein & Hesson, 2018.
25. Ainsley & Soboroff, 2018.
26. In 2018, officials in the Trump administration thought it would be a good idea to give parents this binary choice. Hirschfeld Davis and Shear, 2019, refer to a "discussion paper about possible reforms . . . had been circulating in the top ranks of officials at DHS, ICE, CBP, and the State Department" (p. 332).
27. McCausland, 2018.
28. Jordan & Dickerson, 2018; Yan, 2018.

29. Hirschfeld Davis & Shear, 2019, p. 294.
30. Soboroff & Ainsley, 2019a.
31. Attanasio et al., 2019.
32. Committee on Oversight and Reform, House of Representatives, 2019.
33. Amnesty International, 2018.
34. Yee & Jordan, 2018.
35. Stillman, 2018.
36. Thompson, 2018b.
37. Clark, 2018.
38. US Department of Health and Human Services, Office of the Inspector General, 2019.
39. Jordan & Dickerson, 2019.
40. Jacobs, 2019.
41. "Editorial: The Government," 2019.
42. Soboroff & Ainsley, 2019b.
43. US Department of Health and Human Services, Office of the Inspector General, 2019.
44. Well into December 2019, discrepancies were still appearing in the numbers being reported of families separated since June 2018; Washington, 2019.
45. Ferriss, 2019.
46. US Government Accountability Office, 2021.
47. Gerstein & Hesson, 2018.
48. Hirschfeld Davis & Shear, 2019, p. 292.
49. Moore, 2019b.
50. Hagg, 2019.
51. *A.P.F. et al v. United States of America*, 2020.
52. Montoya-Galvez, 2020.
53. Government Accountability Office, 2020.
54. US Department of Homeland Security, 2020.
55. Shear & Janno-Youngs, 2019; US Department of Homeland Security, 2019.
56. Reilly & Carlisle, 2019; Acevedo, 2019.
57. *Ms. L v. ICE*, 2019. The court defined the class as,

> All adult parents who enter the United States at or between designated ports of entry who (1) have been, are, or will be detained in immigration custody by the DHS, and (2) have a minor child who is or will be separated from them by DHS and detained in ORR custody, ORR foster care, or DHS custody, absent a determination that the parent is unfit or presents a danger to the child.

Parents with a criminal history or communicable disease, as well as those apprehended in the interior, were excluded from the class. The court later expanded the class of parents eligible for relief to those parents who were separated on or after July 1, 2017, to apply retroactively to include the first known pilot of this policy.
58. Montoya-Galvez, 2019.
59. Jordan, 2019.
60. *Ms. J. P. v. William P. Barr fka Jefferson B. Sessions*, 2018.
61. *Ms. L v. ICE*, 2019, pp. 45–46.

62. Jordan, 2019.
63. Sullivan & Qiu, 2018.
64. US Customs and Border Protection, 2018a.
65. US Customs and Border Protection, 2018b.
66. Grinberg et al., 2018.
67. Images of the original letters and their translations are available at http://grassroot sleadership.org/blog/2018/06/letters-inside-officials-threaten-them-transfers-16-women-detained-hutto-speak-out. Information was made available by Claudia Muñoz, co-executive director of Grassroots Leadership, Inc., January 21, 2022, personal communication.

6

Hiding Boys in Therapeutic Detention

The detention of parents and children had been going on since 2014, and the separation of children from parents was fully underway in 2018. So too, but unknown to many, was the detention of teenage boys in therapeutic residential centers under a contract with the Office of Refugee Resettlement (ORR). The boys somehow found themselves in the custody of ORR, sometimes on the mere rumor or supposition that they were gang members, had gang tattoos, wore gang colors, or flashed gang signals. Even disclosing, honestly, to counselors and therapists that they had been coerced by gangs in their native El Salvador, Guatemala, or Honduras to rob, threaten, or beat someone made them subject to detention as a threat. How this category of boys was created and how it was that they came to have prolonged stays in detention—8 months on average but for over a quarter of the kids up to 2 years—was a concern that the New York Civil Liberties Union (NYCLU) took on.

The NYCLU filed a class-action lawsuit, *L. V. M. v. Lloyd (1-18-cv-01453)*, in the federal district court of the Southern District of New York, which was heard by Judge Paul A. Crotty on behalf of immigrant teens detained in New York State by ORR.[1] The teenagers' releases had been significantly delayed because of a policy implemented by the Trump-appointed ORR director that required him to personally review and approve the release of any detained immigrant child who had ever been in a heightened supervision placement while in ORR custody.

Just hours after taking office as the director of ORR in March 2017, Scott Lloyd had adopted the director-level review policy without so much as an analysis of the cases or even a thorough count of the kids in his custody and how they would be affected by the policy. His policy was intended to move immigrant youth who disclosed some gang ties into detention. More often than not, the youth was apprehended and placed in a secure detention facility before being transferred to residential treatment facilities. He was also "working to enhance our day-to-day consultations" with Immigration and Customs Enforcement (ICE), which would turn into an arrangement that would not only violate the confidential notes from therapy sessions but would

Through Iceboxes and Kennels. Luis H. Zayas, Oxford University Press. © Oxford University Press 2023.
DOI: 10.1093/oso/9780197668160.003.0007

also facilitate the transfer of youth into adult detention as soon as they turned 18. Lloyd said he acted in response to concerns about criminals coming across the border. "There definitely were policy changes," he said in 2020. "I could see there being no downside to just sharing information."[2] Well, he was wrong, and his error was damaging young lives. In a deposition in May 2018, Lloyd said his only sources of information were reports in the news of immigrant youth involved in criminal activity, mostly gang-related. Even though ORR is responsible for protecting immigrant children and placing them with approved sponsors, the policy that ORR director Lloyd instituted led to children in New York being detained beyond a lawful period. It was, as Judge Crotty would later write in his decision, an "unlawful agency behavior" that was at the "zenith of impermissible agency actions" and that "the Court cannot turn a blind eye to Plaintiff's suffering and irreparable injury."

Any reasonable professional would know that it would be humanly impossible to review and approve hundreds of cases promptly, each with voluminous records from law enforcement and clinicians on the ground, not to mention unique aspects of the cases that were seldom black or white. Operating from ignorance about immigrant children, Lloyd also used his office for a personal religious campaign to block young immigrant women from accessing safe, legal abortions, even in the case of rape or incest.[3] In a *Washington Post* article, Lloyd said, "I suggest that the American people make a deal with women: So long as you are using the condom, pill or patch I am providing with my [Title X] money, you are going to promise not to have an abortion if [it] fails."[4] If his imposition of reviewing every case to determine release was not enough, Lloyd went a step further a year after implementing the policy. In April 2018, ORR forged a formal memorandum of agreement with ICE that would permit ORR to share private and confidential details about children in its custody.

As anyone might expect, ORR's policy of director-level reviews resulted in the indefinite and unlawful detention of hundreds of teens. Since the policy had gone into effect, impacting more than 700 teenagers in ORR facilities, only 12% of these had been released to adult sponsors. In contrast, the year before Lloyd's appointment and his policy, more than 90% of children in ORR custody had been released within a month and a half. Children were held in custody well beyond the appropriate time, but Lloyd argued that the policy of reviewing the cases of immigrant children who had been held in heightened supervision placements was necessary to assess their "dangerousness." But

Lloyd got it wrong: ORR already had in place a thorough evaluation process through which children could be placed with their family sponsors.

The NYCLU asked the court for a preliminary injunction to ensure that the youth be promptly released and reunited with family members. The NYCLU wanted to end the cruel policy that gratuitously prolonged the separation of immigrant children from their families and upended their lives. Children, the NYCLU opined, were being detained at the whim of a director with little expertise and consideration of the children's welfare or their anxious families and sponsors. On April 9, I received a call from the NYCLU attorneys heading up the case. Would I help them as I had done in *R.I.L-R v. Johnson* and *Flores v. Johnson* 3 years earlier? My job would be to review cases and policies and provide my opinion on whether ORR policies and practices met common standards of child welfare practice. These topics were squarely in my area of social work competency, so I signed on with the NYCLU as a pro bono expert witness.

The 25-page petition for a writ of habeas corpus contained the names of defendants, recognizable to me from the press—Lloyd, Trump's choice for director of ORR; his deputy director, Jonathan White; their boss, Steven Wagner, the acting assistant secretary for the Administration for Children and Families of the Department of Health and Human Services (DHHS) in which ORR is housed; and Alex Azar, Trump's secretary of DHHS. Listed as defendants were two others. One was an ORR field specialist, and the other was a person I did not recognize but whose affiliation I knew. That name was Jeremy Kohomban, president and CEO of Children's Village in Dobbs Ferry, New York, a well-known therapeutic residential facility about 20 miles north of mid-town Manhattan. I had been on the Children's Village campus numerous times as a social worker in the 1970s and 1980s. For 21 years, I had driven past Children's Village nearly every day on my way to work in Manhattan and the Bronx. Although I had never heard of Kohomban, I was very skeptical about someone so deeply entrenched with and enriched by the Trump ORR. Kohomban's communications team regarded him highly as an advocate "driven by the belief that every child, regardless of age, deserves a family, and he is outspoken in his recognition of the social justice antecedents that drive child welfare and juvenile justice."[5] Youth deserving to be with families yet being separated from them in collaboration with a tyrannical, insensitive regime just did not add up for me. Other non-profits were enriching themselves through ORR, such as Southwest Key at $1.39 billion and Baptist Child and Family Services at $948 million.[6] Neither agency had a stellar history in providing for immigrant children, making it unsurprising that they were first in line with hands out. Kohomban was later dropped as a defendant in the case, and Children's Village would continue to make millions but with a blemish on its reputation.

Reading the lawsuit raised the question of why a residential treatment facility was being used as a detention center when it was intended for children in need of serious psychiatric, emotional, and behavioral disorders. A standard definition of a *residential treatment center* (RTC) is a facility with round-the-clock structured and coordinated therapeutic programs, often customized for each child's needs. Unlike a psychiatric hospital, the RTC provides important care for children after an acute episode or pattern of psychological problems. The idea is to get kids ready to re-enter their families and communities. Education is important so that the child doesn't lose learning time. In its definition of an RTC, ORR includes "non-coercive, coordinated, individualized care, specialized services and interventions." Moreover, ORR acknowledges that assignment to an RTC occurs *"at the recommendation of a psychiatrist or psychologist or with ORR Treatment Authorization Request approval for an unaccompanied child who poses a danger to self or others and does not require inpatient hospitalization"*[7] (emphasis mine). That is, a child had to have significant behavioral or emotional problems to be placed there.

If an RTC was being used to provide therapeutic services to young boys, then what were the clinical indications for placement there? And if ORR was operating on the basis that an RTC should be non-coercive, then why was it considered a secure placement for these teens? According to ORR, placement called for strict security measures and a low staff-to-unaccompanied-children ratio to supervise the youth to control disruptive behavior and prevent escape. Service provision is tailored to address an unaccompanied child's individual needs and to manage the behaviors that necessitated the child's placement in this more restrictive setting.

As its primary mission, ORR is responsible for protecting unaccompanied immigrant children and placing them as safely and as expeditiously as possible with approved sponsors. Like most federal government agencies, it does not do the direct casework itself but rather contracts with private organizations, often non-profits like Children's Village, which have experience in feeding, sheltering, educating, treating and nurturing, and providing services of all kinds that children need. It is these agencies that connect the children with their parents, grandparents, aunts, uncles, older siblings, and fictive kin. The last resort is a state's foster care system, which sometimes happens. The contractors' key objective is to make sure that children are placed in safe environments and to determine whether safety background checks are conducted on the families, home studies, and other issues. Of course, ORR's gravest concern, a worry felt by contractors also, is the possibility of placing children in homes where they might be abused, neglected, killed, or trafficked.

At the heart of NYCLU's lawsuit was the policy that the ORR director personally review and approve the release of any detained unaccompanied immigrant child who was or had ever been placed in heightened supervision while in ORR custody. The NYCLU argued that the director-level review policy was causing extraordinary delays. In any large organization with numerous employees and contractors, delays and other interruptions, big or small, will occur. But when it comes to human lives, those of teenage boys from Central America who might be unlawfully detained for indefinite periods, the problem arises from mere inconvenience to life and death. The NYCLU asked Judge Crotty to issue an order to release the boys promptly and reunite them with their families or with other sponsors, usually first-degree relations.

When the NYCLU filed its lawsuit, the boy who was the lead plaintiff, L. V. M., had been placed initially in a high-security facility because of baseless charges that he was a gang member. His caseworkers had determined that L. V. M. could be returned to his parents' care, and a judge agreed that he was not a danger to anyone. Even though L. V. M. was moved to a less restrictive setting and a judge had pronounced that L. V. M. was not dangerous, he remained in custody for an additional 8 months.

The request from the NYCLU was that I review cases of teenage boys being held in Children's Village and provide a professional assessment of recent ORR policies and practices. Specifically, my job was to evaluate the detention and release policies and practices of ORR and to describe the harms that children face from prolonged detention. ORR policies are governed by legal requirements and best-practice principles in the detention and release of children in institutional settings. The Administration for Children and Families of DHHS, which oversees ORR, provides guidance on the many possible settings and situations a child in its custody must receive.[8] ORR may place children in a *shelter facility*—a residential care provider facility with programs administered on-site in the least restrictive environment—or in therapeutic or transitional foster care. Therapeutic foster care is usually a trained foster family for unaccompanied children with exceptional needs that cannot be met in regular family foster care. Transitional foster care is typically short-term foster care for kids under 13 years of age, sibling groups with one sibling under 13 years of age, pregnant or parenting teens, or unaccompanied children with special needs. Sometimes, the youth can go to a group home, which is a provider facility that specializes in caring for specific populations with 24-hour staff. Group housing can also be with parents who house 4 to 12 unaccompanied children.

Under the classification of shelter, there were other subcategories with definitions that were important to understand for the work I was conducting. There was a *residential treatment center*, which is, according to the Administration for Children and Families that includes ORR, "a sub-acute, time-limited, interdisciplinary, psycho-educational, and therapeutic 24-hour-a-day structured program with community linkages, provided through non-coercive, coordinated, individualized care, specialized services and interventions." RTCs provide highly customized care and services to individuals following either a community-based placement or more intensive intervention, with the aim of moving individuals toward a stable, less intensive level of care or independence. The policy is that ORR uses an RTC at the recommendation of a psychiatrist or psychologist or with its treatment authorization request approval for an unaccompanied child who poses a danger to self or others but does not require inpatient hospitalization. Therefore, to place an unaccompanied youngster in residential treatment there would have to exist a documented need and, possibly, a diagnosed emotional or psychological problem attested to by a mental health professional. A therapeutic residence was not intended for the placement of a minor based on allegations of being affiliated with a gang. Lloyd's ORR was violating its practices.

Then there is *secure care*, a facility with a

physically secure structure and staff able to control violent behavior. ORR uses a secure facility as the most restrictive placement option for an unaccompanied child who poses a danger to themself or others or has been charged with having committed a criminal offense. A secure facility may be a licensed juvenile detention center or a highly structured therapeutic facility.

Staff secure care refers to a

facility that maintains stricter security measures, such as higher staff to unaccompanied children ratio for supervision, than a shelter to control disruptive behavior and to prevent escape. A staff secure facility is for unaccompanied children who may require close supervision but do not need placement in a secure facility. Service provision is tailored to address an unaccompanied child's individual needs and to manage the behaviors that necessitated the child's placement in this more restrictive setting. The staff-secure atmosphere reflects a more home-like shelter setting rather than secure detention. Unlike many secure care providers, a staff secure care provider is not equipped internally with multiple locked pods or cell units.

My dive into the documents I had been given found three major things that were troublesome. First was that the director-level reviews of release decisions for children did not conform to best-practice standards in the child welfare and human services field. In fact, it was highly unusual for a human services or child welfare agency to elevate large numbers of release decisions to senior management for review and sign-off. Only in very rare circumstances, involving truly extraordinary circumstances (for example, where a minor discloses a history of a serious violent crime such as rape or murder) would a decision be elevated for senior staff or headquarter personnel stationed some 250 miles away to review and determine whether to approve these releases or not. There were exceedingly few cases that required decision-making of this magnitude.

ORR's published policy guide leads one to understand that the agency's guidance regarding release was in line with best practices in the field. That guideline tasked ORR's local federal field specialists to make the ultimate release decision, determinations based on recommendations received from case managers, clinicians, and psychiatric specialists. Federal field specialists are charged with conferring with and listening to trained professional staff who know the child in question well; have spent copious numbers of hours talking, assessing, intervening, and assessing again; and are in direct, daily, in-person contact with the child. These individuals provide significant inputs. The field specialist's role is to coordinate among the various stakeholders and render the ultimate decision. These are consistent with policies and practices whose aims strike an appropriate balance of sufficient levels of vetting and oversight with rendering the best decisions promptly. For instance, the policy allows the field specialist to remand a case back to the case manager and case coordinator for more information or order a home study and review the findings of that study before issuing a final decision on release. And because all the relevant professionals, including the ultimate decision maker, are either directly in contact with the child and/or the potential sponsor or relatively proximate to the child, this process maximizes the chances of decisions being made quickly and efficiently.

After 40 years in social work, I knew from experience and the scientific literature that an organization's placement decisions, including the decision to reunify a child with their family, should be a collective process involving the knowledge, skills, insights, and discussion of a team of professionals representing different disciplines who were closely associated with and had first-hand knowledge of the child. These teams are typically led by human service professionals who coordinate the teams' discussions and decision-making. The aim is to "bring something to build hope on in often desperate situations, regardless of the specific treatment method used."[9] In arriving at decisions about the child's future care, such as whether the care provided in the family of origin will result in better outcomes than continuing residential care, social workers and other professionals must observe the need for both thoroughness and speed. Carelessness, delays, and poor decision-making are likely to cause harmful delays in placing or releasing children from residential custody.[10]

The new policy requiring headquarters review was flawed because it removed discretion from field staff who were either in direct contact or in close proximity to the affected child and, instead, situated the decision-making authority with the head of a large agency, who is far removed from the affected child. I also imagine, based on my experience working with similarly large organizations, that the effort to prepare and submit files for review by such a senior-level actor was undoubtedly a time-consuming process. The removal of decision-making authority to high-ranking agency officials distant from the children was contrary to best practices and had led to delays that prolonged children's separation from family as well as the time spent in highly restrictive custodial settings. These delays could cause severe, potentially irreversible harm for this population of already vulnerable immigrant children. This was an instance in which the distal nature of the decision-making and the delay of weeks, and possibly months, in conveying the decision to release or retain failed to meet the best interest of the child and the least restrictive environment requirements.

None of the children whose cases I reviewed and who were elevated to the director-level review exhibited behavior—either during or before custody—that presented the sorts of extraordinary circumstances that would warrant elevation of release decisions to senior management of such a large agency. As mentioned previously, only very rare and serious cases would justify elevation to these high levels. I was concerned that Mr. Lloyd made the decision to institute this policy without understanding its full impact or the potential for significant harm it would inflict on the children the policy covers.

The second major question I had about why a sophisticated organization like ORR with decades of experience across multiple presidential administrations would institute such a flawed policy was answered as I discovered new information. That information led me to conclude that Scott Lloyd was unable to provide any useful guidance because he was simply unqualified to hold the position of ORR director. Lloyd did not appear to have the qualifications to make the kinds of determinations that he was calling for. Not only did he not understand child welfare and mental health principles, but he also did not understand or appreciate how unprepared he was to make decisions on releasing or retaining a young person in ORR custody. Reading Lloyd's testimony to Congress and familiarizing myself with the ORR guide and the FAQ on director-level release decisions, I did not find the professional credentials or experience necessary to make decisions on children's clinical conditions and readiness for release or risk of harm determinations. Lloyd was an attorney with no previous history in the child welfare or child mental health system. He did not hold a professional degree in a human service or psychological field. According to his testimony, he had not even practiced family law, which might have provided some expertise. He had no experience in interprofessional collaboration in child welfare or mental health or with the many and varied mental health professions that populated both the child welfare and mental health systems. I raised concern about Lloyd's qualifications to make decisions that overruled those of psychiatrists, psychiatric social workers, case managers, and others with relevant expertise working with the youth. I had concerns that Lloyd was overruling his subordinate staff who had made recommendations to approve or disapprove releases of youth. It appeared that Lloyd was making assessments about whether the child in question posed a level of danger without the credentials to do so. Determining the risk of harm a child poses to themselves or others is a central issue in the fields of social work, human services, and child welfare. Professionals trained in these fields would employ their experience, knowledge, skills, consultations, and other tools in making these types of determinations.

The third major conclusion I drew was that the director release review policy was causing children in ORR custody severe harm. Delay in releasing teenagers was hurting them. The best place for developing children is at home with their families, the cornerstone of society and the basis for healthy human development. When families are separated, the effects on children are known to disrupt emotional, social, and cognitive functioning. What's more, the damage caused by ruptures from parents and siblings leaves long-lasting and sometimes permanent emotional and psychological scars. The American Academy of Pediatrics had urged caution to "ensure that the emotional and physical stress children experience as they seek refuge in the United States is not exacerbated by the additional trauma of being separated from their siblings, parents or other relatives and caregivers."[11] In a 2016 report, the Advisory Committee on Family Residential Centers of the Department of Homeland Security asserted that "the separation of families for purposes of immigration enforcement or management, or detention is never in the best interest of children."[12] It was not uncommon to see children and adolescents engage in deliberate self-harm, suicidal behavior, and voluntary starvation and show severe depression, sleep difficulties, somatic complaints, anxiety, and post-traumatic stress reactions.[13] The sense of indeterminacy in detention is a major contributor to negative health and mental health symptoms. The deprived conditions of detention—in which children cannot experience developmentally normative activities, events, and milestones—also affects peer and family relations.

The children whose files I reviewed were suffering from separation from family and the highly restrictive nature of their custodial settings. Among the documents I reviewed were case records of 107 adolescent detainees, voluminous records that contained information on the date of apprehension, locations in which the youth were held before arriving in New York State, medical conditions, and, most importantly, notes made by social workers, psychiatrists, psychologists, case managers, and other staff. Clinical notes contained daily updates, "significant incident reports" (completed by care providers to report and document any serious incidents while in care), and weekly and monthly team case-conference notes in which therapeutic staff gave updates on each youth. These notes were the most informative of all since they provided a comprehensive narrative of the person's behavioral and emotional progress over time as well as updates on the vetting of family sponsors. From them, I could glean any preexisting psychiatric or emotional problems, how they were alleviated or exacerbated by the experience of

detention in the therapeutic residential center, and the disorders and problematic behaviors that emerged from the detention itself.

Given all these issues with the policy itself and how it was adopted, it is no
surprise that the additional layers of review had contributed to significant
delays in the rendering of release decisions. Based on 107 cases that were
the subject of Lloyd's imperious review process, the average length of time
for a final review by the ORR director was approximately *35 days from the
time it was received in Washington.* To be clear, this was the review period,
not the length of the detention. While the average review time was 35 days
from the moment a boy's record hit Lloyd's desk, some reviews took significantly longer. One case took about 86 days to be reviewed by ORR, another
117 days, and another 142 days.

In two cases where Lloyd denied release, there was a lack of coherence between reports about a minor's behavior in the therapeutic setting and the decision that he made. In both cases, Lloyd based his decision on the potential
for violence. Yet, in neither case were there indications of antisocial, aggressive, or other behaviors that might justify a decision to reject the release of a
minor detainee. There seemed to be no connection in my opinion between
the director's denial of release and the assessments of psychiatric and social
work personnel who knew the detained child. The two cases were those of
Carlos and David.

Carlos, a 16-year-old male from El Salvador had been admitted into ORR
care in mid-July 2017 and denied release in early January 2018, a period of
over 5 months. Carlos's record showed that he had a history of sexual abuse
in his childhood, one of the most psychologically devastating experiences
a young person can experience. The reason given for Lloyd's denial was so
that the young man could continue "gang prevention interventions." Yet,
a psychiatrist who treated the child in October 2017 wrote bluntly that "I
cannot find any clinical basis to determine that the patient is at risk for violence in the community. On the contrary, he seems to be violence averse. . . .
Observed behaviors have not been violent." A significant incident review in
early August stated that Carlos made verbal threats to another detainee but
did not act violently. Another significant incident review a week later reported that he again made verbal threats to another youth and kicked a door.
Most other incident reviews showed verbal threats and bravado or that
Carlos was the target of bullying by another detainee. That is the extent of
the violence reported in the documents I reviewed. In another incident, he
expressed fear that gang members might try to hurt or kill him. A case review

dated November 21 concluded that "Minor has matured[d] since his arrival to the program and has shown progress in his behavior and interaction with others."

David, also 16 and from El Salvador, had been involved with immigration detention since, according to available records, late 2016. He had experienced multiple placements and transfers. The case record revealed too that he suffered some mental health problems and was diagnosed with disruptive mood and dysregulation behaviors, depression, and anxiety. It would have been easily discernible by any clinician working with adolescent boys that behavioral problems like David's often mask a major depression. The care record was clear about the progression in his behaviors from defiance, threats, and damage to property to improved, well-regulated, even insightful behavior. David was referred for release in early August 2017 and transferred to another residential treatment center first while awaiting a response from the ORR director in late August or early September. Reports showed that he had had ongoing self-harm incidents at the first treatment center that culminated in a suicide attempt and psychiatric hospitalization in September, followed by a denial of release in mid-October. The reason given was that he needed "additional time in ORR custody without aggressive behavior incidents/significant incident reviews before he can be determined safe to release." The problem with the reasoning is that his behavior was self-directed, not other-directed, and that it was born of the frustration of the delay in setting a discharge date.

In yet another case, ORR seemed to drag its feet intentionally over releasing a boy who was approaching his 18th birthday. His case record showed that staff at Children's Village had become alarmed that, as the clock wound down to his birth date, he would be transferred to an adult facility. Then the record ended abruptly on his birthday. No one on the legal team knew what happened to the young man, but most of us surmised that he had been turned over to ICE and sent to an adult detention facility.

Several other cases demonstrated the problems with director-level reviews. There was the case of Mateo, a boy who was introduced to ORR in 2015 when he entered the United States. It appeared that he was then released to his sponsor but arrested in 2017 for having a BB gun. When admitted to Children's Village in March 2017, Mateo had some behavioral problems, which continued intermittently. The problems consisted mostly of not getting along with peers in the facility because he could not relate to them. But there were no significant behavioral or other problems in the files I reviewed. Still, it was not until February 2018—nearly a year since he arrived at Children's Village—that a memorandum was sent from the field specialist to ORR's deputy director, stating that the child did not pose a risk of flight or danger to the community. The memorandum was heavily redacted in my copies, but one could infer that the field specialist had recommended release. But it was not until early March 2018 that the ORR's deputy director sent an email indicating that Lloyd had approved Mateo's release. At that point, that young man had spent nearly 1 year in custody.

Another example of the impact of poor decision-making on a detained minor appears in the case of Ricardo. An incident review revealed that one evening in early February 2018, Ricardo had engaged in a sexual interaction with a female staff member, which the document listed as "sexual abuse." Striking about this case is that Ricardo was admitted in late October 2017 and was recommended for release by social workers in the residential treatment facility just days before the New Year. Yet he remained in placement. In late January 2018, an Administration for Children and Family staff member wrote that "This release is now overdue." Still, no decision was made. The sexual abuse occurred a few weeks later. Poor communication and decision-making that led to delays set the stage for the abuse. Had ORR leadership listened to the treatment facility's professional staff and ORR staff on the ground—people who were closer to the child—and allowed them to use their best judgment and make decisions, the incident might have been prevented.

Yet another example was that of Julián who had suffered a gunshot wound by police in his native El Salvador in August 2016. After surgery, he fled to save his life. He and his family had also been terrorized by MS-13 gang members. Julián entered the residential center in late June 2017. He made very good progress behaviorally, according to the documents, and was eligible for protection for a severe form of human trafficking. This boy had experienced significant trauma in his life, having endured threats by gang members, a gunshot wound, and a risky flight through Mexico to the United States. Despite the reports of positive responses to therapeutic interventions, it was not until February 2018 that a memo from the field specialist to ORR appears to recommend release. But it was another 12 days before ORR Deputy Director Jonathan White wrote an email communicating Lloyd's approval for Julián's release. Given the severe traumas experienced by Julián that left him at heightened risk from the harms associated with detention and family separation, such delays in decision-making served no child welfare purpose and were harmful to the child.

Finally, the handling of another case raises very serious concerns about detention and the nature and delay in decision-making for release. Simón was first admitted into immigration holding in Homestead, Florida, in the second week of February 2017. Two months later he was moved to New York State and into Children's Village, where he spent some time in staff secure then moved to shelter level in June. Simón's record shows that he was suicidal at times, and this naturally raised the concern of staff. Despite improved behavior that allowed him to be dropped from staff secure to secure and then to a shelter, it was not until mid-March 2018 that he was approved for release. This suicidal boy, eligible for protection under the Trafficking Victims Protection Reauthorization Act of 2008,[14] appears to have spent *over a year* in detention in one form or another. As a clinician, I am left with questions about whether the suicidal behavior was a function of the detention process that was mixed with his preexisting psychological condition.

Thinking back to the cases of those boys and how they responded to their detention brings to mind the words of Behrouz Boochani: "[E]very prisoner creates a smaller emotional jail with themselves—something that occurs at the apex of hopelessness and disenfranchisement."[15]

Of course, it is possible for qualified professionals reading these case files to disagree about a particular release decision. But a group of child welfare and mental health professionals would likely agree that, in the examples I cited, Lloyd's decisions were contraindicated. He seemed to disregard the case records and his staff's recommendations. In many cases, Lloyd did not appear to explain his reasoning or provide any meaningful guidance to his staff on what further steps they could take to ready a child for release.

The deterioration in behavior seen in some of the boys seemed to be reactions to detention, accumulated stresses and traumas, and frustration. In several cases, the boys' behaviors would fluctuate. At first, youth might show some resistance to therapeutic and administrative staff's input and feedback. This is a typical adolescent response to authority, part of the developmentally appropriate internal struggle between autonomy and conformity. Then, as the adolescents accommodated to the routines and practices of the therapeutic environment, their behavior improved, as noted by staff. However, when frustrations occurred, such as when they missed a phone call with a parent or waited long periods for release despite being informed that they would be joining their families soon, behavioral reactions occurred. In most adolescents, this resulted in verbal threats and braggadocio, or destruction of property possibly. In the rare instance in which an adolescent has serious problems with physical self-regulation, violence occurred in fights, assaults, and other provocations. The unsettling behavior was concerning but not always sufficient in intensity and duration to warrant a step-up to secure placement or extended detention. They were reactions to their circumstances, and clinicians' notes confirm it. Lloyd's decision-making process on cases of youth far removed from his office was not just bad child welfare practice. It contributed to additional harm to the child. Even in cases where Mr. Lloyd accepted the recommendations of his staff, the need for his review was not clear and took much longer than is necessary.

Lloyd was not the man to direct ORR. When the crisis he created with the unaccompanied children was at its height and the government needed to solve it, Lloyd was sidelined at the request of more experienced people around him. Lloyd's misguided ideas, actions, cluelessness, and myopia confirmed what I later read in Jacob Soboroff's book, quoting a career ORR official: that Lloyd "couldn't put out a small grease fire," never mind a global cataclysm.[16]

In June 2018, Judge Paul A. Crotty ruled that L. V. M. and others had adequately demonstrated irreparable injury and likelihood of success on numerous claims and ordered ORR officials to end the director-level review policy. In November, the government conceded that the director review policy was illegal. Within weeks, Lloyd was removed as ORR director and reassigned to another office that still gave him control over access to healthcare for detainees. Giving the responsibility of healthcare access to a crusading anti-abortionist was another perplexing decision made by an administration that was driven by ideology and not science or best-practice standards. In June 2019 Lloyd left the administration.

Two years later, a compelling story written by Hannah Dreier appeared in the *Washington Post*. Dreier's story followed a boy named Kevin who had spent 856 days in detention. He had crossed the Rio Grande with his 18-year-old sister on an inflatable raft. Federal agents sent his sister to an ICE detention center until she could be deported. At 17, Kevin was transferred to ORR. Encouraged to go to therapy and tell his therapist everything, Kevin did so. Unbeknownst to this boy, Steven Wagner, who was heading ORR at the time of Kevin's detention, told Congress that the agency would request that its contract therapists "develop additional information" about children during "weekly counseling sessions where they may self-disclose previous gang or criminal activity to their assigned clinician." If a child relayed any information about their involvement with gangs or drug dealing, therapists were required to file a report within 4 hours, to be passed to ICE within 1 day. The agency instructed personnel to tell children that it was essential that they be honest with staff in their meetings and sessions. Dreier told of the use of children's confidential therapy records to justify keeping the youth in detention. The records followed Kevin from one detention facility to the next, and therapy notes became part of his permanent files, accessible to the next custodian of the child. "Intimate confessions, early trauma, half-remembered nightmares," wrote Dreier, "all have been turned into prosecutorial weapons, often without the consent of the therapists involved, and always without the consent of the minors themselves, in hearings where the stakes can be life and death."[17] As I finished reading the story, shutting the laptop cover, I wondered how many of the kids in *L. V. M. v. Lloyd* had had the same thing happen to them.

Notes

1. *L. V. M. v. Lloyd (1-18-cv-01453)*.
2. Dreier, 2020.
3. Anwar, 2019; Levintova, 2019.
4. Siegel, 2017.
5. Children's Village, 2022.
6. Cohen, 2020, p. 39.
7. Office of Refugee Resettlement, 2015.
8. Details can be found at https://www.acf.hhs.gov/orr/policy-guidance/children-enter ing-united-states-unaccompanied-guide-terms#Shelter%20Care
9. Forkby & Höjer, 2011.
10. Beckett et al., 2007.
11. American Academy of Pediatrics, 2017.
12. US Department of Homeland Security, 2016.
13. Afifi et al., 2013; Fazel et al., 2014; Newman & Steel, 2008; Silove et al., 2007.
14. The William Wilberforce Trafficking Victims Protection Reauthorization Act was passed in 2008 and was intended to strengthen federal trafficking laws. It added provisions that govern the rights of unaccompanied immigrant children who enter the United States. The law was passed with broad bipartisan support after careful consideration and debate. The bill was recently reauthorized in 2013. For more, see https://www.congress.gov/110/plaws/publ457/PLAW-110publ457.pdf
15. Boochani, 2018, p. 12.
16. Soboroff, 2020, p. 272.
17. Dreier, 2020.

PART II
THE HUMAN COSTS

7

Studying Families, Hearing Their Stories

Up to this point, I have tried to describe what I saw, heard, and learned since 2014 about the state of affairs facing migrant children and mothers. From the time I began visiting Karnes to evaluate families for asylum claims, I was working with a limited base of research on others like them. One useful source of knowledge was case reports presented by mental health clinicians at meetings or told to me individually. Another source was stories in respected news outlets, reports not based on research but that nevertheless provided insights on the topic. There was circumstantial evidence that children were showing signs of psychiatric disorders and that kids with preexisting psychological and learning problems, such as autism and developmental delays, were having even more difficulties in detention. The clinical anecdotes and news accounts made many good points about the effects of detention.[1] But they were stories and clinical reports and could not replace scientific studies.

Another source of information for my clinical work and teaching was research in related areas, such as studies on children of incarcerated women, immigrant children who had not spent time in detention, and children in mixed-status families in which parents are undocumented and some of their children are US citizens.[2] There was also research on refugees detained in Australia, Britain, and Canada who fled war and famine in the Middle East and Africa and escaped mostly by crossing dangerous seas.[3] But how generalizable are findings from countries with immigrants from different continents and cultures to those who come to the United States in search of asylum? To what extent, if any, do the findings from those studies apply to immigration detention in the United States? People from diverse cultures and environments differ widely, even when they have some common experiences. For example, Central American families in US detention centers have their reasons for emigrating and possess social, cultural, religious, linguistic, and other characteristics that make them different from refugees half a globe away from North Africa and the Middle East. Another set of differences that might limit how much we can glean from other countries is that US legal standards and immigration practices differ from those of other countries

Through Iceboxes and Kennels. Luis H. Zayas, Oxford University Press. © Oxford University Press 2023.
DOI: 10.1093/oso/9780197668160.003.0008

and may have a distinct impact, limiting what we can assume about the post-detention developmental, physical, and socioemotional experiences of children held in US facilities.

There was plenty of evidence accumulating that detention does psychological harm to kids and parents, damage that could take a lifetime to resolve or heal, even with adequate intervention. Furthermore, thousands of children and parents were now living in communities across America, attending school, worshiping, working, establishing homes, and receiving healthcare. Because they are not children with typical developmental experiences, local healthcare providers, teachers, and government officials may not fully appreciate the effects of migration and detention, leaving a lot of room for misunderstanding and misinterpretation. Research had to be done, and it had to be focused on issues that would be useful to educators and mental health and health professionals.

I decided to do a study that addressed the mental health effects of detention on children, as well as the strength, grit, and resilience of the youth. It needed to be a study that could help inform others serving these families. The project that I designed in late 2017 and that was originally funded by the National Institutes of Health in 2018 was only to interview children and mothers who had been held in detention. But the landscape had changed from the time of the proposed study—Karnes was now holding fathers and sons, family separation had created a new group of children, immigration policies were changing rapidly, detention centers were filling, private prison companies were making a great deal of money, and Trump's border wall was moving slowly. The nature of the families that were being held, and in some cases separated, changed the characteristics of the families we wanted to study. So, I adjusted the study design to include fathers with children and not just mothers and kids. The revised study would include detained and separated families. The project that hit the ground in early 2019 had the same questions, but they were now being asked to a wider swathe of people seeking asylum. Other parts of the project didn't change, such as the age of children to be enrolled or their countries of origin. When it was completed, the study contributed to the development of the conceptual model in Chapter 8 and the discussion of stress and trauma in Chapter 9.

The research team was made up of undergraduate and graduate students and was led by a doctoral-level project manager from the University of Texas at Austin. Since most of our interviews would be with Spanish-speaking Central

American women who survived experiences that would be best disclosed to other women, interviewers were bilingual Hispanic women. Locating parents to speak with us and consent to having their children interviewed as well could not happen inside of detention; the government would not allow it. Detainees cannot consent to participate in research studies even if they wanted to because they are in the custody of Immigration and Customs Enforcement (ICE) and do not have the freedom to make any decisions. We had to find them once they were out of detention, which involved connecting with community-based service organizations that served previously detained families, connections crucial for doing community-based research. We made contact with local and regional legal aid agencies and other non-profit social service providers. We reached out to churches, schools, and community activists. Our list was fairly long to start with because we knew some would not be able to help us or might decline. There was another source, the community grapevine: meeting families who might know other families who had been detained and might agree to be interviewed, who in turn might introduce us to other families.

Earning the trust of community partners and families who had been detained, even separated, was paramount for my team and me. Just because we were doing what we considered meaningful humanitarian research didn't mean much to people who had had unpleasant experiences with government entities. Our credentials as part of a trustworthy but public institution earned us some credibility, but that's it. It got us *to* the door, but not necessarily *in* the door, with partner organizations and families. Trust had to be earned at every step of the way.

Our key partner became the Refugee and Immigrant Center for Education and Legal Services (RAICES), which defends the rights of immigrants and refugees and empowers them. As a 501(c)(3) non-profit agency, RAICES provides free and low-cost legal services for residency and citizenship services, asylum, removal defense, and Deferred Action for Childhood Arrivals. Relevant to the topic of this book is that RAICES provided legal services to over 4,700 detained children, including thousands held in a tent city in Tornillo, Texas. At the San Antonio bus station, RAICES helped more than 9,000 adults and 12,000 children released from detention to understand their legal rights.

Another place we met many families was the Migrant Resource Center opened by the City of San Antonio in March 2019 at 400 North St. Mary's Street to help with the huge surge of migrants arriving from Central and

South America, Cuba, Angola, Democratic Republic of Congo, and Haiti. Every day government buses delivered large groups of women and children to the Greyhound bus depot, just half a block away from North St. Mary's, where RAICES and other non-profit agencies helped migrant families find their way to destinations all around the country. The good city of San Antonio had converted a storefront space with a kitchen and storage area into a reception and resource center operated by the city's human services department, emergency management department, and other city departments. We got to know the resource center well that summer.

The center was run by an indefatigable city employee, Joe Van Kuiken, who welcomed my team heartily. An Army veteran with special forces and airborne experience and a master's degree in international affairs, Joe was always on the go, multitasking and managing two or more conversations at a time—and all without flustering. I asked about his work there. Joe had been working 12- and 13-hour shifts since the center opened, often 6 or 7 days a week. Joe and others would get in at 7:00 or 7:30 in the morning and didn't leave sometimes till 9:00 at night. He never seemed tired or jaded; he wasn't serving in the military now, but he felt he was still "serving in other ways." After the military, Joe had worked in the San Antonio city council and mayor's office for about 5 years. "Then I went to the migrant center and was there for 7 months," he told me later.

> I walked into the place every day and it was a struggle to just get through the day, to make sure that things that needed to happen, happened. You've got organized chaos going all around you. That for me was the catalyst to changing jobs. It was the kind of environment I like working in. I'm not built to work behind a desk.

Besides managing the chaos of people coming and going, there were medical emergencies almost daily, and migrants had to be taken to a hospital some blocks away. One moment that stood out for Joe was when a volunteer noticed a young mother holding an infant. "That baby looks very lethargic," the volunteer observed. Joe and his team got the baby to the hospital in time to save its life.

While providing material help was the bulk of the staff's work, giving migrants an outlet became part of the job, too. Staff gave out coloring books and crayons, and kids started expressing themselves through their coloring. Joe recalls a drawing someone found that was quite graphic. They asked around to find out who the artist was, and a young boy stepped up. Asked about the drawing, the boy told Joe and those around him that the drawing showed when his dad and a bunch of migrant men were grabbed just before they got to the border and had hoods put over them. The boy saw the men hit the migrants' heads with the butts of their guns. "From what we know," Joe concluded, "it was cartel men grabbing young guys for manpower as labor and drug mules. Many of the women were sexually assaulted."

The center had the support of local non-profit groups such as the Sueños Sin Fronteras de Tejas, the San Antonio Food Bank, the Interfaith Welcome Coalition, and Catholic Charities. RAICES and American Gateways provided legal advice. Nearby Travis Park Church, established in 1946 and led by the belief in the power of "unconditional love and justice in action," offered a place for migrants to sleep at night. The church relied on volunteers who brought cots and covered the church 24 hours a day. The city's fire department stood by doing "overwatch," a military term Joe used meaning watching over another group and supporting them during critical times. "It was a herculean effort," he noted, giving credit to the people around him.

The center would close on October 25, 2019, after serving more than 32,000 migrants seeking asylum. Local non-profit organizations resumed the services they had once offered to migrants, before the large surge of that summer. However, the Migrant Resource Center and all its partners had undertaken the critical, sacred work of helping lost people find their way to safety. Long after the center closed, I asked Joe what stood out to him the most or what random thought came to him after all the people and situations he had seen. Joe paid tribute to the honesty and trustworthiness of the migrants this way:

At the center, we provided cell phones to be used freely by migrants. They were placed on the counter in the front, available and accessible to everyone. Some staff worried that the phones might get stolen. Yet, we never had a cell phone that was stolen. There was one time when someone from the airport called us and said, "Hey, we have one of your phones here. One of the immigrants gave it to us and was beside themselves that they had accidentally put it in their pocket when they rushed off to the airport." The person from the airport said, "The migrant asked us to call you to give back the phone before they boarded their flight." We never had a thing go missing. Such a lesson in human behavior.

It was very clear in the spring of 2019 that detention and even family separation were not deterring desperate families from coming. We learned that Customs and Border Patrol (CBP) and ICE were processing families quickly and sending them to places like San Antonio, where they could take buses or airplanes to different parts of the United States, travel sponsored by families living in those distant locations. It is a tribute to the amazing young women on my team that they went wherever they needed to locate families for the study. Through their efforts, we came to meet and talk with many families who had been detained, sometimes ripped apart and reunited, and were now settled into communities. We interviewed families in their homes, in the secure offices of our partner agency RAICES, at the University of Texas at Austin, in the corners of public libraries, in the din of the Migrant Resource Center and bus depot, through video connections like Zoom and Skype, and by telephone. By going wherever we needed to go to find families, we came to know parents and children who had been released from *hieleras*, *perreras*, and detention, sometimes mere hours before we met them.

Through extensive efforts, we interviewed 83 families for the study. A total of 84 adults and 83 children—72 mothers, 9 fathers, 2 grandmothers, and 1 great-aunt were interviewed. Fifty-one families were from Honduras, 23 from Guatemala, and 9 from El Salvador. The parents' average age was 34 years and ranged from 22 to 56 years. About 38% of the parents were single, 39% were married, and the rest were divorced, separated, or widowed or did not say. There were slightly more boys in the study than girls, 42 boys to 41 girls. The children's average age was 11 but ranged from 7 to 15 years.

This chapter and the ones that follow introduce some of the children and families we met in the study. The stories are presented in their own words; some of the stories are short vignettes and others full-length profiles. The stories highlight the struggles and achievements, defeats and triumphs, losses and gains, moments of weakness, and moments of exceptional courage.

Our first visit to the Migrant Resource Center was July 3, 2019. The temperature in San Antonio was in the mid-90s to upper 90s. I was accompanied by graduate student Tatiana Londoño, who immigrated from Colombia with her parents as a child, and Hilda Torres, an undergraduate student at Texas at the time and herself an immigrant from Mexico. After parking near the bus station, we headed directly to the resource center. That day, and every other day my team visited, the center was filled with the energy of optimistic immigrants waiting out their time to leave on a bus from the Greyhound station to another city or the airport.

The migrant center was made up of two large rooms. To the left as you entered was a counter bearing sandwiches, bottled water, juices, and other packaged treats. Behind the counter were City of San Antonio emergency workers and dedicated volunteers answering questions and planning for who would leave next, knowing who was expecting a call back from a family member to whose home they would be going, arranging for sleeping quarters for the night, and tracking the time that families needed to get to buses for their trips that would sometimes take 2 days. They were the embodiment of altruism. In the other room were tables, perhaps a dozen, each occupied by parents waiting, waiting, occasionally admonishing their children or offering them something to eat. On most of our visits, the center was crowded with families whiling away the time before heading out to the loved ones waiting for them in distant cities. It was a busy place with children from Guatemala, El Salvador, Honduras, Africa, and Haiti running around and playing as their parents talked with staff about their plans.

It was a noisy place, too. Children playing under tables and chairs, chasing one another, or sliding toys between your feet added to the din. The languages and volume at which the immigrants spoke were varied, lively, and energetic. We were interrupted by adult immigrants asking questions, questions that elicited such answers as "The paper says that you have to appear in immigration court in Elizabeth, New Jersey, on the first Tuesday you're there" or "No, that's in a different state" or "Yes, Baltimore gets cold in the winter" or "Michigan is here and we are here [pointing to a map]." The air of relief that everyone there was safely in the United States was palpable. And the atmosphere was full of hope.

Striking to me was that the Haitians were holding cell phones and talking and laughing in their conversations. Not so the other migrants in the center. As I mingled among them and asked questions, I learned that most of the Haitians, especially those with telephones, had migrated to Mexico via air travel (or buses in some cases) from Chile. They described flying to Santiago from Haiti and working from 6 to 9 months, saving their wages to make their way to the border. During their stays in Chile, they were able to afford the cell phones that were almost non-existent among the other migrants.

Tatiana wandered about the room to meet families and make small talk. Hilda did the same. It was our first time at the facility, and we were conscious of simply greeting people and getting a feel for the place where we hoped we would engage families to learn about their experiences crossing deadly lands into the arms of US immigration. From where I stood and watched, the migrant women were talking with my two students easily, eagerly. I knew that our efforts to meet families and hear their stories were in good hands.

Two young men from Honduras, one of them a father traveling with his 6- or 7-year-old son, showed me their airline tickets. They wanted to clarify if they were traveling to the same place or different places because the two places had such similar names: New York and Newark. I clarified that they were going to cities that were near each other but separated by a river and a bay. The two young men smiled and laughed, embraced each other, saying, "We'll be able to visit each other." They thanked me politely and walked away patting each other on the back. But almost as soon as the conversation ended, I began to feel that I had given the men a little too much hope by saying that the cities were close. After all, my description did not stress the actual distance between Newark and New York; it did not, I thought afterward, give them a sense of the magnitude of the sizes of the cities and the width of the Hudson River and Newark Bay, not to mention the ground in between. Perhaps, I thought, if they came from one of the many small towns that dot the countryside of Honduras, their conception of where they were traveling to might be based on smaller cities and narrower rivers, like ones I had seen in my travel in Honduras and Nicaragua. Still, their happiness settled my doubt.

Near the entrance of the migrant welcome centers was a bank of four molded chairs, like those you might find in most public waiting rooms. There I met The Girl with the Cast. I saw the cast rising from the exposed toes to just below her knee. It was a new cast judging by its condition, the kind any American kid who'd broken an ankle playing soccer might have gotten at a local hospital. No one had signed this one yet. The 13-year-old Girl with the Cast sat next to her mother on a bench in the welcome center on North St. Mary's Street.

The girl's mother saw me looking at her daughter's casted leg and smiled. That gave me the opening to sit next to her without wanting to intrude or disturb her or her daughter. Neither mother nor daughter seemed interested in joining with other mothers and girls in conversation. She engaged easily with me when I sat down, asking what country she was from and nodding to her daughter's cast.

"Guatemala," the mother answered with a soft smile and an openness to conversation. There was a shy and modest manner to her. I judged her to be in her late 20s or early 30s. After so many years talking to women and men who had made the dangerous journey through Mexican deserts and violent countryside, I learned to subtract some years from the age they appeared to be. People age quickly during a migration—hunger, thirst, fear, violence, worry, vigilance, exhaustion, sleeplessness, blazing sun and blistering heat, physical assaults, seeing human remains, kidnapping and captivity, and deprivation. Migration accelerates the wrinkles of the face, the hunched back, the gait that might have the hint of a limp. We began with some pleasantries about the heat outside and the coolness inside the welcome center.

Within minutes, her 7-year-old son came to tell his mother he wanted to play with the small truck that other boys had. "Juega con ellos," she told the boy, encouraging him to play with the other boys if he wanted to play with the truck. He went back to following the boys and truck around the crowded floor. The fact that the other boys spoke Creole and he spoke Spanish didn't seem to matter to her son.

As I often do, I asked how long her trip to the border took.

"It took us 23 days," she said. "It would have been sooner, but we were held for ransom for 12 days by the *coyotes* and other men." The trip had begun well as they traveled through southern Mexico, mostly by bus. After a few days, the bus they were riding in at the time was stopped around dusk by a group of armed men, Mexican men, she said, identifying them by the way they spoke. On boarding, the men pointed their firearms at the passengers, all of them migrants from Central America. After intimidating them and taking the small amount of money they could from the scared men and women, the robbers instructed all the adult women to get off the bus. Outside were other men who took the women into the dark, in separate directions and raped them. As she described the episode, the mild-mannered woman spoke in the third person, shielding herself from whatever emotion she felt describing the experience. She made sure to tell me that her daughter was not assaulted by the men. Of the 12 or so women who were taken off the bus, two never boarded the bus again. The bus ride continued in silence.

Several days later, she recounted, they were nearing the US border when the *coyotes* turned against them. For the next 12 days, the group of migrants was held in a safe house of some kind and extorted by the very people who had escorted them all this long way. The *coyotes* had cell phones that they distributed to the migrants.

"Llamen a sus familias y pídanle más dinero para completar el viaje. Si no, aquí los abandonamos" ("Call your families and ask them for more money to finish the trip. If not, we will leave you here"). The migrants called their families back home and instructed them to wire the ransom. It took nearly 2 weeks before all the migrants received the ransom money from their families and handed it over to the *coyotes*, and the journey proceeded again.

Loaded on the back of a flatbed truck, the group of migrants, estimated by the mother to be 20 to 30 men, women, and children, continued. At some point in the journey, the truck was pursued by Mexican police. There was no way in my conversation with the mother to estimate the speed of the chase or what the road conditions were. She only knew that they held on tightly to the sides of the truck. At one point in the pursuit, the drivers and *coyotes* lost sight of the police and stopped the truck. Everyone was told to get off. The police were closing in, and the *coyotes* needed to move faster.

The *coyotes* yelled at them to get off the truck, to jump. Some migrants moved quickly, she said, but others didn't or couldn't. Her daughter was one of those who was squeezed among others and could not move fast enough as the *coyotes* became more panicked. One of the *coyotes*, seeing that the woman's daughter could not move quickly enough, simply pushed the girl off the truck with great force. It was in this fall that the girl's ankle was severely broken, a compound fracture that, fortunately, did not break the skin. The protrusion of the broken bone ballooned into a large lump. The girl could not walk. The mother despaired as her daughter wailed in agony, her younger son standing stunned nearby. She held on to their meager belongings, trying to comfort her crying daughter and bewildered son.

Then, she said, "tres ángeles aparecieron" ("three angels appeared"). Three Honduran men, fellow migrants on the truck, came back to where her daughter lay writhing in pain. The men lifted the girl into their arms and carried her.

With the din of the welcome center, and tears clouding her eyes, I could not hear clearly her muffled words or follow the trajectory of her story. But what I heard next was that the men, she said, carried the girl for a long distance until they saw a farmhouse or empty barn in the distance. Was it a quarter mile or more, miles perhaps, that the three angels carried her child to safety? I never learned that part of the story. Upon arriving at the empty farm building, the men gently rubbed and kneaded the girl's ankle to reduce the swelling and reposition the protruding bone in its place. They had nothing to kill the pain, and her daughter, the mother said, endured the pain bravely. While one of the men worked on the ankle, the two other men searched for sticks and branches, anything, to create a splint. The mother offered pieces of string, cord, and cloth to hold the splint in place. After the splint was complete, the family and their three angels slept. They set off to the north at daybreak. Hungry, tired, and thirsty, they persevered.

I asked about how her daughter came to have such a professionally made cast as she now wore. From the Mexico side of the Rio Grande, they saw that the river current was too strong for any of them to cross, especially a girl in a crude splint. They watched anxiously for border patrol officers on the US side. Finally, a CBP boat saw them on the bank of the river, and the Honduran men waved frantically to the agents on board. Because they were still in Mexico, the agents waved them away, to stay in Mexico. But the three angels watching over the family pointed to the injured girl. The agents took note and maneuvered the boat to the huddled group. Seeing the girl's condition, the agents hurriedly brought the migrants on the boat, navigated to a waiting SUV, and quickly took the family to a medical facility. There the girl's ankle was X-rayed and put in a cast. The mother cried in relief.

"What happened to the three men who helped you?" I asked.

"I don't know," she answered. "I never saw the angels again."

Two months after that initial visit, Hilda returned to the welcome center and the bus stations, this time with Jamie Turcios-Villalta, an undergraduate student at the University of Texas who was born in Canada to Salvadoran immigrants. It was a Friday in September 2019, the end of a school week early in the fall semester, when Hilda and Jamie headed to San Antonio in the early morning. They parked a short walk away from the migrant welcome center. Downtown San Antonio, like other Texas cities settled in the 1700s, has narrow streets and small, concentrated blocks where most places are just a short distance away. The sounds of construction, cars, and people getting to work were familiar ones. Inside the migrant center was the relative calm of people chatting in conversational tones and resting after a long journey. The only noise came from children at play. Staff members arranged water bottles and bananas on the counter for families while they waited to leave San Antonio and put behind them the sorrows of their recent detention. It was much quieter than the visit several weeks before.

Hilda and Jamie greeted the staff and volunteers. The waiting area was filled as usual with plenty of chairs, tables, and a play area for the children. At that time of the morning, there were only a handful of families, mostly with children too young for our research protocol. More would probably arrive throughout the day; that's what the team had seen in previous visits. Joe Van

Kuiken, always friendly, inviting, and informative, explained that the center was not seeing as many families as it had at the beginning of summer. Joe's comments were presaging: A month later the City of San Antonio shut its doors, permanently. But that was not known to the two young researchers when they visited that day.

A migrant father approached Hilda and Jamie. In Spanish, he asked who they were, seeming to think they were lawyers. He said that he fled Venezuela with his wife and children, pointing to his country on a wall map of the American hemisphere. Gesturing toward his wife and young children who were sitting with their luggage, the man explained that they had used their entire savings to get out of Venezuela. They had taken several buses and flights before arriving in Mexico. They arrived penniless but happy to have escaped the economic nightmare that was Venezuela. His story, Hilda wrote later, is age-old, a reminder that immigration is about family, and it will always be about family. The man thanked Hilda and Jamie for taking the time to learn about the experiences of migrants and the hard decisions they make when leaving their countries. He returned to his family and their luggage.

Without prospects to interview at the migrant center, the bus station was the next place to locate families who fit our study eligibility. Operated by the Greyhound bus company, San Antonio's station has the feel of most such places: worn, hard seats and plenty of air conditioning to fight the San Antonio heat. It gave relief to everyone, even if the uncomfortable chairs were designed to discourage you from staying too long. The scene was no different from past visits: volunteers and staff from local non-profits busily helping families get ready for their buses—it might be 24 hours before the next one. About 15 mothers sat patiently in a section cordoned off from the rest of the station, their children restless and impatient.

Volunteers from a local church organization helped orient families, examined their travel documents and bus tickets, and made sure no one missed their bus. Hilda and Jamie received reluctant hellos from the volunteers who had grown very protective of their charges, women and children, some fathers, who had gone through so much and just wanted to get to their relatives. The volunteers' suspicions were allayed when Hilda and Jamie offered to help. Everyone appreciated the value of a couple of extra hands. Help was needed at intake, just collecting information on forms. It required that families provide information to get them on the right buses as family units. Many of the 15 families were scheduled to leave on the next bus, about an hour's wait. One mom with a child had a 4-hour wait.

That family, Martina and her son Jorge, sat near the back of the family section, away from the rest of the group, wearing matching dark green sweatshirts and blue jeans. The mother and son agreed to recount their story of migration and detention. They moved with Hilda and Jamie to the farthest row of seats, away from the rest of the group, to ensure privacy. Martina and Jorge did not want to be more than one seat away from each other. Understood. It would soon become clear why they wanted to remain so close. Hilda began the conversation with Martina in a chair close to a window that let in the daylight. Past them, they could see buses coming in and out of the station.

Martina was in her mid-30s with a tired body and a face worn from struggles no one but she could ever really know. Dark crescents of exhaustion hung below her wide eyes. Even her hair looked tired in a scrunched bun set low on the back of her head. She had been released from detention just hours before arriving at the bus station. Domestic violence and threats of death by her children's father were the push that set her on a journey out of Honduras. She had lived in fear and torment. She knew that a better life for her children and herself could be possible if she came to the United States; but it meant money, and she didn't have enough.

On a typical workday, Martina's brother would call to chat, more often than not urging her to leave and come to the United States with him. In one of his last calls over a month before the interview took place in the bus station, he offered to pay for her journey; but his means were limited—after crunching numbers, he could only finance the travel for her and one child. Here, at last, was an opening to escape the savage life with her abuser, but it came at a steep sacrifice and the need for a quick decision. Martina knew that such a chance could be fleeting and unlikely to come around soon, if ever again. It was the focus of conversation that night at home with her children—a 3-year-old daughter, two twin 11-year-old sons, and two sons, 18 and 19. Her heart was heavy, forced to choose one child of five. These are the choices most parents don't have to make, one of those choices that cannot be understood; any amount of speculation by others does not come anywhere near what a person feels. The elder sons knew that they needed to stay and provide for the siblings left behind, especially the 3-year-old. It was too much for just one older brother to handle alone, and it was decided that both would stay. Jorge's twin said flatly that he would not; he was happy living in Honduras. With that, Jorge stepped up and agreed to go with her. It was decided. Martina called her brother and accepted his offer. Joy at his end of the line, tears on hers.

As Martina told of how the decision for her and Jorge to travel alone was made, Jorge gazed down at his lap, fiddling with the crucifix on the chain around his neck. His eyes told of something deeply painful. Slowly, Jorge spoke about the decision that no parent or sibling should ever have to make. With his decision, Jorge left not just siblings but a twin brother linked to him in ways that only twins know. Martina chose to accept her children's and Jorge's courageous decision.

"Duro," Martina said, describing how hard it was to leave her children behind. Her voice cracked, and tears rolled down her cheeks. "Very hard because to leave one's family is the saddest thing there is," she said, adding "It is sad." Martina wiped away her tears, her voice cleared up. She was offered a break from the conversation, but Martina declined. Maybe the offer of the break was actually for Hilda who was feeling Martina's heartache as if it were her own. She was aware, though, that the volunteers nearby might see Martina cry and intervene. Martina resumed her story.

Travel through Guatemala was not bad, boarding pickups and buses. Mexico was another matter, where wiles were needed in abundance. Martina and Jorge had to hike long stretches by foot to get around the Mexican police. Migrants along the way warned Martina that the police would stop and board buses for documentation. A minor issue could result in the police taking Jorge from her. The group she traveled with did not encounter the *federales* and paid a car to take them the remainder of the trip to northern Mexico. It would take 16 days in the car, driving slowly and evading police that might appear on the roads. Police were the biggest obstacle, with their reputation for corruption and capricious actions. Mexico was following an anti-immigration policy at the time, and deporting Central Americans was very common. It was a fearsome prospect for Martina's group, but there was no turning back. The anxiety among the group was shared, and they voted at one point in the 2 weeks of car travel to hole up somewhere for a few days, "Para que estuviera buena la pasada" (colloquially, "till the coast was clear"). They could not travel through Mexico without encountering checkpoints, but they knew, too, that the checkpoints were left unmanned at the end of the workday.

Upon reaching the Mexican–US border, Martina, Jorge, and their fellow travelers walked some miles for a place where they could enter the Rio Grande. The *coyotes* they paid knew exactly where and when to cross. When they did, the group was apprehended by CBP agents, friendly ones. The officers asked the group what they were looking for. "A dream of safety," someone said, speaking for the others. The CBP officers instructed the group to get inside the cars and offered them water, then took them to a nearby *perrera*. Stories of friendly agents were not typical. The most common ones included discourteous, abrupt, unfriendly agents. On the ride to the *perrera*, Martina felt a sense of certainty that she and Jorge would be allowed to stay and reunite with her brothers. She had a chance of staying in the United States without having to wait in Mexico like so many others under Trump's "stay in Mexico" policy.[4] Soon, though, Martina learned the cost of possibly staying on American soil—her son was taken from her—despite a federal court order to the government that families were not to be separated. It was Martina's worst moment.

"I felt awful that maybe, because of me, my child was suffering cold, hunger, and needed my warmth, and the warmth of his brothers. I only blame myself." Thinking that her child might be experiencing the same misery as she threw Martina into excruciating anguish. Martina's voice quavered at this point of the story, and tears flowed again.

Perrera officers were far stricter than the ones who arrested her. They would not let migrants sleep, insisting that migrants do what they were ordered to do. Martina was forced to eat bean burritos that were not fully cooked. Meanwhile, CBP agents called people's names for deportation. She felt that as long as her name was not called it meant that there was a chance; "no news is good news." If she were being deported, it would have happened by now, Martina reasoned. Still, as the clock ticked, her optimism and hope rose and fell. What was happening? Would she be able to stay?

Her separation from Jorge lasted 5 days, mercifully. Narrating their saga through tears, Martina told how happy she was once she saw her son, quickly hugging him to give him the warmth she dreamed he had been missing all those days. After reunification, they were transferred to a detention center in south Texas. She felt better and safer there, with her son by her side. It was a blessing when they were fed breakfast around 7:00, allowed to eat whatever and as much as they wanted. Mother and son received medical care: Martina for tonsil inflammation and asthma, Jorge for chickenpox he contracted there. Later, she was allowed to call her brother for 2 minutes, so she needed to use her time wisely. "We are here. You must get Jorge and me bus tickets. This is what we'll need." It was an affectionate and efficient 2 minutes. He agreed and assured her that he would be paying close attention to his phone for any calls from ICE. Hearing her brother made her feel more secure.

Martina's credible fear interview (CFI) took place in the south Texas facility. The results of the hearing were positive: She could seek asylum, elating Martina and increasing her gratitude to the United States. The joy was short-lived, though, when lawyers in immigration court challenged her positive CFI. "Are you sure you were given a positive CFI?" the government lawyers asked, sternly and repeatedly. "Yes," she said, four times. "¿Estás segura?" ("Are you sure?"), the officer asked once again, seeming to try to break Martina. "Si, estoy segura," she affirmed. Whether it had been a game or a test, the outcome was that Martina signed some papers, and the following day her brother was notified to buy her tickets. At about 5:00 in the morning on the day of our meeting, Martina and Jorge were told they were leaving. Her brother had acted instantly when notified. A monitoring device was placed on her ankle, the well-known *grillete* (translated literally as a fetter, it is commonly thought of as a modern-day shackle). There followed some lectures about what she needed to do after release. By 8:30 a.m., they departed the detention center and were dropped off at the bus station.

Tired, worn out, but grateful, Martina was emotionally frayed, nostalgic but excited to be on her way to her brother's place. However, no amount of distraction or a positive outlook could keep Martina's thoughts far from the children she left in Honduras.

"Since I crossed the river, I haven't heard anything from my children. That alone has been hard for me, not being able to talk to them. But we will arrive at my brother's home on Sunday at one in the afternoon. I can speak with my kids and then I will be calm." Martina sobbed so powerfully that her words were hard to understand, she was hunched over as if the pain had all accrued in her chest. Martina and Jorge sat closely, tightly. Their embrace and tears told of the painful sacrifices that desperate families must make when leaving home, saying goodbye to the people they love, fracturing their families. Their journey and their losses reinforced the closeness between them. It was time now for Martina and Jorge's interviews with Hilda and Jamie to end. Jamie showed them on her cell phone their destination in Pennsylvania. Martina gasped at the long blue line that would take 24 hours to complete. "El viaje no ha terminado" ("The journey is not over"), Martina said as she reached for Jorge's hand. Martina and Jorge had undergone what most people will never have to endure, and their journey wasn't even over. They were alone but would soon be with family in Pennsylvania. Others back home were counting on them to make it so that one day they would all be together again.

The bus pulled out of the station carrying Martina and Jorge and their hopes for an unknown future.

Notes

1. For examples, see Gogolak, 2016; Hylton, 2015; Phippen, 2016.
2. For research on children who have lived in prison with their mothers, see Byrne et al., 2012; Foster & Hagan, 2013; Murray & Farrington, 2005; Nesmith & Ruhland, 2008.
3. Detained children had high rates of psychiatric symptoms, including attachment disorders, self-harm, suicidality, severe depression, regression, delays in reaching developmental milestones, physical health problems, and post-traumatic stresses (Australian Human Rights Commission, 2014; Bronstein & Montgomery, 2011; Burnett et al., 2010; Cleveland & Rousseau, 2013; Crawley & Lester, 2005; Fazel et al., 2014; Kronick et al., 2015; Lorek et al., 2009; Mares & Jureidini, 2004; Mares et al., 2002; Newman & Steel, 2008; Opaas & Varvin, 2015; Steel et al., 2004; Sun et al., 2017; Zwi et al., 2018).
4. The "Remain in Mexico" policy, officially known as *Migrant Protection Protocols*, was an immigration policy put in place by the Trump administration in January 2019. The policy required migrants seeking asylum to remain in Mexico until their US immigration court date.

8

Stages of Central American Immigration

From history books, news clippings, reputable online sources, existing research, and my clinical work and funded research, a pattern of Central
American migration emerged. The pathway that Central American migrants
took to arrive at the US border was unique to each person and family. But,
as a whole, their individual journeys had many things in common, such as
what prompted them to leave and how they got to the United States. Almost
invariantly, they felt pushed out of their countries. In sociology and migration studies, *push* factors are conditions that make living at home impossible
or extremely difficult, usually because of rampant violence, insecurity, and
government corruption, making it an *involuntary* migration decision.[1] (*Pull*
factors may be family, jobs, education, healthcare, and better quality of life.)
The many migrants I met say, nearly unanimously, what many other men and
women told researchers Mark Lusk and Georgina Sanchez Garcia, "I did not
want to leave my country."[2] With conversations, interviews, reading, and reflection, a conceptual model began to take shape.

   The model of Central American migration that emerged is comprised of
four stages. The first stage is *pre-migration*, comprised of the circumstances
that triggered their flight. The second stage is the *mid-migration journey*, the
passage across international borders and rough situations. The third stage
is labeled *detention* and begins the moment they set foot on US soil and are
taken into custody by US immigration officials. The fourth and last stage is
post-detention when families are released and begin the processes of settlement and adjustment to life in the United States. It doesn't imply that life is
no longer complicated. There is still a court hearing in the future when the
government will make a determination on their asylum claim. At the time
that I wrote this book, the typical court date was several years away for most
asylum applicants. For them, the waiting is flush with anticipation and hope.
It is a challenging, long-term situation; but life must be lived, work done, and
children educated. The activities of daily life take up most of the conscious,
waking day; but the date of the immigration hearing, and its outcome, looms
out there in the distance.

Through Iceboxes and Kennels. Luis H. Zayas, Oxford University Press. © Oxford University Press 2023.
DOI: 10.1093/oso/9780197668160.003.0009

The four stages of immigration include layers of strains, stresses, and traumas through which countless, nameless masses of migrant children and parents have passed. I use the word *stage* intentionally to denote the section of a journey that is not necessarily bounded by time. *Stages*, as I use the term, implies a predictable trajectory, a sequence of experiences. Stages are spaces, terrains, and paths that every migrant crosses, irrespective of time or distance. Migrants may follow the same stages, but each individual has a unique path and set of experiences. All the immigrants whose stories I heard had these stages in common, and their stories were as different as their fingerprints. It is for this reason that I eschewed the term *period of migration* because of its connotation as an interval, a segment circumscribed by time. Indeed, each stage has a time period of days, weeks, months, and maybe years; but the time to arrive at each stage is different for every migrating family. The stage might last days for some families, weeks for others, and months for those moving more slowly or beset by hurdles. Along the same lines, I decided against the term *phase of migration*, for it does not denote a sequential process, a pre-dictable trajectory, and may imply constrained periods of time. The choice of the term *stages of migration* can be debated, but it serves the purpose of conceptualizing the entire process.[3]

Breaking apart the long path to asylum into stages helps interrogate each stage with a critical eye to find ways to study it and its constituent parts. Each stage can be examined closely and solutions framed. Focusing on the individual and family allows behavioral scientists to explore the *layers of pain* represented in each stage, the piling on of stressors on top of stressors, traumas upon traumas, the accumulation of physical challenges and psychic pain. Even with these layers of pain, some families and individuals undergo the migration process and survive, maybe thrive, physically and emotion-ally. From both those who succumbed to the journey and those who thrived, clinicians and scientists can search for *sources of protection*—social, psycho-logical, emotional, and communal strengths, resources, coping tactics, and strategies—that balance, ward off, or prevent the challenges they face. For researchers, the layers of pain and sources of protection yield knowledge for study; for clinicians, the layers of pain and sources of protection represent points of intervention and treatment.

Figure 8.1 depicts the four stages of this process. To understand the model, there are some assumptions and characteristics that apply to all stages. Each stage is assumed to have (a) a starting point, (b) movement across a space in an unspecified time, (c) rising and receding levels of intensity, (d) an

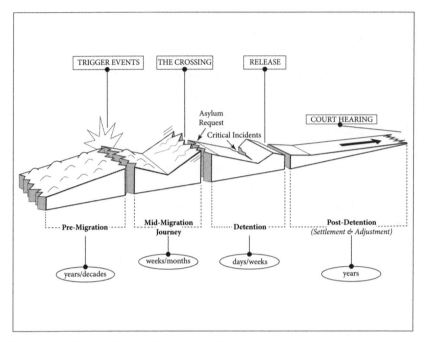

Figure 8.1. Stages of Central American Migration

endpoint, and (e) a threshold event. The pre-migration stage is shown in the figure as having an indeterminate starting point and the post-detention stage as having an unknown endpoint. Each stage has some general time frames, but these are approximate. The slope in a stage signifies a heightened intensity, a growing magnitude of fear, intimidation, hope, or sense of anticipation, anxiety, tension, even physical exertion. The intensification occurs before a threshold is approached, and threshold events are different for each stage; but all stages have one. For example, the pre-migration stage's threshold is the incident or event that was the proverbial "last straw" in a family's life that motivated or triggered the act of leaving, such as a threat, assault, murder, or other act of coercion. The threshold represents the liminal moment before the next stage. The threshold at the end of the mid-migration slope is the "Crossing," the final act of passing into the United States, the culmination of their migration dream. In the detention stage, the threshold at the end is the "Release," which is itself preceded by a slope of anticipation and waiting. In the post-detention stage, the slope is unknown because it is of much longer duration, and the threshold—the appearance in immigration court at a future date—is distant, real, yet virtually imperceptible.

Figure 8.1 comes with a caveat: It does not represent migration in all parts of the world. Instead, it is limited to the migration of families from Central America seeking asylum in the United States during the second and third decades of the 21st century. Every continent and epoch in history have migrations that are distinct, whether it is the reason for emigrating, the nature of the migration journey, or the immigration into the receiving country. Thus, it will have looked different for the refugees of Europe in the late 1800s and early 1900s who came by steamship to Ellis Island in New York and the refugees from Vietnam in the 1970s under protection of the US government.

The *pre-migration* stage may have existed for decades, but usually it has escalated in direness in the months, maybe year, before the critical decision is made to leave, as shown in Figure 8.1. Events and forces from even a century before may still be reverberating in families and communities and contribute to the painful decision to emigrate. Colonization, slavery, genocides of Indigenous people, and civil wars have occurred in each of the three Northern Triangle countries of Central America. And while it may seem to be in the past, historical trauma lives on in the descendant families and communities and is no less important in understanding today's immigrants. *Historical trauma*, that is the accumulated, intergenerational experiences of emotional and psychological injury to families and communities, is part of the collective experience of many immigrants who want to put behind not just the present injustices but the painful memories of loss. You will meet one such family in Chapter 14.

Indigenous people of the Northern Triangle countries must be considered in their own right when discussing pre-migration conditions. El Salvador, Guatemala, and Honduras, and other Central and South American countries, share histories of highly complex and sophisticated pre-Columbian civilizations. Sadly, like Indigenous people in what is now the United States and other parts of the Caribbean and Central and South America, the Mayas have a tragic history of conquest, colonization, and genocide. Much of their vulnerability comes from poverty and their linguistic and cultural differences from others in their countries. A list of the historical traumas of the Northern Triangle countries starts with colonization by Spain, genocide of Indigenous peoples of the isthmus, and the enslavement of African people. The three countries fought wars of independence followed by oppressive governments, abusive military actions, civil wars, and massive loss of lives. When Mayan people in the highlands of Guatemala were thought to be giving harbor to leftist insurgents, scorched earth government actions destroyed 440 of their villages between 1981 and 1983 and killed or "disappeared" about 150,000 Mayas. In El Salvador, the memory of 1932 still lives on from the traumatic period of *La Matanza* ("The Massacre") when the Mayas rebelled against the government. As Erik Ching and Virginia Tilley write,

> Many people today will claim that the military government . . . outlawed indigenous dress and language. But if not banned outright, indigenous identity was thought to have been targeted through terror; when the army troops swept through the insurgent regions, "all those of a strongly Indian cast of features . . . were considered guilty." On the roads, people in "Indian" peasant dress were shot on sight, and in some areas indigenous campesinos were rounded up and machine-gunned by the hundreds. After tens of thousands of indigenous deaths in a matter of weeks, the Indians reputedly abandoned their ethnic identity, including their language and traditional dress, in order to survive.[4]

Human labor has been exploited in Central America for over a century by private companies from the United States and Europe that confiscated the lands and sacred sites of Indigenous nations to reap the bounty of the earth and its natural resources (fruits, vegetables, and ores). Rival American fruit companies—Cuyamel Fruit, Standard Fruit Company, and the United Fruit Company (which evolved the ubiquitous *Miss Chiquita* company mascot)—made Honduras the original *Banana Republic*, a pejorative term implying corruption and instability. But the term reflects the reality of the massive control that American companies, particularly United Fruit, had over the economies and governments through their close ties to the military strongmen who ruled Honduras, El Salvador, Guatemala, Costa Rica, Nicaragua, and other countries in the region. When labor uprisings occurred, workers were killed en masse, their villages abandoned at the point of a gun or burned to the ground, leaving no trace that people once lived there.[5] The exploitation, oppression, and genocide continue in quieter forms today.

With the effects of long-ago national traumas, the pervasive violence of the present that inexorably constricts the lives of people of the Northern Triangle countries makes it impossible to support a family, work, run a business, and raise and educate children in any safe way. Threats may have begun in some distant period, but they have crept up on the family and are now at their doorstep. Not all of it is traumatic, but it is very stressful and growing. Finally, there is a trigger event or events, shown in the figure with a blast icon, that forces families to see emigration as their only option. The trigger point can be a singular event—a rape, an assault, the death of a loved one, an ultimatum—or it might be the increase in stress, tension, fear, and feeling as if the violence is imminent. This begins the planning for a journey of months, weeks, or just days. The mounting tension is shown in the model by a slope, and the trigger is the peak, the threshold, that starts the journey. Almost always, there is no turning back.

To get into the minds of parents who would place their children and themselves in such deadly situations as to travel under the conditions they do, we have to understand what drives families from Central America and other countries to send their children north, alone or with parents. Of course, a prime mover is the desperation brought by gang violence and insecurity.[6] Central American gang violence has made the three countries of the Northern Triangle some of the deadliest countries on earth. El Salvador and Honduras have the distinction of having the highest rates of female homicide in the world.[7] Intentional homicides in El Salvador as reported by the World Bank make it one of the most dangerous countries in the world, with 52 residents murdered per 100,000 people.[8] In the Americas, it is followed by Honduras (39 per 100,000), Belize (38 per 100,000), and Guatemala (23 per 100,000). To grasp how dire the conditions in these countries are, we have to look at the rates in neighboring countries such as Costa Rica (11 per 100,000), Panama (9 per 100,000), and Nicaragua (7 per 100,000). The United States, by contrast, has a rate of intentional homicides of 5 per 100,000. Hondurans and Salvadorans who had experienced more than one crime were 10% to 15% likelier to intend to migrate than their countrymen who had not suffered multiple victimizations.[9] A 2017 survey of voters in Guatemala showed that a quarter of respondents had been asked by police to pay at least one bribe and 66% believed that all or at least more than half of all politicians were corrupt.[10] The aunt of a 6-year-old girl said that gangs were everywhere in El Salvador. "They're on the buses. They're in the banks. They're in schools. They're in the police. There's nowhere for normal people to feel safe."[11]

Governments' inability to respond to the dire needs of the people of El Salvador, Guatemala, and Honduras only makes life worse. Lacking money and political will, leaders of these countries cannot stem the violence, unchecked bribery, and embezzlement. With underfunding and theft, the state treasuries are depleted. Funding for education, public transportation, police and fire departments, social and health services, and other public goods and services is undermined. It's axiomatic that weak public institutions cannot protect citizens, prevent crime, or prosecute them. Without the capacity to enforce laws and to finance government efforts, Central American countries will remain porous to criminal trafficking.[12] Poverty, hunger, unemployment, and ineffectual governments and infrastructure add to the push forces for leaving.[13]

Increasingly being recognized as a push factor for migrants are the effects of climate change in Central America. Rising temperatures, droughts, and heavy rainfall are disrupting crop-growing cycles, destroying the agricultural sector that makes up more than 30% of the work in El Salvador, Guatemala, and Honduras. Coffee, the most important cash crop, is only one of the agricultural products damaged by climate change; others are cane sugar, beans, and rice that, like coffee, thrive in a narrow range of temperatures. Extreme temperature variations leave devastation in the field and on mountainsides and force families into debt or selling their land and other valuables to survive. Migration is one means of survival.

This book is filled with the pre-migration stories of families who were pushed from their countries when they did not want to leave. To illustrate briefly the pre-migration conditions facing one family, I turn to the story told to us by Ian and Santino, his father.

"In my little town, I never went out. I was afraid of the police," Ian, 10, told us. The town where Ian and his sister and three brothers grew up was plagued by corruption and poverty. His father Santino had a college education and was a college professor. He was mistakenly thought by his community to be a man of wealth. The perception that others had of Santino as having money made him a threat to political figures in his town and a target of opportunity for thugs. Santino knew that the chances were high that he and his family would be victimized, sooner or later. Indeed, the extortion began, just the first wave of many that would follow. The decision to leave came swiftly; he would leave behind a career that brought him prestige and that could influence a generation of young Guatemalan students. Santino worked around the clock to put together the things he would need to make it to the U.S. First, he moved his wife and children to his in-laws' home where they would be safe. It was agreed that Ian would go with him,

although the announcement troubled Ian. As the oldest child, he was naturally protective of his siblings; they were very close. He wasn't given a lot of
time to prepare or to say goodbye to everyone. Despite a range of emotions,
Ian followed his father's lead. They migrated together.

With the first step of the emigration, a process of crossing lands and
encountering new and strange experiences is launched. Typically, the migration crosses interior political and geographic boundaries—towns, cities,
departamentos (country subdivisions similar to states or counties), and
mountains and valleys. The first threshold as shown in Figure 8.1 is the passage by foot, car, or bus across an international political border into another
country. If the migrant is from El Salvador or Honduras, the first international threshold is crossing the border into Guatemala. The next international passage occurs for Honduran, Salvadoran, and Guatemalan migrants
when they traverse the border into Mexico. These can be stressful moments in
the early days of the odyssey—abuse, extortion, arrest, and detention. Even if
migrants comply, they might still be repatriated to their countries, and most
migrants are not stopped; they start the process of survival all over again.
There have been joint efforts by governments of the Northern Triangle countries and the United States to convince people of the potential dangers of migration. Billboards, radio and television announcements, and social media
blasts have not worked.[14] Those who intend to migrate are not deterred; neither the dangers nor the likelihood of being detained and deported stops
them. The reasons are as old as the ages: Better to die emigrating than to die
of starvation or murder.

The second stage, depicted in the figure as the *mid-migration journey*,
includes challenging terrain and experiences with people of all kinds.
Traversing Guatemala and Mexico can take weeks or months, and, like
other stages, there are stressors and traumatic events, as well as moments
of supreme compassion. Children traveling in family units and alone may
be victims of or witnesses to beatings, abductions, rapes, imprisonment,
murders, and life-threatening medical problems.[15] Their stories recall soci-
ologist Leisy Abrego's words: "Sadly, these cases of horrific debasement and
devalued humanity are happening daily."[16]
    Some of the experiences during the mid-migration period can be rela-
tively low in stress, such as families that can afford bus travel to the US border.
Most migrants, however, endure great hardships. Even with the occasional

and random kindness of Mexican citizens and officials, pastors and charity groups, and strangers who are lifesavers and guardians, most families encounter stresses that can range from moderate to traumatic. Recall the mother in Chapter 1 who left El Salvador with her daughter and son with the help of a costly but loyal *coyote*. Terror was part of their mid-migration process: In Mexico, the migrants were attacked by rival smugglers who killed their *coyote* in their presence and held them hostage for nearly 2 weeks in an empty warehouse under squalid conditions and without electricity, potable water, sleeping mats, or means of escape. Only after paying additional ransom was the group escorted to the border. Many of the cases in this book describe the mid-migration journey, but here are just a few examples.

Back to Ian and Santino, who joined a group of immigrants, led by a *coyote*, in December 2019 and arrived in the United States in January of 2020. During their time in Mexico, Santino worried about Ian. He knew about cartels and other outlaws who targeted children, and he was especially troubled because they were alone and could not rely on anyone to help them, even their fellow travelers. He held his son tightly through the entire trip. Each night, Santino paid to stay in rooms with others in the group. The *coyote* would not allow anyone to leave the room. They were transported by a bus and made two stops before arriving at the US–Mexican border. Santino recalled that he was asked to show documentation to the Mexican officials but not the American immigration officers. If you are able to pay off the Mexican officials, Santino said, you can proceed to the border without further questioning. Experiences like theirs were common, yet some mid-migration journeys were frightening, others deadly.

Another boy, Miguel, from Honduras, told of his mid-migration trek across Mexico and to the Rio Grande. Eight years old, Miguel differed from other immigrant children we met. His vocabulary was rich, and he was a natural storyteller, even on a telephone interview. During and after the migration with his mother, they discussed what was happening to them and where they were headed, a seemingly rich communicative relationship. At first, Miguel struggled to recall the details of his experiences for the interviewer, but after a while he was able to place feelings associated with moments in their journey. His voice was soft, in sweet juxtaposition to the harsh realities of his time in detention. He began the telephone conversation with an apology, fearing he would inconvenience or disappoint us, because "I always forget about the time in my life when I first came to the United States." Perhaps it was modesty or innocence speaking because soon we recognized his crisp memory.

Miguel left Honduras with his mother but didn't really grasp what moving to the United States meant; he was young, and the decision was made hurriedly and without much discussion. Miguel recalled how sad and bereft he felt knowing he would have to leave behind his family. The day came quickly when he began the journey north with his mother. They took several buses to get as close to the US border as they could but still had to walk miles to find the spot by the Rio Grande where they would cross. Miguel said they walked carefully to avoid the deep gashes that could be inflicted by sharp thorns of cactus and the painful scrapes of hard limbs of bushes that lived in the dry desert conditions.

Thirty-three-year-old Eduardo's reason for leaving Honduras was a conflict with government officials regarding a property he owned. The endemic corruption and unfairness of those with government authority made Eduardo fearful of being jailed or killed. With the guidance of a few friends who knew the journey, Eduardo set out with his then 13-year-old son, Christopher, and traveled through Guatemala and Mexico. But it was not easy. Christopher suffered repeated bouts of vomiting on the entire passage north, which intensified Eduardo's own suffering. "I don't think I slept during the whole time," Eduardo said. In Matamoros, the Mexican police extorted 10,000 pesos (approximately $470), threatening that if the money was not given, they would be deported back to Honduras.

The mid-migration journey culminates—days, weeks, or months after leaving home—in the threshold labeled *The Crossing*. It is the moment that the migrant passes onto US soil somewhere in Arizona, California, New Mexico, or Texas, the physical and emotional space between the mid-migration journey and just prior to the stage labeled *Detention*. The slope in the second stage of Figure 8.1 reflects the emotional and physical exertion and growing excitement that their journey, or at least the mid-migration stage, is nearing its end. As the United States appears within reach, whether measured in miles, days, or hours, the migrating family approaches it with awe, apprehension, and hope. It is the next trial in the journey, one of extreme risk and certain arrest on the other side, whether it is the Sonoran Desert, the Rio Grande, or an international pedestrian bridge or checkpoint.

The Rio Grande was cold at that time of year and the current sent a shock of fear throughout Ian's body as he inched closer to the frigid and unknown waters. As with other major stops throughout their journey, a fee had to be paid to secure a spot on a boat to cross into the U.S. Santino made the payment. Ahead of them was another group of migrants being herded onto boats that didn't appear safe for the number of people that were boarding. Yet they continued to be pulled across the steady flow of the water. Fear began to overwhelm Ian as his turn came to get on the boat with others. He wondered if he would make it across like everyone else. Without hesitation Santino wrapped his arms around Ian and shielded his view from the treacherous Rio Grande. Hunched over and unsure of what was happening, Ian buried his face into his father's body, focused on the secure warmth of his father's protection, until they reach the U.S. side.

Young Miguel and his mother made it across the Rio Grande like so many others but with their own unique experience.

He saw people crossing, swimming, or using their own flotation devices. Miguel told of a mix of emotions when he stood at the riverbank, one was fear so overpowering that he felt a choking sensation. He imagined crocodiles in the river. There was no time to think, he had to enter the river. Others told him to leave behind the things he was carrying. "They would do no good and only make crossing harder," they said. It was indelibly one of the hardest moments in the long walk with his mother. He would have to toss aside his backpack, with its drawings of little cars, that had been a gift from his grandmother to see him through the trip. It was too significant a memento to discard in a lonely, unnamed place somewhere along the Mexican riverside. It was a precious gift from his grandmother, and he had to let it go. The emotions hurt. Maybe, Miguel thought to assuage himself, some other boy would find it and cross into America with it.

The Crossing is the step that begins the stage labeled *Detention*, which is characterized by arrest and internment. This stage represents the period wherein physical confinement is controlled by Customs and Border Protection (CBP) or Immigration and Customs Enforcement (ICE), and emotional stresses are imposed by detention policies and practices, often overseen by employees of private prison contractors. The stage involves physical indignities, credible fear interviews, loss of autonomy and regulation of one's family, threats, and waiting for the system to grind through its steps to release or deport. It is the stage in which the twin costs of detention trauma—deprivation and threat—are levied.[17] The period in detention, typically days to weeks, sometimes months, begins with holding in *hieleras* or *perreras*, followed in most instances by extended stays in family residential centers where the prospects of deportation, interactions with insensitive guards, and the corrosiveness of incarceration continue the damage of the pre- and mid-migration experiences.[18] It is part of the dehumanization of detention.[19] For many families, the separation of thousands of children from parents during the family separation policy that began in 2017 wreaked additional suffering. Some children were never reunited with parents or other suitable guardians, adding psychiatric insult to the bruising migration.[20]

> When Ian and his father reached the other side, they had no time for a sigh of relief. Border agents advanced towards the group as they reached the U.S. side, and Ian felt sheer panic rising in him as he realized police were nearing. He sat at the front of the boat and was the first to be seen by the oncoming agents. His breathing sped up and he was filled with overwhelming fear. Immediately, CBP officers detained the man who was helping them cross and held families in the group, telling them to relax, that they were now in the U.S. Their group was moved to under a bridge where they stayed, wet and cold. The agents took down names and assigned everyone a number and took away all belongings and valuable items. For over an hour, Santino, Ian, and others waited as the agents collected more groups and filled a bus that would take them to a *hielera*. Santino saw families freezing when they arrived. He and Ian too were very cold after being in the river and stripped of their jackets. They were detained in the *hielera* for three days and moved to a *perrera* after. Neither father nor son got much sleep in the *hielera* and only had pieces of Mylar sheets to warm them. Ian missed his mother. In the *perrera*, they were given dry clothes, a place to sleep, and more food.

Miguel's story after crossing the Rio Grande is similar to that of others who spoke to me and my team. On the other side of the river CBP officers met them and Miguel, his mother, and the others who crossed. They went to a *hielera*.

> Miguel's body shook from fear, he said. The *hielera* was packed with "so many people" besides all the agents in their CBP uniforms. One particularly sadistic agent seemed to take pleasure in telling Miguel that he was going to be separated from his mother, pulling him by his shirt, like a worthless doll, as tears streamed down his face. The guard told Miguel that he would be

placed in a *hielera* just for children. He couldn't eat and became sick from hunger. Food was given but it tasted raw to Miguel.

The *hielera* was cold and crowded with children, and they sat idly with the ceiling lights on day and night. Miguel befriended another child and they kept each other company and supported. An older boy bullied Miguel and hit him, leaving him bruised. Miguel cried at night, not knowing what would happen next, not being able to sleep on the cold, hard floor. He remained in the same dirty clothes of his journey. There was no shower, and he couldn't stomach brushing his teeth in the dirty and smelly bathroom. "I don't think they ever cleaned it," he said. One of the children in the *hielera* told Miguel that he and the others would be sent to a shelter next. With my mom? Alone? Miguel worried and cried.

Miguel was separated and moved to a shelter where he was vaccinated but didn't know why. Miguel thought that everyone else was given only five while he was given eight shots. In the shelter he was able to shower and go to school. A teacher told him that it would be a short stay and he would soon join his mother. A day or so later, after a bumpy bus ride, he was taken with other children to another place with glass walls and chairs where they sat. But it wasn't long before he saw a group of women coming toward them. Miguel first saw his mom through the glass wall and felt relief. They were able to shower and eat food before heading off to their new home in Texas. Unlike other children, Miguel did not spend any time in a detention center.

Eduardo, who fled Honduras with his son Christopher, recalled his disappointment at the US border where he had expected better treatment at the hands of agents who represented a country that followed the rule of law. They crossed the border in May 2018, at a time when the family separation policy was at its peak. Like so many other families, they were separated, split in detention centers in Texas and New Mexico. Eduardo remembers clearly a CBP agent telling Christopher, "You will not be able to see your parents." Eduardo wept as he recalled some of the darkest moments. Surrounded by other fathers who told him stories of their own migration journeys, including getting kidnapped in Mexico, Eduardo was there when a father died by suicide after they were not able to find his child. It was a profoundly troubling moment for Eduardo as he wondered how deep the man's anguish must have been to end his life before knowing exactly what happened to his child. Eduardo's separation from Christopher was the most difficult experience of all, he said, 2 months without any communication.

For some families, the time spent in a detention center can have many serious untoward effects on both children and parents. The caustic prison environment can lead to outcomes like children's regression when they revert to behaviors from an earlier phase of development. It was in full view to me in a visit to the South Texas Family Residential Center, an ICE facility in Dilley, Texas, operated by CoreCivic, a private prison company, where I evaluated a young girl detained with her mother.

> The request for my clinical assessment had come in June 2015 from an attorney. There were disturbing reports that the girl, Erlinda, now 8 years of age, was insisting on being breastfed by her mother, Clara, 24. The two fled Honduras because of physical abuse by Erlinda's father. Clara described an occasion in which he threw a hot iron at her but instead hit Erlinda, leaving a scar. Adding to this, Clara was harassed by *maras* who insisted that she pay them an *impuesto de guerra* (war tax) from the small earnings she made selling candy on the street. She was warned that "only *mara* girlfriends could have blonde hair" and that she should not dye her hair. Clara said that her uncle was killed by the *maras*. Erlinda said she saw "My father yell and hit my mama. He came home drunk. I cried a lot." Asked about why she sucked her mother's breast since she was no longer an infant, Erlinda said that "I feel like a baby when I suck her breast." It did not matter to her what other people thought or said. In the interview, Erlinda would act at one moment like a younger child and at other times assume the behaviors of a child of her chronological age. Other mothers told Clara that her child was too old to be suckling. Clara felt ashamed and ineffectual. In my presence, Clara and Erlinda were very affectionate with each other and Erlinda sat on her mother's lap at one point. Some of the tests I ran showed Erlinda to be perfectionistic with obsessive tendencies. She scored in the clinical range for anxiety, depression, social withdrawal, and physical complaints of psychological origin (i.e., somatization). Most days Erlinda thought of herself as "bad" and preferred to stay away from people or anything that reminded her of what happened to her because the world was "really dangerous."

Regression like Erlinda's is not uncommon when children experience excessive stress and adversity. According to Clara's narrative, her daughter's regressive behavior appeared to be a reaction to the conditions of migration and detention. Erlinda had suffered multiple losses, leaving only her mother as a source of attachment. Complicating this picture was Clara's inability to manage her daughter's behavior. Her own guilt for disrupting Erlinda's life, and her inability to return home for fear of the violence of her husband and the *maras*, had diminished her ability and strength to be firm while empathic with her daughter. Perhaps also Erlinda's regression was a reflection of Clara's own psychological regression to a time when she could protect and care for her daughter as she did when she was a breastfeeding mother. Only through psychotherapeutic exploration could the possibility of a symbiotic regression be confirmed and treated.

The Release is the threshold that ends the third stage. But before the release there is the waiting, growing anticipation and wavering hope that they will be allowed to reunite with families in the United States. The slope in the model, like the stage, represents the uncertainty, the mounting tension of getting out. Release is so close that detainees are, in Behrouz Boochani's words, "Waiting in sweet anticipation/Waiting as we scent the fragrance of freedom."[21] The moment of the release begins the fourth stage of the migration process, *post-detention*. It begins with the family's release or repatriation to their home country, if they have not met the criteria for being allowed to remain in the United States. The immediate post-detention process continues as families travel to their destinations, travel that can take several hours by air or bus or even a few days by bus to a distant point in the United States. The determining factor is what sponsoring families can afford. The release typically includes a notice of when they must return to immigration court for an asylum hearing, often years into the future. The court hearing will determine the family's fate—to stay or be deported. Still, it is more restful and productive than previous stages.

Not shown in the conceptual model but underlying it are two processes—*Settlement* and *Adjustment*—that occur simultaneously and interactively, nurturing each other. By identifying them as two processes, I do not mean to imply that they are separate or sequential. Instead, one cannot exist without the other. Settlement may ease adjustment, and adjustment eases settlement.

Settlement signifies the literal settling down into life in the United States. Settlement is characterized by receiving shelter, usually staying with extended family while the new arrivals get a financial footing. The parent and children may eventually move into their own home and go about the tasks of enrolling children in school, finding employment, and learning the community through shopping and walks around the neighborhood. Finding a church community and engaging with a congregation or parish eases the settlement process. Friendships form and networks build that provide social support and practical tips such as referrals for schools, medical and dental providers, best stores and parks, inexpensive clothes, and all the things needed to live. In time, community integration occurs through social circles and recreational organizations. Parents' employment prospects dictate many of these settlement processes, and through jobs new friendships are forged.

Whereas *settlement* refers to the physical and material aspects of the post-detention stage, *adjustment* refers to the psychological adaptation and functioning of children in their new lives. Adjustment encompasses the families' functioning as a unit and its general health and well-being. Adjusting is a lifelong process that doesn't end, and it involves many psychological and social processes. Belonging is one of them. *Belonging*, as Lauren Gulbas and I defined it in our work on immigrant youth, is the "transformative, meaningful experience through which people derive both their identity and an emotional connectedness to their social and physical world."[22] It is a basic psychological need to have a social place in the world in which one feels like "I fit in. I belong." Belonging is an emotional attachment to a new environment, even one that does not perceive you as legal or in which your legal status is indeterminate. Attachment to places and people is a natural part of being human, the intense connection to the social and physical world. We need social connection; it helps tie us to one another in ways that make us feel safe, accepted, secure, and comfortable. As the asylum-seeking child grows, belonging becomes critical to successfully navigating a complex social world.

Belonging takes on new and maybe painful meanings for children who confront an immigration system that declares their illegality and liminal status and then forces them to wait, suspended and uncertain, in that status for years before a court hearing. Still, living must go on—school, friends, jobs, family. Of this positioning, poet Marcelo Hernandez Castillo, once an undocumented child, says

> When I came undocumented to the U.S., I crossed into a threshold of invisibility. Every act of living became an act of trying to remain visible. I was negotiating a simultaneous absence and presence that was begun by the act of my displacement: *I am trying to dissect the moment of my erasure.* I tried to remain seen for those whom I desired to be seen by, and I wanted to be invisible to everyone else.[23]

Another process of adjustment that the immigrant child will undergo, inescapably, is *acculturation*, that is, the adaptation to the new culture and its environment. Acculturation is the process of acquiring elements from the new culture, the one outside the home and beyond parents' influences. The immigrant child has left a familiar, if feared, life in Central America and is now living in another cultural environment, one which is dominant in the new life. Children learn and adopt—sometimes intentionally, sometimes unconsciously—the new ways, values, languages, social skills, even cognitive styles of the new world as they acculturate. Almost universally, children acculturate at a faster pace than their parents, sometimes causing conflict in the family. The language, behavioral, and value preferences that children make may strike parents as unappealing and at odds with their beliefs and values. Parents may feel that their children are abandoning their cultural heritage, maybe even deserting them. But it does not have to be that way. Acculturation is not a zero-sum game as some parents might fear. As children identify with the new culture, there is not necessarily a corresponding loss of identification with the original culture. It is a highly complex and rich emotional and psychological blending of the old and new that makes them bicultural.[24]

The psychological adjustment of children and parents is a deep one, not easy to access and often as unconscious as it is conscious. And it takes, possibly, a lifetime. Young Miguel's narration about his settlement and adjustment period after migration and detention is instructive.

Miguel feels okay in his new school compared to the one he attended in Honduras but knows he has a lot to learn in English. Still adjusting, Miguel made sure we knew that he is scared of getting on school buses, afraid of being taken away to a detention center or *hielera*. Miguel knows everything that happened to him was a troubling journey and he has the insight to know that his fear of the school bus is connected to the fear of buses that took him to detention. Fortunately, a sympathetic neighbor now drives him to school to lessen his anxiety about riding the bus to school. Miguel has scary dreams at night. He doesn't like Halloween and it makes it harder to sleep. But at the same time, he feels he is a better person after living in the U.S. His family tries to go out as much as they can. Miguel misses his grandparents, although he communicates with them often on his computer. Talking to his grandparents on the computer and going out with his parents makes him feel happy and he feels good knowing they work to send some money back to his family in Honduras. "My strength comes from my mom," he says, grateful that she is always there to support him.

Almost a year since his immigration, Ian showed a keen sense of the world around him and the adjustment to America. Just minutes before his interview, Ian's father, Santino, sent us his son's cell phone number, quite an achievement for a boy who had left everything behind. On the first ring, Ian picked up and spoke confidently, unafraid, and interested in what we were going to ask. Father and son were now settled, and Santino was actively pursuing his asylum claim so as to bring the rest of his family soon. Ian was enjoying school immensely and excited about learning English. He was making friends in school and feeling more integrated with them.

For Eduardo, settlement had been challenging but gratifying. He now worked in Florida as a roofer but drove back and forth to Texas every few weeks to be with Christopher. It was the only work he could find after the coronavirus pandemic struck. Our telephone interview with Eduardo took place late one day, arranged at a time after his dinner. His was the voice of a tired man, someone with hard work and with even heavier responsibilities that he carried alone. Still, Eduardo wanted to participate, and there weren't better times we could connect.

His brother had already come to the United States a few years prior and was able to help Eduardo settle. With the only open job in Florida, Eduardo arranged with his brother to have Christopher live with his uncle and family. Eduardo felt nothing but gratitude for his brother's support in caring for his son. Eduardo and Christopher spent time together when they could, walking, shopping, dining out. Eduardo's focus was on Christopher, and he only slightly mentioned his wife and kids in Honduras, who he also supported financially. Eduardo ended the interview by saying slowly, as if lingering on the thought of the forces that pushed him to where he was now, "I didn't know the suffering we would experience in the States." He was undergoing his adjustment just as Christopher was acculturating to live in America.

Immigrant children in every developmental epoch—early childhood, middle childhood, and adolescence—undergoing each stage of the migration process will experience it differently, see it from their individual vantage points, and interpret it in their own way. Children at all ages face stressors, some helpful for survival and health, some not. Migration and detention—in the case of separations in 2018 and other times—compound the challenges of development during childhood and adolescence. Displacement, suffering, physical exhaustion, mental anguish, and adjustment to lives in new environments are among the many trials. Migrant children who were detained and, sometimes, separated from parents are, despite tenacious parental support and their innate strengths and resiliencies, at heightened risk for psychological distress in comparison to immigrant children who have entered the United States through visas and children in general community settings. Stresses and trauma build up with toxic effects, as I discuss next.

Notes

1. National Immigration Forum, 2019.
2. Lusk & Sanchez Garcia, 2021.
3. It is worth noting that models and frameworks on migration exist. See, as examples, Clauss-Ehlers, 2019; Miller & Rasco, 2004.
4. Ching & Tilley, 1998, p. 122.
5. Bucheli, 2008; Jonas, 2013; Leonard, 2011. This discussion was enriched by a 2022 training guide produced by Oscar F. Rojas Perez, David G. Zelaya, Nancy Herrera, and Manuel Paris for the National Hispanic/Latino Mental Health Technology Transfer Center, Universidad Central del Caribe, Puerto Rico.
6. International Organization for Migration, 2020; World Food Programme, 2017.
7. Geneva Declaration on Armed Violence and Development, 2015; United Nations High Commissioner for Refugees, 2015.
8. World Bank, 2018b.
9. Hiskey et al., 2018.
10. Zechmeister & Azpuru, 2017.
11. Thompson, 2018a.
12. Meyer & Taft-Morales, 2019.
13. Human Rights First, 2020; Sweileh et al., 2018; World Bank, 2018a.
14. Hiskey et al., 2018.
15. Bean et al., 2007.
16. Abrego, 2014, p. 55.
17. McLaughlin et al., 2014.
18. Pierce, 2015.
19. Salerno Valdez et al., 2015.
20. Crea et al., 2018; Ramel et al., 2015.
21. Boochani, 2018, p. 56.
22. Zayas & Gulbas, 2017, p. 2464.
23. Hernandez Castillo, 2020, p. 19, original italics.
24. I provide a full discussion of acculturation in *Latinas Attempting Suicide: When Cultures, Families, and Daughters Collide* (Zayas, 2011).

9

Stress, Trauma, and Children's Development

It became very clear to the most casual observer that detention was harming kids, having immediate effects on their psychological health and well-being. Children who had survived long journeys in relatively good health weren't doing well in detention even when they were held with mothers for 2 to 3 weeks. Parents had run for their lives and their children's lives, and now mothers were distraught by the guilt that they had brought their children from one nightmarish situation to another, despite having no choice. No amount of logical reasoning about their decisions relieved the guilt they felt. Separation anxiety seemed to afflict children of all ages when their mothers were out of sight for quick runs to meetings inside Karnes. Children were losing weight, according to some mothers; and the kids' joie de vivre waned, some reverting to infantile behaviors. Teenagers worried about not seeing family again, about their education, and about the loss of their autonomy, a key part of adolescent development in which they elaborate skills essential for engaging with the world outside the detention. Unlike adolescents in most communities, the teens now had their development put on hold in confinement. One teenager told me that he would rather take his life than return to his hometown and face the gangs that had tried to recruit him. Complicating children's development were the disrupted family roles and dynamics in detention. Parents, the persons who children most need to perceive as strong, protective, and comforting, are reduced to vulnerable and helpless adults. Infants and children who live in prison with their mothers often have more maladaptive social interactions, academic failure, and emotional outcomes.[1]

Entire family systems can show mental health distress and disrupted family patterns, like those in the Zaragoza family that I met in 2014. Josefina and her three daughters had been in Karnes for over 5 months when we met. Josefina was trying very hard to maintain a positive attitude. Her oldest daughter, Bianca, 16, confirmed it by saying, "My mother acts strong so we

Through Iceboxes and Kennels. Luis H. Zayas, Oxford University Press. © Oxford University Press 2023.
DOI: 10.1093/oso/9780197668160.003.0010

can feel better." I met the family twice over the span of a month to evaluate the girls for their attorney.

Bianca described a nightmare that recurred about twice a week in which "I'm walking near my house in El Salvador at nighttime. I sense someone following me. Then someone grabs my shoulder and I wake up." The nightmare came directly from an assault in El Salvador by two drunken gang members. "They followed me and tore off my clothes," she said. "I was violated by their kisses all over my body." Another intrusive memory came from a home invasion by some men who put a gun to her mother's head. Bianca wanted closure from the nightmares and memories, but they persisted. Threats from detention guards that the sisters would be separated from their mother added to their pain. There was no separation policy at the time; it was just the cruelty of insensitive guards. On a measure of traumatic symptoms, Bianca scored in the clinically significant range on both anxiety and post-traumatic stress. More importantly, her scores at the second evaluation had jumped more than 30 percentage points from the first administration of the instrument.[2] Similarly, Bianca scored in the clinical range on a measure of depression the second time she completed it.[3] Both instruments showed a worsening in her mental health. Bianca's affect was exceptionally flat and her mood depressed. It was a worrisome trend; the detention at Karnes was causing deterioration of her mental state. She wanted to be released but not without her mother.

Her sister, Alma, the second child in birth order, was a month shy of turning 14. Alma was petite and seemed to shrink and not be noticed. The constant smile on her face, to please and avoid conflict, was a poor attempt to disguise her fear. The uncertainty about her mother's status—because her mother's credible fear interview had been denied—weighed heavily on her. I had to shorten the interview with Alma to avoid any harm but not before she completed the same measures of depression and trauma that Bianca had also completed. Her scores on depression were unremarkable except that they rose from the first administration to the second. In the measure of post-traumatic stress, there were signs of mild dissociation, a mental process in which the person disconnects from the world around them.

The youngest sister, Fátima, 11, also kept a smile that covered the fear that lurked behind it. The smile turned quickly to tears when I asked about her stay at Karnes. Fátima's scores on anxiety and post-traumatic stress symptoms were nearly three times higher in the second administration than in the first. Fátima's dissociation score was higher than her sister's, indicating that she too dissociated as a way of coping in the prison environment.

Detention was taking a toll on the three sisters and mother who carried classic signs of trauma: recurrent and distressing memories, nightmares, dissociative reactions, prolonged psychological distress, avoidance of people or other reminders of the trauma, intrusive and distressing thoughts, and memory lapses. No one was spared in this family. To what extent were the clinical conditions supported or sustained by other family members? We may never know, but in a family system no one suffers alone. The entire system suffers.

Detention is a major childhood stressor, even when the period of detention is brief.[4] Two distinct and destructive elements exist in detention—deprivation and threat—that create the conditions for psychological, emotional, and behavioral disorders.[5] *Deprivation* robs children of the typical, expected, and developmentally appropriate interaction with a wide and complex world, such as riding bikes to school, making change at the candy store, interacting with teachers and coaches with different personalities, and making and losing friends on the playground and at school. *Threat* represents the sense of an immediate or ongoing menace to the child's physical integrity and psychological security. Deprivation and threat bring about the developmental arrests, regression, and psychological reactions described earlier.

Even threats and deprivation that might seem insignificant bring with them undue strain. This was shockingly revealed to the world in November 2016 when the GEO Group (GEO) at Karnes detention center banned the use of crayons by children.[6] It was a cruel and petty act by a $2 billion global security and private prison company that had made over $60 million operating Karnes. GEO complained that children playing with crayons in the waiting room had caused "property damage" in the form of crayon markings on tables when kids went off the paper or book they were marking. The damage was said to have occurred while mothers were meeting with their lawyers in private rooms. Immigration and Customs Enforcement (ICE) staff blamed staff and volunteers from non-profit organizations that brought the crayons and coloring books for children. What's more, the center would now restrict children to a 9-foot-by-5-foot rug in the visitation room on which they could play with toys, and they were not permitted to take toys off the rug or into meeting rooms with their parents. Every parent of a toddler and preschooler knows that you can't confine them to such a small space.

Another group at high risk in detention is children with preexisting illnesses or disabilities. Like Romeo, the nearly blind teenager in Chapter 2, disabilities are not a direct result of migration or detention but can be exacerbated by them. Some disabilities are easy to spot, such as blindness and hearing impairments, Down syndrome, cerebral palsy, and other physical debilities acquired at birth or through an illness or accident, such as paraplegia. Other disabilities may not be evident at first glance, such as asthma and other respiratory disorders, diabetes, or congenital heart anomalies. Some disabilities take more time to identify, such as intellectual-cognitive limitations that may include dyslexia or below-average intelligence, reading, and speech and language processing. Intellectual and cognitive disabilities are conditions that can throw into question the person's capacity to answer questions posed in credible fear interviews or medical encounters. This is what I encountered in an evaluation of a teenager for his asylum case.

Matías was a 16-year-old Salvadoran male who entered the United States with his mother in May 2016. He grew up on a small farm where he was expected to help his mother and siblings with chores. Matías reported that he was threatened with death by the *maras* if he did not join them, but he did not tell his mother because he did not want to worry her. In our interaction, Matías engaged quickly. He had good short- and long-term memory, and his mood and affect were appropriate to the situation. There were no signs of emotional problems. He did, however, show signs of problems in visual–motor integration. Matías held the pencil in his left (dominant) hand but did not demonstrate much skill with it. His reproductions of unique figures that I presented were scattered or crowded, and some of the figures did not resemble the figures placed before him. Matías worked slowly, bent over with his face about 7 to 8 inches from the table. In a test of concentration and capacity to follow instructions, he showed a tendency to be impulsive. Matías had clinically significant levels of generalized anxiety and hyperarousal and showed evidence of post-traumatic stress such as intrusive thoughts, sensations, and nightmares. While some scores indicated sadness, unhappiness, and loneliness, his presentation did not show signs of chronic or short-term depression. Matías's exceedingly high scores on sexual distress suggested that he may have been the victim of sexual abuse, something to which persons with intellectual limitations are susceptible. Matías had a difficult time with questions that required the application of metaphors or abstract thinking, such as the meaning of "feeling dirty inside." His thinking tended to be concrete. Overall, the picture was of a moderate level of intellectual-cognitive limitations that could have been due to any number of things, such as inadequate environmental stimulation (e.g., low level of educational attainment, impoverished home and social interaction), neurocognitive deficits of the brain (e.g., congenital, exposure to toxins such as lead or mercury), or even traumatic brain injury sustained through injury or abuse.

This clinical impression took me back to an ICE report I had seen in his record that doubted Matías's truthfulness and implied that he was evasive in answering questions posed by the immigration officer. Based on my interview and tests, it seemed that Matías may not have understood fully the questions but tried to answer them truthfully and earnestly. For example, the immigration officer asked Matías, "If you are sent back to your country, do you fear that you will be persecuted or tortured?" Matías's response was one that the immigration officer doubted. Given my findings, though, I wondered if Matías understood the term *persecuted* and maybe even the word *tortured*. Both are words that an elementary or middle school student might comprehend, assuming a child of average intelligence and comparatively good education. (Matías said he attended school until the age of 11, which may have translated to about 5 years of schooling and probably of low quality.) Yet Matías told me he left school because he had been threatened and harassed (i.e., persecuted) by the *maras*. He knew they would beat (i.e., torture) him or, worse, kill him if he had stayed or was sent back. Thus, it appeared that Matías understood the *experience* of persecution and torture but not the *words*. Likewise, compound questions were confusing to him and were probably amplified by the anxiety-producing, high-stakes interview. If Matías were to complete a full neuropsychological evaluation in a supportive and calm setting, we would get a better picture of the extent of his limitations. My report to his attorney and immigration court recommended that Matías be interviewed again by immigration officials while taking into account his intellectual-cognitive capacity. Furthermore, I recommended that Matías be released to his father in Miami, Florida, where he could receive educational services for his possible disability and mental health therapy for his post-traumatic stress symptoms. Matías had come this far in life. His intellectual, cognitive, or perceptual limitations were balanced by strengths in social skills, personality, and a willingness to work that would serve him well in work and friendships. Matías's future, if given a chance, could be a bright one.

The family separation policy imposed by Donald Trump in 2017 and 2018 had its own particular contribution to the experience of deprivation and threat. Under family separation, the sure signs of the psychological damage to children—not to mention the anguish and damage to their parents' own mental health—were appearing everywhere. Once outgoing kids were quiet and unresponsive or refused to eat or bathe. Panic attacks were reported, sometimes so intense that children had to be hospitalized. Some showed moments of fugue-like states, out of touch with their sur- roundings, even seeming to process information more slowly than their parents remembered. Nightmares and night terrors were symptoms of trau-matic separations. Children became inhibited, withdrawn, irritable, sad, and fearful. Developmental trajectories were thrown into chaos, battering and dysregulating children's stress response systems. Diagnosable mental illnesses like separation anxiety, generalized and social anxiety, depression, and reactive attachment problems were correlated to the reign of terror on families.[7] To be separated from their parents, children were tricked into eating a treat or playing with other kids, only to return to find their parents missing. Devastated, kids felt that parents had abandoned them willfully or that they were being punished for some misdeed. On top of the already fragile psychological conditions of separated children, there was restrictive detention that hastened the damage to children's psyches.[8] In some cases, separated children in detention were not allowed to touch each other, and staff members were prohibited from touching children under the age of 4, a developmental epoch when physical affection from primary caregivers is vital.[9] It came as no surprise when the inspector general for the Department of Health and Human Services issued a report in September 2019 that said "intense trauma" was common among children in the Office of Refugee Resettlement facilities but especially acute in children who had been "unex-pectedly separated from a parent."[10] They were riddled with "fear, feelings of abandonment and post-traumatic stress." The children cried desolately from acute grief. These were signs of impaired attachment and bonding, incipient mental disorders, and impediments in normal development; and whether the symptoms were transitory or permanent, they were the vestiges of mal-treatment at the hands of the government. Family separation leaves no one in the family untouched; children, siblings, and parents suffer alike.[11]

Tragic family memories and regrets live on, passed from one generation to the next—referred to as *intergenerational trauma* or *historical trauma*.[12] The passing of trauma from parent to child is unintentional and often outside of the conscious awareness of the parent. The transmission process results in disrupted interpersonal attachments, inadequate coping abilities, and family interactions that may be dysfunctional. Intergenerational transmission, at its essence, affects those closest to the individual, leaving vestiges of the past that cannot be shed.[13] It ripples across generations, and the accumulation is seen in how the behaviors and emotions are displayed by children and the children's offspring. Individuals with problems in behavioral and emotional self-regulation that stem from a history of childhood stress and trauma become parents, and their struggles are transmitted to their children who are the observers and recipients of their parenting.[14] Even when mothers suffer trauma before their children are born, the impact on their offspring is seen in children's abilities to, say, modulate their responses to a frightening moment even under safe conditions (such as the presence of an adult or a barrier between them and the fear-inducing stimulus).[15] And these responses are independent of whether their children have had their own traumatic experiences or not. The mechanisms of transmission remain unclear, but some of the maternal signals may come behaviorally and unconsciously.[16] It may take a combination of individual and family therapy to end the transmission cycle in a family.

One way to understand how traumatic loss, especially sudden, inexplicable, and extended separation, damages young children, we have to look at the most crucial and fragile of human relationships—the parent–child bond.[17] When nurtured, supported, and sustained, the parent–child relationship confers long-term health and mental health benefits to children, shaping the patterns for future relationships and educational and occupational performance. In infancy and toddlerhood, especially during the first 2 years, the need for attachment and the safety and nurturance of a "secure base"—mommy, usually—is at its peak. With sustained sensitive and responsive parenting, infants and children will develop secure attachments to their primary caregivers. It is through this essential, universal human connection with parents that infants and children learn to modulate, control, and regulate their emotions. The consistent, predictable presence of a parent instills in the child an expectation that comfort will come soon. Witness in everyday life how children run to their parents' arms after a separation of a few hours. When that relational bond is suddenly ruptured—as it was for many children by the family separation policy of 2017, 2018, and well into 2019—insecurity about their parents' loyalty follows. Separation anxiety is the best-known response after a breach of the parent–child bond. The separation is so intolerable that children worry, cry, behave oddly, regress, and, in rare cases, lose functional abilities, such as bladder and bowel control. A recollection by research assistant Jamie Turcios-Villalta of an event in her workplace during the zero tolerance policy period is illustrative.

In the spring and summer of 2018, as the Zero Tolerance Policy and practice of family separations grew, I interned with the [Refugee and Immigration Center for Education and Legal Services] team at the Karnes Detention Center, putting in a few days a week. While there, I was a witness to the immediate repercussions of separation and detention on immigrant children and parents.

At the beginning of the summer, Karnes held only mothers and children. Within a few weeks, I settled into the rhythm of the work and the daily routine. Entering the facility on my scheduled days, my every move was watched vigilantly by the GEO employees. At each visit, we would put our cell phones in the locker, present our identification and special access form to the front desk, and go through a metal detector. Everything was scanned and searched to ensure we had no recorders or other restricted items. My nerves were always on edge during this process but would settle once we entered the visitation room, the only room we were permitted to be in within the entire facility. Families, all in the same clothing, a sweater, blue jeans, and white sneakers, would often be lined up, already waiting for us. I would set up the station before we would begin our day of preparing families for their credible fear interviews, intakes, and *charlas* [talks]. They were busy days, and we tried our best to meet with as many families as possible.

But even that familiar routine changed. Without announcement, mothers and children were transferred from Karnes to other facilities in the middle of the night. There were no families to work with for a few days as news of family separations spread across the nation. Karnes was later designated as one of the reunification facilities for separated families. Slowly, fathers and their sons filled the center. The work picked up again, but with fathers instead of mothers. The majority of the fathers had been held in adult detention centers or jails for a month or longer with little or no information as to where their children had been taken. Children were put in shelters around the country with almost no contact with their fathers. The separation ate away at the fathers. Many of them told of the hopelessness they felt, not knowing if they would see their children again or if they would ever be released. Others shared the pain and shame of being shackled while detained. One man said, "Nunca he hecho nada malo en mi vida. No soy un criminal." ["I've never done anything wrong in my life. I am not a criminal."] They now had to rebuild relationships with their children while fighting to stay in the country.

One day in July of 2018, as I completed paperwork, I watched a 6-year-old boy doing what any child his age does in a play area. His father was escorted to meet with an attorney in a room about six feet away from the child. The child looked up and, not seeing his father, began to cry uncontrollably. Between his sobs and catching his breath, the boy called for his "papá." Moved by his passionate wails, I hugged the child and took his hand to lead him to his father. Since their separation and reunification, the father said, the child panicked when he was out of his son's sight. I know children reacted differently to their parents' absence, although most 6-year-olds can tolerate the separation. But the boy's frantic, disconsolate lamentation, from deep down, was unlike any I had ever heard from a child. He had endured such a traumatic separation that it seemed it could never be righted.

Children who have been separated may ask "Why did you leave me?"—not understanding that the might and reach of the US government were far greater than the power that their parents wielded.[18] The separations leave children doubting their parents' love and devotion. They may avoid or resist reconnecting with parents from anger and fear of further rejection. The avoidant-resistant child rebuffs the parents, a "you-rejected-me-now-I'll-reject-you" dynamic. Avoidance reduces the chance of conflict and the possibility of any further repudiation by parents. Videos and reports that were broadcast at the time of reunification of separated children in the summer of 2018 revealed children's damaged bonds and impaired behaviors. One video aired in July 2018 by the American Civil Liberties Union caught the heart-wrenching scene of a Honduran mother reuniting with her son after months of separation.[19] She and her husband fled gang violence in Honduras and sought asylum with their two children separately: the father with their 3-year-old son in April and the mother with her 5-month-old daughter in May. Caught by immigration officials, the father was told to sign documents in front of an immigration judge; but when he returned, his son had been sent to another facility. The boy was placed in a foster children's facility in Grand Rapids, Michigan. After 3 months, the video records the moment that the mother is seeing her son for the first time.

"My love," the mother cries at the start of the 32-second video segment, trying to hug and be hugged by her son. The boy is seen trying to get out of her hold, looking away, arms dangling at his side with no seeming effort to reciprocate her hug, and his body leaning away from hers. His face is expressionless, neither distressed nor happy, flat, maybe a little bewildered. He was avoiding contact.

"I am your mami, papi. I am your mami," she repeats, as the boy pulls away and breaks free of her hold. He sits before her, appearing confused momentarily. "What's wrong with my son?" she asks her husband, who is holding the daughter he has not seen in months. As the mother seeks her husband's answer and comfort, the boy crawls toward his father and between his father's legs, away from both parents. He stops to look back with the same dazed look. When his mother, still sobbing, approaches him he continues to crawl toward an exit door.

"What happened?" the mother asks no one in particular. "Papi, come with me," she tells her son, but he keeps crawling away from her. "My son is traumatized," she weeps. "My son is traumatized."

The child who at reunion is ambivalent doubts the parent's love and faithfulness but does not discard it the way the avoidant child does. The ambivalent-resistant child fears another abandonment and looks for minute signs of rejection or just the hint or perception of rejection by the parent. At times, ambivalent-resistant children engage in positive interaction with parents but can quickly become angry and retreat for self-protection. Even when parents respond, ambivalent children are not comforted. A video documentary produced by *The Atlantic* titled "The Separated: Children at the Border" has a vivid example of this ambivalent attachment reaction.[20] The boy, perhaps 4 years old, and his mother are seen in a shelter after being reunified, seeming to be mending their relationship in the wake of forced separation. But in one scene their dialogue reveals the boy's underlying anger, resistance, and ambivalence. The boy is crying on a bed, his mother sits on the bed to comfort him.

SON: I want to go to jail. (Cries, hands over his eyes.)

MOTHER: You want to go there?

SON: You don't love me. (Crying, hands covering his eyes.)

MOTHER: Who told you I don't love you?

SON: You're not my mother anymore. (Crying inconsolably with hands covering his eyes, and his mother calling out his name several times.)

MOTHER: (Voiceover, spoken sadly) The separation was so long, my son has changed so much. With so much trauma. "I don't want to be your son. I'm not your son," he said.

For this young boy, bedtime may have been fraught with fears, anxiety, and complex attachment reactions. He and his mother at times appear to have an intact relationship. But as the documentary progresses, it seems that the boy is still confused about why he was separated from his mother and why she didn't do something to prevent it, protect him. Settling time in the evening as bedtime approaches is where his doubts surface and reveal the still lingering misgivings about his mother's devotion. For some reason, as yet unknown, the vulnerability associated with bedtime seems to be a trigger for his psychological reaction. For the mother, this seems particularly perplexing as during other times of the day their relationship seems in many ways to be integral but still mending. To her credit, the mother speaks to him soothingly. What meaning does sleep or bedtime have for him? What might have happened at night during the time he was somewhere else in the care of strangers? How did sleep or bedtime become so emotionally loaded that he strikes out in sudden anger and denunciation of his mother and her affection after showing what appears to be a normal attachment earlier in the day?[21] A clinician working with this boy and his mother would explore the connection, if any, to bedtime and the origins of his reaction. In time, he may recall and be able to vocalize the things that he underwent while separated from his mother. The mother's words and tone are warm and soothing to the child, which will benefit them both. Any clinician who works with them will need to help the boy unearth the past and process it emotionally and cognitively. The clinician will need to support the mother in responding to the boy's feelings in a way that repairs the attachment relationship, rather than further stresses it.

Not all kids were reacting avoidantly and ambivalently. They were showing their reactions to the traumatic separation in other ways. A 5-year-old Brazilian boy, separated from his mother for 50 days, acted differently; he was not the son she remembered.[22] Like the avoidant boy at the Houston airport, the Brazilian boy stood frozen, aloof as his mother hugged him and cried. Once settled in their new American home, the boy pleaded to be breastfed or hid behind a sofa when people visited or became highly anxious when his mother left his sight to go to another room. These were familiar indicators of regression, fear, and separation anxiety. Like other children I met in my work who had witnessed their parents' arrest, many became frightened at the sight of police in uniforms.

Children incorporate their experiences of migration, detention, and separations in their drawings. They will also incorporate lived experiences in their play, such as the 3-year-old who pretended to handcuff and vaccinate those around him after reunification with his mother. I encountered such a moment while visiting Purdue University's campus in Fort Wayne, Indiana, in September 2018. There a local preschool teacher told me of a group of her students playing leapfrog. What caught her eye was that they were all wearing hoodies with the hoods covering their heads and their faces barely visible. She asked why they were playing leapfrog in their hoodies. "That way *la migra* can't see us," the children replied. Playing at handcuffing, vaccinating, and leapfrogging with hoodies as disguises helped them make sense of the scary things they didn't fully understand.

One observant father who had fled Honduras with his 3-year-old son, leaving behind a wife and daughter, told NBC News of his son's reaction to reunifying after 2 months apart.[23]

The only thing that I knew is that he was in a shelter in Arizona, nothing else. I would lose my appetite when I was thinking about him. I would go to bed thinking about him. I would stay up until dawn and I wouldn't sleep. I felt desperate not having any news about him. Not being able to caress him. Kids need love from their parents.

They gave me one video call when I was detained. He wouldn't talk to me. I would talk to him and he would only stare at me. It's like he felt resentment towards me. My own son wouldn't talk to me or smile. It felt horrible. He would look at me as if I wasn't his father. He must think that I abandoned him. He must think it's my fault. When I was reunited with my son, he would only look at me and cry. He wouldn't talk to me. He was sad. He probably thought I had abandoned him. It has been difficult to gain his trust like before. I was so happy to have my son with me. I was happy to hold him in my arms again like I carried him when he was born.

I came here because we were in danger. There's no safety back home. I wanted a future for my son. My family back home is afraid to be in Honduras. But they're happy because my son and I are reunited again. I worry about the trauma that this separation could cause. I worry about how this will affect my son's growth. I pray to God that I'm able to stay here with my son. I hope to be able to enroll him in school so that he can have a better future.

The quality of these early separations and their repair, if they happen, will be evident in how individuals regulate and control negative emotions across life.

Secure adults manage the inevitable distresses in life and seek people around them who can acknowledge their distress and offer comfort and support. They feel secure in themselves and possess constructive coping strategies. Adults whose early-life disruptions are never resolved or treated will generally be more anxious in the face of challenges. They may avoid others out of a perception that people cannot be trusted to give love. In their insecurity, these individuals may avoid acknowledging that they are in distress, acting in isolation from others to control and reduce negative affect when it arises. They may be more anxious than is normal, and they may tend toward avoidant coping strategies, hypervigilant to the smallest indications that a personal relationship might be lost or that they might be abandoned.

Stress is normal and essential. It helps us develop our coping abilities. Tolerable stress may come from unpleasant moments of embarrassment, a difficult test, or a tense interpersonal exchange at work. A higher level of stress comes from the death of a parent or friend or a severe injury requiring hospitalization or surgery but can be dealt with in time. Typically, we recover from these painful moments, although they are not forgotten. When children face stress, the best conditions are to have supportive, caring adults nearby to help.[24] But the adults must have acquired the capacity to manage their stress responses to comfort the child and model self-regulation.

While there are no studies to my knowledge comparing children in detention who were not separated from their parents to those in detention who were separated from their parents, we can safely assume that the group that was separated will have experienced stress levels far beyond what is positive and tolerable.[25] The levels of stress experienced by the separated children may be similar to other well-known sources of toxic stress, such as physical, sexual, and psychological abuse; family violence; parental mental illness; drug and alcohol abuse in the family; and chronic neglect.[26]

The words *stress* and *trauma* appear extensively in this book. In everyday parlance, the two words appear to be used interchangeably. We might even stretch to say that the word *trauma* seems to have eclipsed the use of the word *stress*. In common language, the overlap may not matter that much. But in clinical and research language they must be used carefully, precisely. Neuroscientists Gal Richter-Levin at the University of Haifa and Carmen Sandi at the Swiss Federal Institute of Technology in Lausanne make a similar argument about distinguishing between stressful experiences and traumatic experiences. Richter-Levin and Sandi write that trauma is

An experience that activates a robust emotional response, which not only acutely changes the choice of a behavioral response, but also induces lasting alterations that would change the response of the individual to a variety of future experiences. Critically, those alterations are pathological, compromising functional capacity, i.e., the ability of the individual to cope later on with daily challenges. . . . People who have undergone a severe experience, may change their behavior in significant ways and, if examined, will exhibit neuronal alterations at different levels of analysis. Yet many of them will continue with what is considered regular daily life and a satisfactory level of day-to-day functional capacity. What this means is that these people do not suffer from a pathology. Somehow, they have managed to cope with the experience. It is, therefore, important to clearly distinguish these individuals' experiences from that of others, who, as a result of being exposed to a similar experience, have lost a significant part of their previous neurobehavioral functional capacities.[27]

Richter-Levin and Sandi conclude that the neural mechanisms associated with trauma-related psychopathology are different from the neural mechanisms triggered by stressful experiences that do not lead to trauma-related psychopathology. Like Richter-Levin and Sandi, I have come to see that in common usage by clinicians, students, and the public the terms *stress* and *trauma* are treated as about the same and that the word *trauma* is applied when *stress* is more correct or descriptive. One could say that "stress is living"; that is, everyday life includes upsetting incidents that are thrown at us and that temporarily dislocate our emotional and psychological balance. The American Psychological Association defines stress as a "pattern of specific and nonspecific responses an organism makes to stimulus events that disturb its equilibrium and tax or exceed its ability to cope."[28] We could say correspondingly that traumatic experiences, as defined by Richter-Levin and Sandi, are always stressful but that stressors are not always traumatic.[29] It means, therefore, that a determination of what is stressful and what is traumatic must be made carefully, using three parameters that Richter-Levin and Sandi identify: (1) the type and degree of stress, (2) the individual's physiology, and (3) the person's subjective perception of the stressor.[30] In effect, the same stressful event will affect people differently because stressful experiences are defined not solely by the conditions of the stress or the number of times it happens but also by the person's physical constitution and how the individual evaluates them subjectively (which involves a cognitive and emotional operation). One person might show moderate irritation to an event that another person finds immobilizing. For this reason, clinicians and researchers need to be acutely aware of the differences between stress and trauma.

Outward indicators of distress are only one part of the problems of children overstressed by migrations, detention, and sudden separation. In children's development, there are "sensitive periods" when the brain is growing and wiring itself. These sensitive periods are then subject to the profound influence exerted by external events in a child's environment. Brain growth and functioning are affected, and consequently so is behavior. In essence, these periods are acutely sensitive to the external experiences and "tell" the neural circuits how to handle the incoming information to make it adaptive for the child.[31] While the most sensitive periods of brain growth are during the first few years of life, it continues throughout childhood. There is emerging evidence that suggests that at about age 10 there is a developmental shift in the underlying brain circuits that may contribute to vulnerability because that age is associated with the greatest recall of earlier trauma.[32] Other research shows that the accumulation of stresses and trauma before the age of 13 increases the likelihood of psychological distress in adulthood.[33] Hormonal changes of puberty may form the trajectories toward risk or resilience. The research supports the understanding of childhood and adolescence as the seedbed for later psychological problems.

Like the proverbial tip of the iceberg, what is happening underneath— the child's brain—is important in the long run because as adversity persists the likelihood of impediments in brain growth and neural development increases.[34] The unrelenting physical and mental stress of facing unceasing and unyielding fear, violence, worry, anxiety, alertness and hypervigilance, and disturbed sleep and rest weakens the body. The body's protective system can be damaged from operating in overdrive for too long, too intensely, and not given a chance to slow down, reset, and restore. That protective system is known as the *hypothalamic–pituitary–adrenal (HPA) axis*, which is activated when the individual is facing a stressful moment, such as a threat or a fear. The HPA axis acts in a coordinated way to increase our alertness, heart rate, blood pressure, concentration, perspiration, and muscular reactions, including the sensation of dry mouth and trembling. Within seconds of a stressful incident, the glands secrete hormones (norepinephrine, adrenalin, and cortisol, which raises the glucose in the bloodstream to give the extra energy to deal with the stress). When the stress is passed, the body returns to a more restful state.

When the HPA axis is stimulated too much too often it is weakened and breaks down. Too much stress and depletion of cortisol and other hormones suppress our immune system and its capacity to fight off infections and illnesses. Memory and cognitive abilities are affected, and high cortisol levels over time can lead to mood disorders. The implacable exhaustion of the stress response system changes the brain's structure, such as wiring circuits in the brain and hormonal systems in abnormal ways that affect the structure and functioning of brain regions known to be essential for self-regulation and other behaviors. Brain regions associated with reasoning, planning, and behavioral self-control and involved in combating fear and anxiety are left with fewer neural connections. The impact on the wiring and architecture leads to poor control over one's stress response systems, making the child overly reactive or slow to calm themselves. Children may feel threatened by or respond impulsively to situations where no real threat exists, such as seeing anger or hostility in a facial expression that is actually neutral; or they may remain excessively anxious long after a threat has passed.[35] Cognitive and behavioral functioning, such as thinking, intellectual abilities, self-regulation, judgment, trust, and social interaction, are diminished, sometimes permanently. Untreated consequences of stress in early life affect adulthood, leaving protective functions of the body open to chronic illnesses such as diabetes, obesity, and other cardiovascular disorders; depression and mental illness; drug use and addiction; and early mortality.[36] Cumulatively, detention and separation, and other insults to the body and mind, lead children and adults to suffer from recurrent and distressing nightmares and night terrors, depression and anxiety, dissociative reactions, hopelessness and suicidal thinking, and post-traumatic stress disorders.

Instead of building a big, beautiful wall running the 1,954-mile length of the US–Mexican border, Trump built a policy wall that was "not made of steel and concrete, but of terror."[37] Once more, Jamie Turcios-Villalta provides a first-hand account of the effects of family separation at the hands of the Trump administration in the summer of 2018.

My job that day was to prepare a fifteen-year-old boy and his father for their credible fear interview. It entailed explaining to them the asylum process and criteria, and the types of questions they would be asked in the credible fear interview. The father was only in his mid-thirties with a tired body and exhausted face from the struggles of prolonged detention. He wore an oversized navy sweater that hid his small frame. He later explained that he had lost a lot of weight in the last few months. The boy resembled his father, they shared the same brown almond-shaped eyes and dark black hair. Sadness could be seen in both their eyes. I asked if they'd been in touch with their family in Guatemala. Both of them shook their heads with obvious emotional pain. No, they had not been able to reach their family in over two months. No one knew whether they had made it to the U.S. or not, and no one in the family knew that they had been separated. Father and son had no money to make an international call and would have to wait until they were released to communicate with their family.

I asked the father if he had a number to reach his wife. The father pulled out a piece of scrap paper from his jean pocket and handed it to me. I ironed out the very worn and wrinkled scrap to make out the number written on it. I dialed the number on the conference telephone and explained that they had only a few minutes to speak with the family. Etched in my memory was the sight of them holding their breath as the phone rang. It took several rings to connect; they seemed to lose hope as each ring passed. At the last, someone picked up.

"*Alo*," a woman's voice said, hesitantly. It was the mother. Her voice filled the room and father and son's eyes opened widely.

"*¡Somos nosotros! ¡Somos nosotros!*" ["It's us! It's us!"] father and son nearly yelled into the speakerphone joyfully, talking over one another. The moment was too big to hold back their tears. I could hear the mother cry on the other end. They became wholly absorbed in the sound of the mother's voice and words. And I became acutely aware that I was an outsider in a poignant and intimate moment in this family's suffering and joyful reunion. As I left the room, the father was recounting their saga and his son was cutting in with details.

This brief moment of reunion, however short, brought some normalcy and reprieve from the toxic stress father and son had already experienced. If only every story of detention could hold a moment like this—a beacon in the middle of darkness.

Notes

1. Byrne et al., 2012; Murray & Farrington, 2005; Nesmith & Ruhland, 2008.
2. Briere, 1996.
3. Kovacs, 2011.
4. Abram et al., 2014; Dallaire et al., 2014; Foster & Hagan, 2013.

5. American Psychiatric Association, 2013.
6. Buch, 2016; Laughland, 2016.
7. American Psychiatric Association, 2013.
8. McLaughlin et al., 2014.
9. Jordan, 2018b.
10. US Department of Health and Human Services, Office of Inspector General, 2019b.
11. Linton et al., 2017; Teicher, 2018.
12. Bakó & Zano, 2020; O'Neill et al., 2018.
13. Bar-On, 1996; O'Neill et al., 2018.
14. Babineau et al., 2022.
15. Stenson et al., 2021.
16. Bosquet Enlow et al., 2017; Dubowitz et al., 2001; Jovanovic et al., 2011.
17. The literature on attachment theory and research is vast. For a useful summary, see Zeanah et al., 2011.
18. Jordan, 2018a.
19. Pelley, 2019; Valdes & Mejia, 2018.
20. *Atlantic*, 2018.
21. I am grateful to Rob Hasson of Providence College for the insight and editorial suggestion on the boy's emotional reaction at bedtime.
22. Jordan, 2018b; Zayas, 2015.
23. NBC News, 2018.
24. National Scientific Council on the Developing Child, 2014.
25. Beal, 2019; Bucci et al., 2016.
26. Shonkoff et al., 2009.
27. Richter-Levin & Sandi, 2021, p. 386.
28. Gerrig & Zimbardo, 2002.
29. Shalev, 2009.
30. Creamer et al., 2005; Huzard et al., 2019.
31. Stevens et al., 2018; Teicher et al., 2016.
32. Pechtel et al., 2014.
33. Björkenstam et al., 2015.
34. McLaughlin et al., 2014.
35. Loman & Gunnar, 2010; Lupien et al., 2009; National Scientific Council on the Developing Child, 2014.
36. Chapman et al., 2007; Evans & Kim, 2013; Finkelhor et al., 2013; Fuemmeler et al., 2009; Hardcastle et al., 2018; Vaughn et al., 2017.
37. Soboroff, 2020, p. 76.

10

I Need to Tell My Story, Too [*]

In the study of migrant families who had spent time in detention, we heard of near-drownings, violence, mistrust, deprivation, sleeplessness, exposure, hunger, threats, and extortion. But we also heard of kindness, generosity, loyalty, compassion, and unnamed heroes. The resolve, perseverance, and unity of the children and their parents and siblings in our study were awe-inspiring despite crippling fear. In some families, one member seemed to be the heroic figure—whether a child or a parent. In other families, each member played a role in survival. What would these experiences do to children's and parents' mental health? In the long run, we will find out. But in the moment of crisis, individuals revealed strengths like those of Atlas in Greek mythology, for they too felt like they had to hold up the sky for eternity, or at least for their families.

We met them at the Migrant Resource Center in San Antonio, people who had faced down extreme adversity. In each stage of the migration, their minds, bodies, and spirits confronted obstacles. Along each stage of their migration, families had destinations and goals. The first was to get out of the danger they were facing at home, making the border with the next country a destination. Traversing Mexico was a series of destinations, each a bit closer to the US–Mexican border. The next destination was the border itself and safety on the US side. Once apprehended, they were held in custody for days, weeks, or months. During the waiting period, release was their next goal. The migrant resource center was a layover after release from Immigration and Customs Enforcement (ICE) or Customs and Border Protection custody. Nearly every day that summer, we saw government buses drop families off on a street corner between the bus depot and the resource center. Children and mothers eagerly entered the bus station knowing that they were that much closer to joining family members somewhere in the United States. Each had a story of joys and sorrows, some tragic. Perhaps it's human nature that most

[*] Case profile contributed by Tatiana Londoño.

Through Iceboxes and Kennels. Luis H. Zayas, Oxford University Press. © Oxford University Press 2023.
DOI: 10.1093/oso/9780197668160.003.0011

people want to tell their stories to somebody, sooner or later—abreaction of memories and events that simply need expression, a burst of release.

The resource center seemed small when filled with the dozens of families that it received every day. During the hot summer of 2019, families huddled in the cramped, humid room or outside on the sidewalk. On most days, mothers sat at tables caring for their babies, while fathers or other relatives gathered information and provisions for the final leg of their journeys. While parents were doing all of this, the older children huddled in the corner of the back room where an old television played cartoons and where toys were placed. There, children socialized freely and made friends, something they hadn't done in some time.

Whenever our research team entered the center, we would fan out around the room to find families who would agree to be interviewed. We looked for children who appeared to fit our study. Often, the room was filled with people who had stories, but their stories would not be heard. Even if they wanted to speak, the timing was not right; their buses were leaving soon. Other families were there after weeks or days from punishing *hieleras* or other confinements. They had come far through impossible odds. They were too tired. Too scared, maybe. Their infants fussed, and older children asked, "When do we leave?" They had places to go, and every ounce of energy was concentrated on getting there. The parents, mothers mostly, would look at us with tired and bewildered eyes and say kindly, "Maybe later if we're still here. I'm just not ready to talk." On most days.

This was not the case today. We got lucky. Not only were there many families waiting, but most were catching buses late that evening or the next morning. There was plenty of time for stories. It was going to be a long but rewarding day for us.

Sitting at a table with a boy she was interviewing, Tatiana Londoño caught sight of another young boy staring at them. Privacy was not possible in the noisy, crowded room, but parents were usually too preoccupied to eavesdrop intentionally. They might catch snippets of conversations, and whatever they overheard was not that different from their own stories. Children were less inhibited. They would approach us to ask "What are you doing?" and then walk away after quickly losing interest. But this boy was curious and did not lose interest like so many others. He stared from afar. Eventually, he approached Tatiana, speaking directly, confidently: "I want to do what he's doing. I want to go next." Told that he could with his parents' permission after this interview ended, he agreed and quickly made his way to his parents to share the news. He was different from the others in the room, not shy or soft-spoken. Quite the opposite. His voice was firm and lively, loud enough to be heard from across the room. He seemed self-assured, as if nothing could dissuade or diminish him. His name was Jorge. He waited anxiously for his turn to talk, staying close to his parents. Weary hope hung in his mother's eyes as she held her youngest boy in her arms. The resource center was serving food for the families, and her husband was in the line.

"Jorge was just telling us about you and how you're interviewing families here. I guess he has decided that we will be interviewed too. My name is Mariela." His mother's calm presence exuded warmth and trust. In a room filled with the voices and cries of children, Mariela leaned in across the table to hear and be heard, while feeding her youngest, Miguel. Our team was always alert to concerns that families might not trust us. After everything they had been through, why would they trust a stranger wanting to "interview" them about the events, sometimes atrocities, they experienced in their migration? But Mariela didn't hesitate. She said, "I spoke to another mom that was interviewed just an hour or two ago. She said it helped to share her story. I want to share mine too. When do we start?" From her self-assured demeanor, we could see where Jorge got his pluck. Like all interviews, the first step was to get formal consent from the parent and assent from the child. Mariela gave consent. Jorge was glancing at his form, curious to know what it said.

"Okay, my turn!" Jorge said as he saw his mother sign the form. Mariela did not have any questions about the study. She just wanted to tell her story to see if, as others before her had said, she would feel better. Jorge had questions, just not related to the study.

"And where are you from?" he asked Tatiana,

"I live here in the US." But that wasn't a simple answer for Jorge. He persisted.

"So then how do you speak Spanish? Do you also speak English?" He seemed amazed and said that he hoped to speak both one day, too. Jorge asked questions about the English consent form. "What does it say here? What about this word? Why don't the words have accents?" But he knew he was digressing from the main purpose of the meeting.

"Yes, I know. Interview first," he said, slumping his shoulders in feigned resignation.

The information that Jorge provided in his interview was framed by Mariela's interview, which almost didn't happen because Samuel, Mariela's husband, returned to tell his family that their bus had arrived and was leaving right away. Within minutes, news came that the bus was not leaving for another hour. Mariela said, "I need to tell my story too."

Mariela sat with slightly closed eyes as if trying hard to reflect on something she had tried to forget. It was April 2, 2019, and she and Samuel had had enough. The *pandilleros* of the 18th Street Gang that controlled their town had come to Mariela and insisted that she store a large vase for them. Mariela couldn't understand why; "Why me?" When she asked them what was in it, they simply responded, "That is none of your business. You have to take it; otherwise, you know what the consequences are." Despite these threats, Mariela knew that she did not want to participate in anything that involved helping the gang. She refused. They gave her 15 days to think it over.

"What kind of example would that set for my children? Would my children then become a part of it too? Probably." Mariela also knew that by not participating, her family would face death one by one until they gave in to the gang's demands. Frightened by the threat, she kept the unusual request to herself. About 10 days later, the gang members appeared at her home and asked if she had made up her mind. Mariela reminded them that she still had 5 days to decide. She knew of countless killings of families when they did not abide by the gangs' orders. She was jittery and fearful, startled and frightened every time she heard the frequent sound of gunshots in the streets. After many tearful nights, Mariela made the difficult decision to leave both her mother and her two older children, ages 12 and 14, behind. She needed someone to take care of her ill mother and knew that her two older boys could look out for each other in the meantime. Mariela recalled it being the most difficult decision she had ever made. But she knew she had no choice. She had already witnessed many others make similarly difficult choices in her town. It had become the norm for parents to ask, "If we have to leave, who has to stay behind? Who has to leave?" she said. There was no time to even consider "Will we make it? Will we survive?"

Without much planning, Mariela and Samuel took their two youngest children, Jorge and Miguel, ages 8 and 5, and left without telling Mariela's mother. To avoid arousing suspicion, they dressed as if going grocery shopping. Mariela and Samuel made plans with a taxi driver whom they trusted but who would be risking his life also by helping the family leave town. To make matters more complicated, the neighboring town where they were to meet the taxi was controlled by another gang. This heightened the danger for the family and the driver—gangs did not allow taxis from one town to operate in another town. Taxi drivers would be killed if they violated these rules. Mother, father, and their two young sons walked in the early morning through the fields with nothing but a purse and two backpacks for the kids. The rendezvous with their driver took place in a remote area of the adjacent town. The taxi driver took them to the town's center—the typical Central American and Caribbean town plaza lorded over by a Catholic church— where he dropped them off safely. Once at the town's center, they quickly hopped on the first bus to the nearby city of San Pedro Sula, Honduras. From San Pedro Sula, they boarded a bus that took them directly to Ciudad Tecun Uman, a town in Guatemala bordering Mexico, placing miles between them and their family. Mariela cried for most of the bus journey. Her thoughts were incessant: "Had I made the right choice? What if I had left my two other kids and my mother in danger?" Would the *pandilla* come looking for Mariela and ask the family where she and her husband had gone? It was an emotion- ally exhausting 20-hour journey to Guatemala.

On arriving in Ciudad Tecun Uman, they spent the night in a local motel, and from there, Mariela called her mother to reveal what she had done. Her mother was shocked but upon hearing the whole story, she absolved and affirmed Mariela: "That was the smartest and only choice you had." Mariela went about making plans for her mother and the two older children to move to another town 3 hours away from their home to avoid being targeted. No amount of planning could be too much. Mariela told Tatiana, "You can't risk it. Once they target you, they target your whole family." She begged her mother to promise that she would never let the boys out of her sight. Mariela recalled wistfully how her two older boys would play outside while she watched them from her porch. Now, she said, nothing is safe, regardless of where one lives in Honduras. As Mariela sighed and stared at the floor, she acknowledged that there was only so much she could do to shield them from the dangers of the Honduran *maras*; but she couldn't help feeling like it was never enough. Guilt washed through her as she spoke. Mariela remained hopeful that her two older children could make the trip to the United States when they were old enough to manage it themselves. For now, she could only cling to that hope.

Jorge's story of their migration began with, "Well, I'm going to tell you the truth. I was scared of the *pandilla*. I was crying." Before Tatiana could follow up with a question, Jorge skipped ahead to their crossing of the Rio Grande into the United States. Tatiana followed his storyline since she knew that children often digress when talking about emotionally charged topics. Jorge was no exception and preferred to talk about how he missed his dog and her six puppies. His grandmother couldn't take care of them, and some of them died. Two of the puppies had recently been stolen by gang members. His face showed the grief of losing his puppies.

"I started thinking weird things," Jorge said about the moment he learned that they were leaving Honduras. "What if we get arrested? What if robbers kidnap us?" He was gripped with fear and uncertainty about what was in store. Jorge recalled being on two different buses for 3 days after leaving Honduras. They had to switch buses because one had broken down from a flat tire and leaked gasoline from under the bus.

"I was very cold and my dad would keep me warm," he went on. Jorge mentioned that as he thought of how cold he was he thought back to his dog. She too would be cold back at home without a blanket. "Who was taking care of my precious dog? Why did I have to leave her behind?" He remembered sitting on the bus, thinking back to when he was given his dog as a puppy. "I grew up with her," he said solemnly. He worried that she wouldn't recognize him anymore if he ever went back to visit. While he knew his family had to flee Honduras and start a new life in the United States, he was struggling to let go of his roots, his home, his best friend.

During their journey to Mexico, Jorge feared every police officer he saw because they might take their money or kidnap them. He kept quiet when they were around. Once when the police stopped them on their way to Mexico, the police asked his father for papers. Jorge heard instead the police asking for money. He was relieved to hear they hadn't taken their money. Still, he feared the officers because he didn't want to be incarcerated or, worse, killed. Since police officers in Honduras were often in cahoots with the gangs, he never felt safe around anyone in a uniform. As he narrated this portion of their journey, Jorge looked around the room, as if making sure there wasn't an officer around. The mental scars from his experience with police officers were evident. Would he ever trust any police officer?

Jorge was also scared when riding the bus at night. He would look toward the mountains and worry that the blood-sucking *chupacabra* would come and get him. (The *chupacabra* is a grotesque, hairless, reptilian-looking animal said by legend and folklore to exist in parts of Latin America, where it supposedly attacks animals and farm livestock, particularly goats, to drink their blood. It gets its name from the Spanish *chupar*, to suck, and *cabra*, goat.)

"My mind is so creative that I would see the three faces of a goat. In the story of *chupacabra* [in Honduras], if you summon the three faces of a goat, you all die. I was worried I had accidentally summoned them." It was one of the most eloquent statements by a child that we recorded in our study. Worried that he had conjured the *chupacabra*, Jorge reported nightmares of the bloody monster killing all the parents on the bus and then all of the children. Jorge added that he had "weird dreams" throughout his journey and thought they came from the worry for the safety of his family.

The first bus broke down at one point, and it was scary to be stranded in the middle of nowhere until a replacement bus could come. The new bus had better air conditioning and wasn't "blowing cold air right at my face." Nevertheless, he still couldn't sleep because he feared the "creatures of the night." Jorge also feared that the bus driver would fall asleep at the wheel. The kindly bus driver assured him that everything was going to be okay. Jorge worried about his little brother, who was throwing up "morning, afternoon, nighttime; all day, every day." He finally slept on the third day on the bus after having a nice warm "café con leche" and once his little brother felt better. When he wasn't sleeping, he would entertain himself with video games on his parents' phone or by watching the scenery outside and making up stories along the way, stories he kept to himself.

The night in the motel was a sleepless one for Mariela. Never had she thought of leaving her beloved Honduras. Her family reveled in their country with its rich culture, sense of community, and abundance of family ties. Like everyone in town, Mariela and Samuel had heard of horrible things that happened to other families who had made the journey to the United States. They were not unaware of the risks they would take in making such a journey. But what other option did they have? As part of their plan, Mariela and Samuel would venture to Mexico first and stay there for a while until they figured out their next steps. At the time, the family could hold special refugee status as Hondurans residing in Mexico. But no manner of legal refugee status could protect them from the possible abuse, extortion, or kidnappings that had already overtaken other Central Americans living in Mexico. It was all too much like what they had already experienced in Honduras. They were hesitant to stay in Mexico but knew that with the resources they had, they had no choice. That night, Mariela prayed that nothing would happen to them in Mexico. Her prayers were in vain: Nightmares were about to become reality.

After spending the night in Ciudad Tecun Uman, the family took a small bus that dropped them off near a bridge that crossed into Mexico. They joined a caravan of migrants walking north, a way of traveling safely without the help of coyotes. Not one official from either side questioned them, probably because they had seen caravans passing since 2018 when hundreds of people gathered at the bus station of San Pedro Sula, one of the largest cities in Honduras, with the goal of getting out of the country. People of all ages walked approximately 2,500 miles from the bus station across three countries to get to Tijuana and San Diego, California. There were reports of caravans of over 7,000 migrants, but they were inflated for political advantage (the true estimate was fewer than 4,000). As the caravans marched, Donald Trump grew apoplectic. He called them an "invasion" and a "national emergency," more reason for his border wall and stringent immigration policies, and threatened to send 1,000 troops to stop them. With such large groups entering its borders, Guatemala had little choice but to open its borders to allow the groups to pass. According to Mariela, they got lucky because a day or two after they crossed, Guatemala stopped letting the *caravanas* through.[1]

In Mexico, Samuel took what work he could to support his family. The pay was paltry; he had to take whatever he could. They withstood all the privations. There were hard times but also good times, Mariela said, adding that they would not have survived the 4 months in Mexico without the help of local people. Still, there were times when Mariela would be "trapped" in their room while Samuel went looking for work. She didn't feel safe with her kids wandering around the home of strangers they had just met. Despite the kindness and generosity of Mexican locals and the hosts who gave them a place to stay, Mariela felt uneasy after all the stories she had heard of kidnappings, assaults, and homicides of migrants in Mexico. They had to be careful, for the sake of the children. Stepping outside also meant the possibility of encountering *la migra*.

In one harrowing moment, she was robbed of all her belongings, including the official document that allowed her to reside in Mexico legally, protection she had waited for weeks to receive. With it, she was able to walk around freely in Mexico. At that abrupt moment, Mariela felt the freedom snatched from her. She knew that the entire family's fate hung in the balance—they could be deported. "After leaving my country and fleeing the violence there, to then come to Mexico and be placed in even more danger and violence? They assaulted me. That is something I'll never forget. I was so afraid." The regret and fear were present in her eyes, her words, her voice. Jorge believed also that their time in Mexico was more difficult than all they had experienced in Honduras.

It was hard for Samuel to work for long stretches of time. The shortage of work and near-constant threats of violence forced the family to move every few weeks to a new town in Mexico. Sometimes short-term jobs would provide the family with housing; other times, they had to find it themselves by knocking on people's doors or paying what they could for a motel. Sometimes Samuel would tell his story at work, and someone would empathize and offer them a place to stay. Sometimes they would move across three states in Mexico in a month, desperately looking for more work to avoid sleeping for too long on the streets. One of their luckiest times was when they were able to stay in a town for 3 weeks, a period of steady employment.

Jorge remembered staying in Mexico "for a very long time," about 4 months. There were racist incidents. A repeated source was the clerk of a grocery store that Mariela frequented. In one incident Mariela was in the store to buy *crema*, a salty creamy buttermilk used to make *baleadas*—a thick flour or corn tortilla put on a charcoal grill and spread thickly with refried black beans and some farmer's cheese and folded like a soft taco. Her request provoked a racist rant from the clerk, who knew the Mexican version of *crema* to be something like sour cream. It was the misunderstanding of two cultural idioms. The confusion between them that day led to "dirty looks" from the clerk every time they entered the store. The clerk would say, "Go back to your country! You can go work in your own country. Stop coming here to take our jobs and our money and to be a burden to us. I know you have that card that our government gives to you—that should be for us! We pay taxes to the government who then gives you that card. The government should be helping us, the Mexicans, not you migrants." Indeed, the clerk was referring to a card that the Mexican government gave to eligible migrants to pay for food and other necessities while they sought stable work in Mexico. Mariela's family, however, was not among those who received the entitlement. She thought other migrants deserved it more than she did since she wasn't planning on staying in Mexico for much longer.

To avoid problems, Mariela remained silent, shopped, and left the store quickly. But with each visit to the store, Mariela felt the clerk's glaring eyes and heard her whisper loudly to her children to "go bother those kids and tell them to go away." In one incident, the clerk instructed her older boy, who was only about 5, to go hit Jorge. Mariela would bear it no longer; she would let no one hurt her children. She confronted the worker, who denied telling her son anything. That was a turning point—the clerk finally ceased bothering Mariela and her kids.

While Samuel worked days and nights, Mariela was often alone with the children, leaving her susceptible to uncomfortable encounters with men who wanted her attention. In one situation, a man went so far as to say to Jorge, "Tell your mom that I'd like to take her out to eat. What's your mom's name? How old is she? Where is she from?" Jorge knew not to respond to his questions. The next time the Mexican guy approached Jorge, he respectfully excused himself from the conversation. Luckily, the husband of one of Mariela's friends approached the man and told him that Mariela was married and wanted to be left alone. The man never bothered Mariela or Jorge again.

After two such incidents with men and other smaller but similar indignities of racism and unsafe interactions, they decided to leave Mexico and continue to the United States. They had little support from family in the United States but had no choice but to reach out to them. Mariela contacted a friend to help with a bus from Puebla to Piedras Negras, a border town. Samuel wanted to call his sisters in the United States for help but knew they would not approve of his decision to make the dangerous journey with his children. His sisters had not lived in Honduras for decades and seemed not to know how bad it was, how desperate people got that they had no choice but to leave. Mariela described Samuel as a proud man who did not want to worry his sisters by telling them of the hell they were living through in Honduras. He kept his decision to leave a secret. But Mariela added that it wasn't just their opposition that kept Samuel silent about his plans. They feared, too, that someone in the family might innocently mention their plans and have it get to the *pandilla*. But they were now in a desperate moment, and he would have to call, even lie to, his sisters. Mariela's voice grew softer as she reflected on the moment, whispering to Tatiana as if she was back in Honduras and the *pandilla* might be listening. Mariela herself felt that if Samuel had told his sisters the truth of what they were going through, they might have supported their decision to leave and sent them money. Instead, Samuel told his sisters they needed the money for medical exams, and they responded quickly with funds. With the money, Mariela and Samuel bought bus tickets for the family. The journey from Puebla to Piedras Negras was long and risky because there was always the chance that the Mexican *migra* would deport them to Honduras. They were stopped as they entered Piedras Negras, but the officer who looked at them suspiciously may have also felt pity when he saw Mariela and Samuel with the two children: "I think that once they see the children, they don't want to hurt them or cause them harm, so they remained quiet." The immigration officers never asked her for her identification.

In Piedras Negras, they entered a small, rugged grocery store to buy some snacks and water. Men loitering in the store stared and whispered among themselves, frightening Mariela. From her description of shortness of breath, feeling her heart "racing out of control," and fearing she would faint—and by her visceral reaction as she recounted the moment—it appears that Mariela suffered a panic attack in the store. As Samuel watched Mariela's panic attack unfold, he rushed her and the children out of the store and began the long walk to the crossing point. A car approached, and the male driver asked, "Where are you going?" Mariela and Samuel responded that they were simply visiting family, but Mariela was nervous. Seeming to notice Mariela's fear of him, the man assured her that he knew where they were going and to not fear him. They could trust him. The man warned them that the area they were in was *caliente*, a hotspot for crime. Although he seemed trustworthy and offered to drive them to the border, Mariela hesitated at first. But she ultimately relented, justifying her decision because there were four of them and only one of him. Mariela trusted her instincts, her gut reaction, and concluded that he looked trustworthy. They got in the car with him. She recalled holding tightly to her boys' hands and theirs gripping hers. They were afraid but hopeful.

As they approached the border, the man noticed something suspicious and said that he could drive them no further. He told them to take a taxi and be taken to a particular *callejón* (alley) where they could jump into the river and cross to the other side. Mariela couldn't swim and became terrified. The kind stranger found a taxi for them and gave the driver instructions. The taxi driver took them to the designated place and got out with the family, now facing the Rio Grande. The taxi driver saw Mariela's terror and asked, "Are you scared?" Mariela nodded, saying she was mostly scared for her children. Without warning, the man looked at the river and back at the family and yelled at them, "Let's go," running toward the river through the shrubs. The driver waded into the shallow part of the river first, reassuring them that everything was going to be alright. From the water, the driver yelled, "Okay, hurry! Time to jump!" And they jumped off the steep riverbank into the deep, fast current of the Rio Grande.

Jorge fell as he followed and scratched himself on a large rock—his shoe came off. He recalled "hundreds of thorns" sinking into the flesh of his bare foot. The pain was unbearable: "It felt like being run over by a bull." He also got a cramp in his foot that made it difficult for him to get up. Seeing this, the taxi driver quickly grabbed Jorge and pulled him to his feet. "We can't stop," he said. Overcome with fear, Jorge began to cry and shake, uncontrollably. "I'm scared! I'm scared! I can't do this!" The taxi driver held Jorge's hand and said, "I will help you. Don't worry. You will be fine." The comforting words did not diminish what would become an indelible memory for Jorge: crossing the river. Even now, Jorge's memory of what he felt at that moment was acute: "I was crying because my mother couldn't swim, and my dad almost fell with my brother. I was scared."

Mariela clawed her way to the surface as she held tightly to Miguel. Jorge kept yelling, "I'm hurt!" and Samuel tried to calm him, reminding him that they were almost there. Suddenly, Samuel, holding tightly onto Jorge, fell into a knickpoint and lost his footing in the river, falling backward into the water with his son. While Samuel's head was not visible, Mariela could see his hands in the water, trying to get up, but young Jorge was completely submerged. Jorge felt he was going to drown, fear gleaming in his eyes as he told the story. He pointed to the scars on his arm that served as a reminder of the traumatic event, jagged lines of scaly scraped skin and dried scabs of blood. His young face was solemn as he stroked his scar with the tip of his finger. He looked up and said, "I now fear the water even more than before." When Mariela saw Jorge completely underwater, she plunged her hand into the water until she felt Samuel's shirt collar and, holding on very tightly, dragged him out, and Samuel pulled Jorge. Jorge slowly emerged from the water gasping for air, feeling faint.

Samuel, terror raging like the Rio Grande around him, said to Mariela, "I can't do this anymore. I'm going back." He dreaded losing his son or that they would both drown. Mariela knew they could not turn back now; they had made it this far. Her fear had turned to courage. In an instant, the taxi driver grabbed onto Jorge to help Samuel, saying, "Let's try to be quiet for a second so I can hear. You might not need to cross the river. Just calm down for one second." Within minutes, as everyone grew quiet, somewhere in the distance they heard the sound of a boat approaching. "Stay put. Everything will be fine," the driver repeated. "Let the boat take you. This is it for me. Goodbye." As he quickly waded out of the water back to his taxi, Mariela looked back to watch him leave, asking herself, "Why would he have done all of that for us?" While the journey was "dangerous, terrifying, traumatic, and something I would never wish upon anyone," she felt blessed to have had those two strangers help them survive it. She said, "Without the taxi driver, we would not be here."

As the taxi driver left, Mariela grabbed onto Jorge; but the current pulled him under for a second time, and his hand slipped away from Mariela's. Jorge resurfaced, but his body was shaking from the shock of almost drowning twice. Mariela held him closely, trying to calm him down. The family pushed their way slowly through the water to make themselves more visible to the boat. They got as far as the middle of the river. The current became stronger, it seemed, the farther they got into the water. Mariela couldn't imagine making it all the way to the other side; she worried they might not survive. Finally, they saw the boat.

"Once we saw the symbol of the USA on the officers' uniforms, we were so happy!" Jorge exclaimed. He yelled and waved at the boat. "We're here! We're here! Help us please!" Watching Jorge call for help, Mariela realized that she was witnessing something she had never seen in her son before: a desperate instinct to survive. The officers asked them to pass the boys first. Jorge quickly jumped on the boat followed by Miguel. The officers saw Jorge unable to stop crying and told him, "Don't worry. Everything is going to be okay now. We will take you to land soon. You will be safe and warm there." Once on the boat, Jorge looked down at the water and couldn't believe his eyes—fish and other unknown creatures were swimming around in the river. "I couldn't believe I was in that water with those scary-looking things." Once the boys were safely on the boat, only Samuel and Mariela remained in the river. While the parents fought the rushing waters, the officers began interrogating Samuel. When asked why they were in the river, Samuel told them truthfully that they were trying to get to the United States. With that, the officers told Samuel and Mariela to get on the boat, too.

Once at the riverbank, the officers drove the family in their patrol car to a location under an overpass. There, they were given plenty of water and juices. The officers in charge of the area told Mariela, Samuel, Jorge, and Miguel that they could relax now, everything was going to be okay. The officers offered the services of an on-site doctor in case they needed it. Mariela was puzzled by the way the officers treated them. "Why are they being so nice?" she wondered at the time and recounted again in the interview. She had heard so many stories about how the American *migras* abused migrants arriving in the United States. Sadly, her wonderment was short-lived when another group of officers, like the ones she had heard about, came to transport them somewhere else. The agents took their belongings, including extra clothes Mariela had brought for her children to wear after crossing the river. Now her children remained soaked in their dirty clothes. The officers threw away the medications Mariela had brought for her children in case they felt nauseous or sick. Mariela pleaded with the agents, but one of the officers, who barely spoke Spanish, responded with "Todo a la basura" ("Everything into the garbage"). The family entered a *hielera* in their wet clothes. Jorge shivered, his lips turning purple. A woman in the *hielera* shared her jacket with Mariela. Jorge laid down on the cement floor with the Mylar blanket that provided little to no warmth and slept for about an hour. While the floor was far from comfortable, he was exhausted beyond anything he had felt before or since. He couldn't sleep more than an hour because he felt "watched" by the officers. Jorge felt like he had to stay up in case the officers did something to harm him or his family. He never felt safe.

Samuel had a different reason for his sleeplessness: he feared that Mariela and the kids would be released, and he wouldn't. He didn't care as much about being detained for longer but worried about how a separation would devastate his children. Samuel also knew that he would become sick if separated from his children. Mariela said about Samuel, "His life had no meaning nor purpose without them. If he couldn't see them again, he didn't see any reason to keep living." Mariela also worried for Samuel because she knew how much he had already done for his family. His removal would leave a gaping hole in their family unit. "Él siempre ha sido muy luchador." ("He's always been a fighter.") Despite the fears of being separated, it never happened. Luckily, the officers respected that they had come as a family unit. Mariela, Samuel, and the two boys came in as a family and left as a family.

The 2 days in the *hielera* were worse than Mariela's wildest imaginings from the stories she'd heard. The officer had told Mariela that they would be released the following day in the middle of the night, and the family spent every minute after that pronouncement counting the hours, waiting for the moment to be released. Every hour felt longer and longer as the clock ticked slower and slower for Mariela, Samuel, and the kids. They were exhausted and cold but couldn't find any comfort in the tightly spaced room whose temperature resembled a refrigerator. The adults were not given food, while the children were given crackers and juice. Once, they gave the children a burrito, still mostly frozen. Jorge only called it a burrito because the officers called it that; it did not taste or look like a burrito. He cried from the unbearable hunger and the intense cold. Mariela tried to comfort him with her body and with reminders that they would be able to eat normal food again. Jorge only responded by saying, "I'm hungry. Yo tengo hambre. Mi pobre pancita me retumba." ("My poor tummy rumbles.") Painful as the memory was, Mariela giggled on reflection of his "poor tummy." Jorge seemed a bit embarrassed at the retelling.

Very early the next day, the family walked out of detention to a waiting van. Everyone felt relieved. They felt lucky to have spent only 36 hours in detention, not days or weeks like other migrant families had. Nothing was certain, but Mariela felt, at least for now, hope and safety. The drive to San Antonio was long, especially since they were traveling in their still damp clothes. The driver kept the van's air conditioner set to a cold level. How they would have welcomed the warmth of the staggeringly hot Texas summer. Mariela's doubt about uprooting her family spiked again. "Why? Why did I do this? Why did I bring my children to these conditions? Did I think this through enough? Is this my fault?" Her guilt, and that of other mothers, was compounded by the loud whispers among ICE officers, "How could parents put their children through such misery?" This was part of sometimes subtle, sometimes overt psychological abuse by immigration officers. Arrival at the Travis Park Church, near to where they now sat, erased Mariela's doubts. Showers, clean clothes, shoes, food—basic things that filled them with relief and joy.

"It was a feeling of peace like a big weight had been lifted from my shoulders." From the church that afternoon they called their family in the United States to ask them to buy the bus tickets from Eagle Pass to San Antonio and then from San Antonio to New York City. Samuel's sisters, recognized by the government as the family's sponsors, had to buy the tickets in advance to guarantee the family's release. Samuel's sisters offered plane tickets to New York City to protect the boys from a bus trip of over 24 hours. Samuel was concerned about the expense and insisted on bus travel.

At this point in the interview, they had about 20 minutes to board. Mariela insisted on finishing her conversation, to complete what she felt she needed to say.

"I feel a peace, a tranquility, nothing compared to how I felt in Honduras or in Mexico. But let's see what will happen." Mariela had been through enough to know that the unexpected could always happen. Jorge's only worry was about New York City and the stories about its dangers. Even the memories of the *chupacabra* didn't worry him anymore. Instead, he looked forward to being with family, sleeping in a warm bed, and eating Honduran food. But mostly, he wanted to feel safe and happy again with his family.

Tatiana walked them to the bus and thanked them again for entrusting her with their story. Mariela hugged Tatiana and whispered, "I'm so glad I had a chance to talk. Thank you for listening to us." Jorge couldn't contain his excitement. From the bus, he yelled, "We're finally going home! *Hasta luego!*"

Note

1. Alvarez, 2019; Long-Garcia, 2018.

11

Sleepless Under the Bridge in El Paso[*]

"Yo sufrí cuando me agarraron aquí en Estados Unidos" ("I suffered when they caught me here in the United States"). After a relatively uneventful journey from Honduras, Genesis described her entry into the United States with this ominous sentence. Once she and her two sons entered the custody of US immigration enforcement, the most harrowing stage of their migration began. First, there was the period of detention. Then there was the time of her sons' debilitating depressions. Now Genesis, 35, and her son, Martín, 13, were telling their story to Hilda Torres and Tatiana Londoño at the offices of the Refugee and Immigrant Center for Education and Services (RAICES) in Austin. Hilda and Tatiana scheduled mother and son with the help of Alexandra Minnaar, a RAICES attorney who directed their Community Immigration Services. A graduate of Northeastern University School of Law, Alex had worked with detained asylum seekers and unaccompanied children for over 10 years. Even when beleaguered by demands on her time, Alex was always available to answer questions, refer clients eligible for the study, and ease those clients' trust in us. Alex and her staff had graciously given us access to a children's room for the interviews. RAICES's offices were private, colorful, and cheerful, optimal for moms and kids to tell their stories in a trusting holding environment, in contrast to the frenzied San Antonio bus station and the Migrant Resource Center.

The story of Genesis and her two sons is a good example of what happens to individuals who survive immensely tormenting experiences. In the heat of the battle, the body calls on stress-response resources to stay alive and persist. People survive by dint of the human instinct for self-preservation. When the external stressors fade, the psychological aftermath begins as the mind seeks to process and purge itself of memories and sensations, and what may ensue is a collapse in the person's mental health.

---

[*] Case profile contributed by Hilda Torres with Tatiana Londoño.

Through Iceboxes and Kennels. Luis H. Zayas, Oxford University Press. © Oxford University Press 2023.
DOI: 10.1093/oso/9780197668160.003.0012

It all began when Genesis learned that Martín was missing school and hiding in one of his classmates' homes. But he was not skipping school willfully. Rather, he was afraid to be in school because gang members wanted him to sell drugs for them. Recruitment was inevitable, a conscription of sorts that a boy couldn't refuse without deadly consequences to him or a family member. Martín's older brother, Gael, 17, was at even greater risk, sooner or later. Genesis herself was under pressure, too, as a small-business owner. Gangs were extorting her, forcing her to comply to stay in business. Anyone in Honduras who owns a business, she told Hilda and Tatiana, must pay an *impuesto de guerra* (a war tax). Refusal, like refusing conscription into a gang, meant threats, beatings, and death. There came a point when she could no longer pay the tax. The gangs quickly noted this development, and one night an ominous telephone call came in, an anonymous male voice that growled, "Atente a las consecuencias si no sigues pagando el impuesto de guerra" ("Look out for the consequences if you don't keep paying the war tax"). That was all the motivation she needed to close her business and consider leaving Honduras. Genesis didn't know what to do next and felt she didn't have the courage to pursue change.

Then, a call came from Adriana, her husband's sister, which changed everything. Adriana disclosed that she was leaving for the United States, to which Genesis replied instantly, "I'm going with you." The planning began in earnest, and Genesis convinced her husband to stay back with their 19-year-old daughter Bianca, who was studying medicine and did not want to abandon her dream of becoming a doctor. It was their only option. In February 2019, Genesis, Adriana, and the three young cousins left by bus, crossing into Guatemala first and then into Mexico. In Mexico, they waited a month, and in late March they made it to Ciudad Juarez; there the two families crossed a dry canal toward the border. Men working on the US side saw them, made eye contact with Genesis and Adriana, and motioned them to a spot where they could cross. The men held open a part of the wire fence for them to pass, another act of kindness.

Thanking the men, the group "walked and walked, and we almost reached the center of El Paso," Genesis said, until a man pointed them out to Customs and Border Protection (CBP) agents. The officers interrogated the group and confiscated their sweaters, coats, gloves, hats, toothpaste, toothbrushes, deodorant, and other things. They spent that night in a *hielera*. Martín said he "shut down" his thinking to overcome the cold, hunger, and fear. From there, Genesis, Gael, and Martín were transported to an encampment, a makeshift detention center of 3,500 people, under the Paso del Norte International Bridge. The camp's perimeter was made of fencing and razor wire, and inside was a large military-style tent.

"Get in there and find a place to sleep," the agent told them and drove off without so much as a "good luck." The family joined the mass of humanity and would stay here for the next four nights. The hardship they had avoided traveling north had now caught up with them.

Genesis and the boys made their way to the rear of the camp, pushing through the crush of bodies jailed there. The place was filled beyond its capacity. They found a spot to stand and claim as theirs. There were two types of ground under the bridge, Martín said. One was dirt and rocks, where they sat, stood, and slept. The other was sandy and more comfortable, but migrants weren't allowed there, only the patrol cars. That night the temperature dropped, and they longed for their confiscated sweaters, coats, and gloves. Gael stood all night; such was the overcrowding. Genesis sat on the ground with Martín's head on her lap. Just before dawn, officers handed out some Mylar covers, and luckily, they got one. Genesis covered Martín with the thin sheet.

News reports coming out of El Paso told of agents who

verbally and physically harmed migrants, forced them to stand for prolonged periods and deprived them of sleep and access to medical care, and had failed to provide the migrants with adequate food and water. Some families were detained under the bridge for as long as four days.[1]

Families with infants had to sleep on the ground without bedding or mats. The *Texas Tribune* quoted a CBP spokesperson as saying that the encampment was "just a transitional facility" where migrants were held for a "couple of hours, [but] it could be 12 hours" and got blankets, food, bathroom facilities, water, and snacks. Those were not the stories being told by newspapers. The spokesperson said that "If all of them wanted to sleep inside the tent, they would be able to. A lot of them choose not to for whatever reason."[2] Was it possible for 3,500 people to fit inside a large military tent?

Challenged by reporters that the time he said migrants were staying—a couple of hours, maybe 12—was inaccurate and more like 2 or 3 days, the spokesperson gave a circuitous answer.

Let's say you get picked up at 6 p.m. and you end up at the river's edge waiting to be transported for a few hours. Then you end up at that [camp] the next morning maybe at 9 a.m. Then you don't get processed because there is a bottleneck until the following day. Did you stay there overnight? Yes, you sure did. So, a lot is just perspective. The sun went down, it came back up. So, for them that's two days.[3]

The dog pound under the bridge, as *Texas Monthly* called it, had, in fact, held people for a month without showers or clean garments, still in the clothes in which they were apprehended.[4] Genesis, Gael, and Martín confirmed these shameful conditions: sleeping on the gravel surface in the open air with only the bridge as cover. All along, the detainees were subject to pigeon droppings from under the bridge.[5]

"We slept for four days with the aluminum [Mylar] blankets on top of rocks," Martín said. "Well, they weren't blankets, but that's what they gave us. We got only two sandwiches in total for the time we were there." His voice trailed off. Struggling to speak, Martín took a deep breath and finished his sentence, "And that was it." He stopped speaking as if all the memories rushing back to him were too much to bear. Tatiana offered him a break from their conversation, but Martín confidently said, "No, let's continue." Nearby, Genesis told Hilda of the experience, her breathing becoming faster and deeper, tears streaming down her face. Recalling the physical pain that Gael had gone through brought on mournful sobs. Hilda offered a break, but Genesis too refused; she wanted to continue, though still in obvious emotional distress.

CBP officials said that they tried to provide relief from the sun, wind, and inclement weather. But all the weather forecasts showed that temperatures in El Paso were dipping to 40 degrees Fahrenheit at night and rising during the day into the upper 90s to low 100s. Keeping people shaded was one thing but keeping them hydrated during a heatwave was another matter. It would be impossible to keep everyone safe with such widely ranging weather and poor conditions; people would die. Immigration officials were just not prepared and did not seem to be trying very hard.

Migrants were often too tired and scared to talk among themselves, sticking to their families. Martín recalled only exchanging conversations with his mother, brother, aunt, cousin, and some other children sitting nearby, chats that helped him forget the awful conditions. They formed a small community around them, solace in captivity: "We became a family with this other lady and her kids. We treated each other like family." Early the next day, they were awakened and told to make a line. Martín was given a juice and a sandwich, and Genesis and Gael only received a sandwich. Officers told adults to drink out of water coolers located around the camp. The distribution of sandwiches created a commotion among the migrants. There was never enough food to go around, so they had to stay alert for mealtime announcements. People got up from their spots to try to get something to eat only to find their spots taken by others when they returned. Chaos and confusion are only natural reactions when people are crowded, cold, hungry, tired, and displaced.

The hardship was taking its toll on Martín, Genesis, Gael, and everyone under the bridge. Martín recalled that when an officer was asked about the migrants' release, the response was, "We have you here like dogs. And you will stay here. This is what happens when you decide to come to our country." Martín's face was red with fury as he told Tatiana of the officers' cruel insults. Martín felt like they were going to be there forever. They were never going to be free. He feared for his life and his family.

Nonetheless, Gael persisted in listening for their names and numbers to be called. At one point, Gael misheard a number, eagerly led his family to the front and was shouted down by a guard. Disappointed, the family walked back to their place only to find that they no longer had their spot or their sheets. Another family had taken everything they had left there, and they were not going to give it back. People under the bridge, Genesis reasoned, were not necessarily greedy or malicious; but after everything they had been through, they were desperate—frantic for a sense of safety, comfort, belonging, even ownership of their scant resources. Under those conditions, everyone had to fend for themselves to keep their families comfortable and warm. That day Martín and his family had to find another spot, much more cramped than the last, and suffer through the night without their blankets or cardboard bedding. They attempted to sleep on the bare rocks. Martín said he "didn't sleep at all through the night because I was cold and felt horrible." They weren't the only ones who couldn't sleep. Martín recalled everyone around him crying out of desperation. Everyone was miserable and scared.

Finally, Genesis had reached her limit. "Love," she called to Gael and Martín, "let's go back. We will tell them to deport us."

"No," Martín replied simply and firmly. "We are already here, and we have to hold on." Indeed, they had all had enough but were determined to press on. "We have made it this far. It has to be worth something," Martín added. Besides, he wanted to meet his *abuela* in the United States. He had dreamt of spending time with her, hearing stories of when she was a little girl in Honduras. As Genesis and Martín debated holding out or giving up, a fellow migrant interrupted.

> Don't do it. You are here already. It's easier for you to get out of this place than from the place that they are going to send you if you ask to be deported. In here, the most you are going to be is four days. That's what they want, to punish us for four days.

The man must have known something because on the fourth day there, he was released, proof to Genesis to stick it out. Her courage returned, and she pushed through 2 more days of grueling waiting.

On the third day under the bridge, reporters began showing up at the bridge, but they were stopped by CBP officers from entering the compound. That didn't stop the migrants from getting their stories out. Desperation was debilitating; seeing the media lifted hope. Migrants ran to the fence and screamed for help from the reporters. Mothers pleaded for babies' milk and diapers. One bottle a day was not enough, with their infants wailing from hunger.

One of those reporters was Bob Moore, a local El Paso freelance journalist covering stories for the *Washington Post*. In an interview with me in January 2022, Moore added insights and information to what we heard from Genesis and Martín. Moore recalled that the detainees were "clearly desperate and calling for help." Even El Pasoans who had lived through immigration tragedies and had rallied many times before were shocked.

Moore told me, "Over the subsequent days, once it was public, that it was out there, members of the community sort of went down there, some using bullhorns to let these folks know they weren't alone, that there were people out there who cared for them." According to Moore, CBP was aware that they had a crisis on their hands. He clarified, "They didn't mean a humanitarian crisis. They meant that our country is being overrun and we need to do something to stop this." CBP and other border agencies were insistent that they did not want to release any single adult men because they viewed it as an admission that they were losing control of the border.

Moore confirmed Genesis's and Martín's description of sleeping on rocks under the bridge. He recalled a moment when a Guatemalan father he was interviewing in a local shelter after release from the outdoor detention center, to show Moore how bad sleeping outside was, called his 5-year-old son over to them and asked the boy to lift his shirt. Moore saw bruises all over the boy's back and legs. A pregnant woman in her sixth month, Moore recalled, had to sleep on the rocks for 3 nights. Moore also confirmed that the night temperatures dropped close to freezing.

"This was under a bridge," Moore went on, "so you have all of these pigeons that have roosted under that bridge for about 60 years, and they do what pigeons do, pooping on these people all night long. That was another one of the details that really stuck with me. Just the abhorrent treatment of people." These unsanitary conditions were worsened by the difficulty of feeding so many detainees. At one point, the food distribution system broke down for several days. Additionally, there were a few portable toilets and cleaning stations but not nearly enough for 3,500 people.

Even for an experienced journalist, the scene of thousands of people—"the crush of humanity under there," Moore said—was deeply moving.

I crossed the bridge several times over the next couple of days, and some of the sounds still haunt me. You are walking over it and you just hear the cries of children. [As] you look over the edge, you could see parents trying to comfort their children. These were people on full display for anybody walking by and stopping and staring in disbelief at what they were seeing.... The really sickening part for me, and in the last couple of years I've seen a lot of stuff[6]—I witnessed the reunions of separated children and covered the terror attack at the Walmart—but that situation under the bridge was still one of the most visceral things that I've seen. To see the lack of humanity in our own government to allow this to go on.... You talk to families and [they said] there were good guys under there trying to help them out. But for the most part this was a policy demonstration by the United States that wanted these people to go back to Guatemala and Honduras, in particular, so that people would see this and decide not to come. It was a deliberate use of cruelty as an instrument of government policy. It was shocking.

Whenever reporters were present, detention officers would call names from a list. But it didn't take very long for detainees to figure out that the names being called were not their names. They were, instead, the names of people already released. It was a strategy to hoodwink reporters and prevent migrants from telling their stories. The journalists asked for detainees who would speak on the record. One woman speaking through the fence into a reporter's camera said that women needed feminine products and sanitary napkins but weren't getting them.

"I saw you," a guard who had witnessed her interview said to the woman. "I know who you are." Rumor spread later, when no one saw the woman again, that she had been locked up and deported. Intimidation was one of the weapons of the guards to halt any communication with the media, and this agent wielded it skillfully.

Finally, on the fourth day, Genesis's number was called, and by late afternoon she was on her way out with Gael and Martín, headed to a *hielera* in Tucson, Arizona, about 320 miles away and nearly a 5-hour drive from El Paso. They rode in government-owned Chevrolet Suburban utility vehicles, a convoy of about six of them in a line. The convoy arrived around 11:00 p.m., and migrants waited for 2 hours before CBP started collecting data on the new families. After fingerprinting, Genesis and her sons were moved to cold rooms with concrete benches, so crowded there was very little space to lay down. Genesis remembered that at least the officers there were friendlier than those under the bridge; they gave the waiting migrants juices and burritos. The floor was cold, Martín said, but more comfortable than sleeping on gravel.

The Mylar blankets provided no warmth or comfort. The bathrooms didn't have doors, and Martín felt uncomfortable using them. Martín's face cringed as he reflected on his experience in these *hieleras*. He was worried they were going to continue living in these places, but his mother assured him they were on their way home. Still, he found himself worrying incessantly: "Where's my aunt? Where are they taking us? Are they going to send me back to Honduras?" Adriana and her child had been allowed to stay with Genesis for a day after apprehension, but she was released with her child from under the bridge before Genesis. Fortunately, Adriana and her child had been sent to New York and were safe, but Genesis, Gael, and Martín did not know that until a month after their release. Still, Martín felt guilt: He had not been able to protect his family, something well beyond his age and capacity to do. He feared that they had been deported to Honduras and that he had lost them forever. He cried as he replayed the experience.

Moving from *hielera* to *hielera*, Martín could not sleep. When asked how he felt being there, he simply said, "Nothing. I felt nothing," accompanied by a facial expression of utter numbness. He tried to dispel the anxiety, fear, and pain that were boiling inside of him. Martín would close his eyes at mealtime, he said, to imagine that what he was eating was tasty; it was the only way he could stomach the food. Who knew when they would eat again? He remembered one *hielera* that had a cart with cookies, juices, and other things; and detainees had options of food and were permitted to grab what they wanted. It was also the only *hielera* that let everyone watch a movie while they waited. In other places, families would just sit in a room with nothing in sight to entertain them or help pass the time. Martín recalled that since there was little entertainment around them, the kids in the *hielera* would talk and try to play with each other. There he befriended a Cuban boy, and together they made a soccer ball from the Mylar blanket they had been given; but when they started playing *futbol*, the night-shift guards yelled at them to stop. As the boys returned to their beds, the guards watched and laughed mockingly at them. The night-shift guards were not friendly. Martín said, "When we went to get juices, they would scold us and not let us do anything. We had to go back to our places. I hadn't played with a child my age in a while. It was fun until it wasn't anymore. I hated being there." Without play, entertainment, or community, there was nothing else to do but to lie down and pretend to sleep, a human need that could not be relieved. Martín framed the mindset of a migrant desperate for sleep but exhausted by fear: "How could you sleep on a cold barren floor when you're afraid and anxious about what will happen next?"

Daytime staff was different, friendlier and more agreeable to letting the children play. The boys were allowed outside in the sunlight to kick the ersatz ball while the guards watched and cheered, enjoying the boys playing. "Nice" doctors would also come to check on them. Martín recalled one time when the doctors brought them sweets, chocolates, and blueberry bars. Besides their conversations with other detained families, this was the only pleasant interaction they had in the *hieleras*.

From that *hielera*, they were transferred to another one where the conditions were pretty much the same, except it had a bit more space. Without windows or doors to see out of their enclosures, detainees couldn't tell night from day. Once, Martín said, his mother told him that they should try and sleep since it was nighttime. As they got ready to sleep for the night, a new migrant and her child entered the *hielera*. The woman told them that it was early in the morning, not nighttime—the day had just begun. Martín and his mom looked at each other with confusion and horror at the inability to know the time of day but, more significantly, at how long they had already been in the *hielera*. Martín wanted to keep track of time, but the disorientation from not having any indication of time or its passing added to his confusion. Without clocks or windows to judge day and night, they began to tell time, roughly, by noting when the workers changed shifts.

Genesis, Martín, and Gael were moved to what would be their last detention location. But it would add to the misery they had endured. There the family was abruptly split up. An officer without empathy in his voice said that Genesis was not going to be with her children anymore.

"Why?" she asked with alarm.

The response was callous: "Those are the rules that you have to follow." Genesis wanted to know where her boys would be taken, but she was just told not to worry, that they would be okay. She beseeched the officers to allow her to keep Martín by her side. She was denied and told that he was past the age limit of 10 years. Even after separation, Genesis would ask to see the boys continually, to no avail. Sometimes guards would play with her emotions. They would say "Wait, we'll go get them" but never produced the boys. What little comfort she could derive was knowing Martín and Gael were together. But with her sons taken from her, Genesis's agony began anew, causing her to stop eating and develop a fever and an intense headache. For 2 long days, the family was apart.

While Genesis disclosed the separation to Hilda, Martín did not mention it to Tatiana. He had effectively avoided the topic until asked a couple of times, "Anything else you want to share about your experience in detention? In the *hieleras*?"

"Well," he said, taking a deep breath. "Actually, there is. They separated me from my mom. They took my brother and me to one place, and my mom to another. I didn't see her for one whole day. I didn't think I was going to ever see her again." It was one of the worst moments of his young life, and it grieved him deeply to reflect on this experience. He said he even became physically sick from not knowing when he would see her again. When separated, Gael and Martín were taken to another place in the same building and given soap to bathe and small towels. "Everywhere I went," Martín said, "I looked into every cell I walked by to see my mother. But I never saw her. I was sad and felt bad. I thought I would never see my mom again." Through the separation, Martín suffered but, he thought, probably not as much as his mother did. The boys were together at least, and she could only wait desperately.

When Genesis was told that her family would be released, her hope leaped. Release day came, and finally, Genesis saw her boys waiting for her in front of the detention facility. "Sentía que volví a vivir" ("I felt I came back to life").

After reunifying, officers took Genesis and her family to an immigration office in Tucson. CBP retook their fingerprints and gave Genesis a document that would permit travel in the United States. She was told to check in with immigration authorities 15 days from the day she was released. However, when she showed up days later, she was told to come back to court nearly 2 years from the date of our interview with her. Genesis realized that 2 years must pass before she knew what her future in the United States would look like. She was not told that she was not allowed to work and that she must enroll her children in school as soon as possible.

Their next stop was at a shelter where they were well treated. Staff and volunteers made sure to call her family and tell them that Genesis and the boys were safe. Even though they would probably stay for 2 days, shelter workers assured them that they could stay for as long as they needed until their tickets came. From there, they were moved to a hotel with other migrants. It was the best 6 days Martín had had since leaving home. There were toys, bicycles, skates, tennis balls, basketballs, and soccer balls. They could go outside of their rooms and were free to have fun; kids were finally allowed to be kids. Mothers talked and watched their children play. At night, kids had to be in their rooms but could stay up and talk, read, and play video games. It did not feel like jail, Martín said. This place was where families waited for their sponsors in the United States to send bus and plane tickets.

Arriving at their family in Tennessee did not disappoint. Martín remembered being in the comfort of the home of Genesis's cousin, wearing clean clothes borrowed from cousins. He liked the cousin's father, who Martín began to call *Abuelo*, a generous man who took the family out to shop and eat. Now he had more than just one set of clothes and could eat until he was full. It was also the first time he had eaten something that made him feel happy and energized.

But then things changed. Once settled down, when life could be lived without the fear, pain, discomfort, indignities, and suffering the boys had been through, the accumulated adversities suddenly sapped Martín's and Gael's physical and emotional strength. Genesis said that Martín and Gael lived through what she called "a shock," falling into a 2-month depression during which the boys stayed in their rooms all day, with no desire to come out or eat. They drank water but hardly took a bite out of the food their mother prepared for them. She would invite them to go help her buy groceries so that they would get out of the house, but they refused. Genesis suffered.

"It broke my heart to see my children not go out. They did not even see sunlight," Genesis added. In desperation, Genesis texted a friend in Austin to see if she could help her out. The friend said that the boys' situation was dangerous and, if it persisted, Genesis could fall into a depression as well. She invited them to come live with her. Genesis was unsure. But waiting for the boys' conditions to "go away" simply wasn't an option anymore. Genesis decided to move to Texas. Martín's new *abuelo* in Tennessee drove them to Dallas. From there, they went to Austin to visit another *tía*, Genesis's friend who was not a biological aunt; but it didn't matter to him. He wanted to be surrounded by the warmth and protection of family. This *tía* was kind to him, and she had a son close to his age whom he now called *primo* (cousin). They decided to stay in Austin. At the time of the interview, Martín and his family had only lived in Austin for 2 weeks.

There is no way of knowing precisely what the boys actually experienced during the "shock" that Genesis described. We may infer that it was a depressive reaction. But both boys suffering the "shock" at the same time? Was it a case of folie à deux wherein two individuals, usually members of a close family, report an identical or similar mental disorder?[7] Without a thorough history and examination of Gael and Martín, independently, I can only infer that they had lived in survival mode during unbearable ordeals. Naturally, their minds and bodies depended on the instinct of self-preservation. During those critical times, individuals function adequately to stay alive; they do it and do it effectively. It is only later, when the crisis is past or resolved—when it is in the individual's "rear-view mirror," so to speak—that the effects are felt, when the body's stress systems break down, as discussed in Chapter 9. Then, living in survival mode becomes dysfunctional, once protective psychological mechanisms recede, no longer being needed. Gradually, stressful and traumatic memories, flashbacks, sensations, and other detritus begin to surface. It is as if the mind pushes the buried, unresolved, unprocessed, confusing, and painful material to the surface, causing the "shock" as Genesis called it. When settled into a secure home, the brothers' months-long depressions surfaced, when survival was assured.

As they wrapped up the interview, Genesis reflected on how tough it was to live in a country where you don't have much family, especially when you have left loved ones behind. "Pues, estamos tratando de adaptarnos. A ver qué pasa en estos dos años que nos dieron de permiso," she added ("Well, we are trying to adapt. Let's see what happens in these two years they permitted us to be here"). She spoke about Bianca, her eldest child, and their dreams of being together again one day. Bianca wants to graduate from medical school and bring her mother back to Honduras, but both women know that it will take a long time.

Martín said he enjoyed having his *primo* around, playing soccer and going to the neighborhood pool. However, he felt like he hadn't made too many friends in the neighborhood; the kids spoke English, went to different schools, and didn't play outside. In Honduras, he would walk home with his classmates after school and play soccer outside of their homes. Now, he was spending much more time at home playing video games. His *tía* would take him and his cousin to the park to play instead.

Although Genesis's family had only been in Texas for a short time, she had already seen a significant change in Martín and Gael. They now enjoyed going to the pool near their home and playing at the park with their aunt. "Están saliendo del shock que ellos tenían" ("They are coming out of the shock that they had"). Martín was excited to start school and had already enrolled and met his teacher, but unfortunately, the coronavirus pandemic delayed them. Martín has asked Genesis often when he will be able to go, but he must wait until he is vaccinated. This process was taking longer than he expected, and he was anxious to begin. Whenever Genesis suggested that they should go back to Honduras, Martín replied, "No Mami, ya sufrimos" ("No Mommy, we already suffered"). Genesis is trying to adapt but feels that she will never make the transition entirely. Genesis marveled that she had left Honduras with a few *lempiras*, and now her dream of bringing her sons to safety had come true. She had persevered even when hope had seemingly abandoned them. She knows that they have some obstacles to overcome but sees also that there are new dreams the family can pursue together.

Notes

1. Romero, 2019.
2. Aguilar, 2019.
3. Aguilar, 2019.
4. Moore, 2019a.
5. Romero, 2019.
6. On August 3, 2019, a 21-year-old man espousing extreme right-wing beliefs against Mexican people opened fire inside of a Walmart store in El Paso. The terrorist attack killed 23 people and injured 23 others.
7. Vargas Alves Nunes et al., 2016.

12

A Mother's Doubt, a Child's Hunger[*]

Psychological distress affecting one member of the family will naturally raise the distress levels of others in the family system; it ripples throughout the family and upsets its balance. Viewed as a system with parts, roles, connections, and interactions, the family is a complex system. Balancing cohesion, identity, and emotional connection with the autonomy and separateness of its members is what families do ideally. All it takes is a negative change in one person's psychological well-being to trigger change in the family's delicate balance. To compensate for the disequilibrium, members step up to assume the roles and responsibilities of the member who cannot meet them. Jumping into these roles is not always healthy, but sometimes it is necessary, especially in critical times. Family systems abhor a vacuum, and members shift organically to fill the absence created by others. Such scrambled roles may lead children to assume parental roles that may suit the family in immediate distress but not after. When the distressed family member wishes to resume their roles, the transition may not be easy as the member who had filled the gap may not know how or want to let go. This issue could be resolved there. But if it isn't, the conflicts and resentments can live on in the family through memories, myths, secrets, childrearing beliefs, bodily sensations, and even silence; a disequilibrium and struggle may be passed from one generation to the next.[1] What's left may be a family cycling through its past trauma across the generations.

Little Walnut Creek Public Library, a welcoming brown building decorated with flags from around the world, was an unfamiliar place for new immigrants who remained fearful of being rounded up by immigration patrols. Families met my team there, knowing it was a chance to memorialize what they had lived through. The Little Walnut Creek Library is located in the Runberg section of Austin, a low-income neighborhood beset by many urban woes: poor

[*] Case profile contributed by Tatiana Londoño with Hilda Torres.

Through Iceboxes and Kennels. Luis H. Zayas, Oxford University Press. © Oxford University Press 2023.
DOI: 10.1093/oso/9780197668160.003.0013

healthcare; inadequate housing; insufficient after-school programming; high rates of unemployment, prostitution, and crime; and low rates of code compliance that left ugly pockmarks of decaying and empty buildings. The library is hard to miss; it sits near a supermarket where families shop regularly. Once inside to meet my team, parents relaxed, some even saying that they would bring their children back. And the family that Tatiana Londoño and Hilda Torres met one day—María Fernanda, her husband Javier, and their 8-year-old daughter, Valeria—was no different. Entering the library, they seemed relieved to meet two young Latinas instead of a trap sprung by immigration officers. Like other families, they now had another resource, one that cost nothing yet could be a lifeline for stirring young minds.

Valeria's eyes were a study in curiosity, of a child ready to explore the world ahead of her, as if she were finally free to do so. But she was skeptical, too. Tatiana offered Valeria snacks and coloring books, but it took coaxing and a glance at her parents for approval. They nodded that it was okay to accept the offerings. After making her choices, Valeria looked at Tatiana and said, self-assuredly and trustingly, "I'm ready to start."

Their migration story began on what seemed a typical day of chores, errands, and meals at their home in Honduras. But it changed quickly when police raided their home, SWAT-style, and arrested Javier. María Fernanda, Valeria, and Pedro, their 16-year-old son, could do nothing but watch, horrified. To their frantic questioning, the police responded with callous silence. They took Javier into custody, "Como cualquier otro delincuente" ("Like any other criminal"), María Fernanda said, without a warrant or reason. They did not get an explanation that afternoon. Days later, after beatings by police and two civilian men, Javier was told that he had been accused by a woman of stealing her bulls. The men who beat Javier, one older and one younger, were her husband and son. María Fernanda collected proof of Javier's innocence: a letter from Javier's boss and a copy of his schedule showing that Javier was at work at the time the cattle were stolen. Javier was released. The welts, bruises, and broken ribs were one thing; the emotional injuries ran deeper, and the humiliation in front of his children was unbearable. Yet the fact that he had survived such an ordeal was at the same time empowering. Javier found the strength to return to police authorities to report the beating by the two men (intentionally omitting the police officers' participation). Surprisingly, Javier prevailed, although, as often happens in places like Honduras, it would be a Pyrrhic victory. Death threats started coming in, and Javier and María Fernanda knew they were not empty ones.

The woman making the accusation, her husband, and her son brought in local gang members, known for killing anyone. In other villages the gangs visited, entire families were murdered.

Javier, 42, and María Fernanda, 40, knew that relocating to another part of Honduras would not guarantee safety. They had to escape. The plan, devised by Javier, was to send María Fernanda along with Valeria and Pedro first. Javier would stay behind for a few days to sell their belongings to help with the costs. Just days after the Feast of the Epiphany in January, a high holy day in Latin America, María Fernanda and her children set out from Honduras. The next 5 months would be harrowing ones. María Fernanda and the children traveled by bus to Ciudad Hidalgo in Chiapas in southern Mexico to wait for Javier. Then, they heard about migrant caravans, a phenomenon that Donald Trump used to monger hate and spread fear about a tsunami of pillaging brown and Indigenous people. While María Fernanda was just learning about them, the *caravanas* had been around for several months, full of desperate people seeking safety and justice from the dangers and violence at the hands of gangs and police, with no recourse. The 2,500-mile trek was arduous and dangerous, but people felt safer doing it in solidarity and with the support of many others. Despite not having arrived as part of a caravan, María Fernanda and the kids mixed in with others. It provided safety but not much else; everything had to be done on the streets: sleep, eat, earn money, urinate, defecate. María Fernanda was utterly uncomfortable; she didn't want her children to have to go through that. She repeated a theme we heard often in our conversations with asylum-seeking migrants: You find both good and bad people along the way. Kind, generous, unnamed Mexicans brought them water and bread during those exhausting and frightening nights.

Seventeen days after his family departed, Javier began his journey north. He met up with María Fernanda in Palenque in Chiapas, where they had moved with the caravan. The journey was hardest on their children, and it was then that María Fernanda's doubts about their decision took hold. She could not bear to put their children through more hardship. Immediately, Javier looked for work and a place to rent. Javier and María Fernanda knocked on doors, some of which slammed in their faces, while others closed as they approached. "Find a job," some would say. If only it were that simple.

"It is something inexplicable, how difficult it is to come down those roads," María Fernanda said about traveling through Mexico. There were many nights spent sleeping on the ground. When they could afford it, they ate; and when money ran out, they went hungry. María Fernanda quickly clarified that they gave what little food they had to the kids. Pointing to Javier, she explained, "He strove to take great care so that the children had their food." Finally, Javier was able to find a job as a construction handyman, earning about $5 a day. Work supervisors took advantage of him, knowing that Javier was in need. But his talent and hard work paid off: Other employers noticed his skills and offered him higher pay if he worked for them. Now, Javier could afford a place to rent. But landlords were hesitant. Turned away yet again, Javier's family spent another night on the street. María Fernanda asked herself—on many occasions—why she had brought her children to this point. Javier's friends in Honduras sent money, and they secured the room that had seemed like such a distant wish. It was just a room of concrete walls, no kitchen, no appliances. The floor was their bedding; their clothes were their blankets. But it was home, a sanctuary.

On the days that Javier worked, María Fernanda and the children waited for him to get home, long days of hunger until they heard Javier enter the room with whatever food he'd collected that day. Days blended together this way. Valeria befriended a neighbor who came home for lunch before re-turning to work. The kind lady invited Valeria into her home for lunch when she could. For Valeria, but not María Fernanda or Pedro, it meant no longer waiting for her father to arrive to have her first meal of the day. The neighbor was at first distrustful of María Fernanda and Javier, "y más a nosotros que nos tienen por lo peor" ("and more of us who they think the worst of"). Through Valeria's friendship and innocence, the neighbor began to offer her food to María Fernanda and Pedro as well. After working a double shift one day, Javier brought home a mini-stove. Using a pan and large spoon lent to them by the landlord, they cooked eggs and beans. María Fernanda and Javier would scavenge through dumpsters for edible fruits and vegetables. With a good washing, these scraps made a meal.

After about 2 months in Palenque, the family found an organization pro-viding Central American migrants monetary aid. A family of four received 6,000 pesos per month, and over the next 3 months, they were able to save 8,000 pesos, enough to get them to the US–Mexican border. María Fernanda knew that, left to his own devices, Javier would just keep working and they would never make it to the United States. The aid they received was their ticket out of there and closer to safety. And with that, 5 months after their arrival at Palenque, they headed north again. It took weeks—long, tiring, hungry, frightening weeks—to get to the border. At times, they could afford a bag of chips and water for Valeria. Sometimes, they were not allowed on buses because they lacked documentation. Just as often as bus drivers turned them away, there was always someone who snuck them onto a bus. When they could not get on a bus, they found a place to stay for a day or two until they could try again. With the continuation of the *caravanas*, Mexican locals were apprehensive of Central Americans. Opinions and news reports circulated on social media, denigrating migrants as invaders. María Fernanda and her family grew increasingly frightened.

As much as Javier tried to protect his family, María Fernanda wanted to give up. She questioned herself, time and again, and felt guilty for putting her family in the predicament they were in. As María Fernanda spoke about her guilt in the library with Hilda, her fingers trembled, and she scratched her head nervously. She looked to where Javier sat in the library, comforted by his gaze. She lamented putting her children in harm's way. María Fernanda grew up with adversity, "That was what hurt me the most, I have suffered since I was little, and I got used to it." Not so her children. There were times when they split the only taco they could afford. Still, they opted to give Valeria their portions. In almost poetic words, María Fernanda said, though she barely ate, "Yo me llenaba mi estómago de satisfacción de ver que Valeria comía" ("I would fill my stomach with satisfaction to see that Valeria ate").

María Fernanda and her son, Pedro, believed they understood their situation more clearly than Valeria. But, in fact, Valeria told Tatiana, she hid her pain and did not cry as often as her mother and brother did. She was determined to be strong for them, an outsized demand for a child of her age but one necessary for their survival. Valeria's strength helped the family arrive near the US–Mexican border in late May. As they made their way down to the Río Grande, María Fernanda's doubts stirred once again. She was ready to turn back when Customs and Border Protection (CBP) officers yelled at the family to stop and return to Mexico. Javier was not having it—they were just too close—and quickly stopped María Fernanda from giving up: "We are already here!" His words did not absolve María Fernanda of the thought that she would never be able to forgive herself if something happened to her kids while crossing. "Ever since I set foot in that river, my nerves got hold of me," she said between heart-wrenching sobs. It was the crucible of their journey, realizing that they had already put their children at risk for so long and, once at the river, there was no turning back.

A CBP rescue boat quickly approached them as officers watched through binoculars from the riverbank. The rescuers put life jackets on Valeria first, then Pedro, and finally on María Fernanda and Javier. María Fernanda recalled friendly CBP rescuers bringing them to safety on the US side where a group of reporters tried to interview migrants before they were taken to the detention facility. But Valeria remembered the CBP officer as unkind and that she had to stop crying because the more she cried, the more her mother cried. Valeria closed her eyes to hold in the tears. And there was worry, too, because her mother was near giving up and returning to Honduras. Would she blurt something out to the CBP agents that would send them back to Honduras? With the insight seen often in children who have gone through the ordeal of migration, Valeria knew they had no choice but to move forward into the unknown. She wanted to show her mother that they needed to keep fighting and that she was going to be strong. She would not cry anymore. They had suffered enough and couldn't take it anymore. She missed Honduras and her family there. It was home. But a new life was ahead of them.

First stop, a *hielera*, packed with hundreds of migrants. Children were crying, mostly from hunger rather than fear, and a young noticeably pregnant woman screamed from stomach pains. CBP officers told the expectant mother that detention was not a place to seek help or mercy. She was sent to another facility. Everyone was interrogated. Javier's paternity was questioned because Valeria did not carry his surname. Officers took Valeria to a separate room, but María Fernanda could still hear their conversation. Valeria was interrogated with questions such as "Where do you live? What does it look like where you live? Did you have any pets? Does your family have clean water? What was their house built of?" She responded as best as a child could. Valeria recalled,

> They wouldn't let me talk to my dad. I would tell them it was my dad, and they wouldn't believe me. They would tell me they would give me all these things, like candy, if I would tell them the truth. They would say he was my uncle and were forcing me to say that. I would just cry and keep repeating to them that he was my dad, and I wasn't lying.

As Valeria told of the interrogation, she pressed hard on the crayon, coloring forcefully, angrily, forgetting the lines she had carefully avoided. Her voice grew softer, and her eyes would not leave the coloring book as she continued telling Tatiana, "They still wouldn't listen and would just yell at me, calling me a liar. After a while, I became really scared of them. So, I hid behind my mom. I couldn't look at them anymore." María Fernanda was willing to do anything to prove that Javier was Valeria's father, and CBP asked for a DNA test, to which María Fernanda and Javier readily agreed.

Detention was cold and crowded. Except for the Mylar sheets, they received nothing for warmth, not even kind words from officers. Everyone felt the hunger, the cold, and the mounting yet stifled desperation. Everyone reached a low point. Children cradled up in mothers' arms no matter their age, the closest to safety and home they could feel. Mothers' comfort and warmth won over the insecurities of what others would say, especially the teenagers who would be concerned, in most neighborhoods, with appearances and the opinion of peers. Warehoused in rooms of unsociable strangers, children did not talk to each other. No one had the energy to engage, even when Valeria could have used a friend to confide in. Seeing people suffer around her gave Valeria another perspective, balancing the inequities. From this 8-year-old girl came statements like, "I wasn't just worried for myself and my family. I was worried about all the children there. It made me so sad to see them so scared and crying all the time. I was worried they were also separated from their *papis*."

But despite her mature insights, Valeria was still a child, recalling being barefoot—cold and dirty feet. The *hielera* place was "awful, creepy, and scary. A really ugly place that no one should ever have to be in." On her face, as she said this, was disgust and horror. They were watched all the time by cameras everywhere including in the bathroom. She wanted to go home. She wanted to be with her father. When Tatiana probed about the detention center, Valeria made it clear she did not want to discuss it. "That's all I remember. That's it. It was just a horrible place. The place that took my daddy away from me. The place that didn't believe me and treated us horribly. It bothers me to think about it more." María Fernanda and Javier were held in the same room nearby, but they could not stand next to each other. An officer told Javier that his family would be separated. This news made Javier physically ill, but the officers did not believe him. His blood pressure rose, and he desperately asked them for water; but they ignored him. Javier had to take matters into his own hands and grabbed water himself and sat down. When Valeria saw her father, she ran toward him; but an officer quickly grabbed her and told her that she needed to stay away from her father. María Fernanda pulled Valeria toward her; Javier continued to look very distressed. María Fernanda went to Javier and hugged him for seconds before a guard yelled, "What part do you not understand? Go, get away from him, go and sit where you were told to sit." No one cared about how Javier felt, and it was agonizing for María

Fernanda and her children to watch helplessly. Officers processed them in different areas according to gender: María Fernanda and Valeria remained together, while Javier and Pedro were taken away separately. María Fernanda would not see her husband Javier for 2 months.

Pedro was placed with other teenage boys in the facility, away from his mother and sister. Valeria recalled her mom sobbing, but she held back tears, barely. Her mother was devastated and deeply worried that she might not see her son again. Everyone else was struggling, and someone had to keep hold of their emotions, Valeria thought. They were detained for 5 days, barefooted the entire time, having lost their shoes in the river. Wet clothes dried on their bodies, and no one cared to give them something dry to wear. Their hunger was neglected; out of desperation, Valeria begged the officers for food. Despite the plea from an innocent child, the two were given no food after being rebuffed by guards. María Fernanda implored, saying, "But my child can't control her hunger anymore" and was dismissed with a dry and harsh, "That is not our problem." María Fernanda offered Valeria a bottle of water, but the child rejected it. The water made her nauseous; she needed food.

Hunger. That is what Valeria remembered most. Emotions about the abusive acts of the officers returned to hunger, not being fed enough. No amount of begging the officers would soften their reactions; they responded by yelling back at her to stay in her place and be silent. Relating her emotions to the many instances of outright rejection by guards, Valeria took a deep breath and let out a sigh, looked over to where her father sat in the library, the father she thought she would never see again.

It did not go unnoticed by others in detention; their fellow detainees were suffering, too. In moments of cruelty, like this one, good people were always nearby, divine interventions that every migrant knew. Migrant mothers, detained, knew the anguish of a hungry child. One of them offered Valeria a sandwich that she had kept from the morning meal. María Fernanda thanked the woman repeatedly and cried tears of relief. She said that the woman simply responded, "Don't worry. This is what I had saved it for. For someone who really needed it." As much as Valeria did not like sandwiches, there was no thought of rejecting this one. Valeria "devoured it happily," she said. "She even wanted to eat the wrapper," María Fernanda joked during the interview, trying to ease the painful memory with humor. After her first full stomach in a long time, Valeria was finally able to have an hour of uninterrupted sleep. But how could one small sandwich replace days of hunger?

Finally, at dinnertime they each got a piece of bread and juice, the meal they would get twice a day for the next few days.

The barbarity of *hielera* bathrooms was widely known and familiar to our research team. The topic of bathrooms appeared in every interview and conversation we had with parents and children. It was a familiar story of no privacy, half walls or no walls surrounding the toilets, and security cameras that captured every personal, private moment.[2] Jammed together, people had to sit near the toilet, the experience unbearable for both those using the bathroom and those able to see it. Children saw others use the toilets, provoking humiliation and discomfort for everyone. The solution was for mothers to form human screens for each other—not much of an improvement but at least an attempt at decency. Nights were restless with the cries of sick children, mothers weeping, longing for their separated children, and the chaos of overcrowding. Sleep, even sanity, was impossible.

Valeria felt many things, mostly hunger and dolefulness at seeing her father taken away in handcuffs, this time not by corrupt Honduran police but by US officials, in the very land where she had been promised safety. They took him to who knew where, she told Tatiana. She overheard the officers tell her mother that Javier was being separated from them. Now telling the story, Valeria's expression had a look of disdain for the officers, even as she intently focused on coloring the princess's dress with a bright pink crayon. Tears welling in her eyes, Valeria remembered wanting to give her father a hug and kiss goodbye, but the officers would not have any of it. "I never saw him again [until released months later]. I only got to tell him quickly that I would miss him," she said.

Javier was offered release but only if he signed some forms, in English. He could not read them. Javier refused to sign documents that Immigration and Customs Enforcement (ICE) and the Department of Homeland Security used in their ruse to send unwitting signatories back to their countries. Seeing his anxiety grow about signing the release papers, the immigration officers applied more pressure. The longer Javier refused, the longer he would be kept in detention without seeing his family. Valeria recalled talking to her father by telephone once she was released, while he was still in detention. The sorrow of hearing her father's sadness and desperation to be reunited with his family was unbearable for her. She knew that their conversations only made him sadder, more disconsolate, more discouraged. She worried that he might sign the papers out of desperation.

Once more, Valeria would force herself to be strong. She would not cry like her mother did so often and, instead, held her mom tightly. Valeria was taking care of her mother. Played out in Valeria's description were the disordered family roles that children who have gone through multiple hardships and indignities in their exodus must assume. Parents can only parent so much before they too capitulate to extreme stress. Family roles begin to change: Young children forced to take care of parents and older siblings, teenagers forced to care for younger siblings and parents, or other combinations of roles that they assume without experience or instructions on how to do it. Humiliated by the times when they were berated, refused, or dismissed and reduced to begging, defecating in open spaces, and rummaging in dumpsters while their children watched, parents could easily succumb, abdicating their roles as the "executive subsystem" of the family system. It is a testament to the strength of families who endure disrupted family scripts that some are able to resume their respective roles as children and parents. Without a doubt, families that return to normal, or at least a new normal in which parents resume being parents and children can be children, will still carry vestiges of the times when their functioning was altered. It may not be spoken of, but the past will regardless be present. Valeria personified this when she told Tatiana that she was nervous about the future after detention. She had a sense that her family would never be the same. The injustice in Honduras, the backbreaking journey, mortifications, and abuses had changed everything.

News finally came that they would be released, but excitement had become an ancient sensation for María Fernanda and Valeria. It felt new and different— and didn't last long. Their cautious joy was interrupted by the credible fear interview (CFI) that María Fernanda had to undergo. It was more of an interrogation of quick rat-tat-tat questions than an interview: Why did you come here? How can you prove that you would be killed? Are you sure about that? How do we know your husband didn't steal the cattle? Why does your daughter have a different last name than her father? Who is your sponsor? And many more intrusive questions. Despite all the pressure, María Fernanda passed the CFI.

Once told that she and Valeria could leave, María Fernanda immediately asked to see Pedro, whom she had not seen since their first day. "What son?" the CFI interviewer asked. The CFI officer was not aware she had a son, although other officers knew. He, too, had been kept in the dark by his colleagues. "What's his name? I'll look for him," the officer said. He was very forthright; he did not know she had another child besides Valeria. Within hours, Pedro was reunited with his mother and sister. ICE had again proved its slapdash record-keeping.

María Fernanda asked if she could say goodbye to Javier but was completely ignored. She continued to ask when she would see her husband again. To shut her up, a guard assured her that he would be released soon. And with that confirmation, the incomplete family was swept into a cold-hearted release from detention. They were driven to a parking lot somewhere in a south Texas city, the name of which she never learned. "Get off," the agent ordered. "Where are we?" María Fernanda asked. She had no idea and no bearing as to what to do or what direction to go. "Well, y'all will figure it out" were the agent's parting words as he laughed and drove away. María Fernanda had been in predicaments like this before, in Mexico and Guatemala; but this was a new place with a new language. She would, indeed, figure it out because she must. With Pedro and Valeria in tow, she wandered about the area, alert to sounds and sights that would lead her to people. Indeed, her wandering brought her upon other Spanish-speaking people. They provided advice and guidance to grab a bus that would take her to San Antonio, where she could find help. They directed her to the bus station, a place teeming with migrants who also had to "figure it out" like her, abandoned there by CBP or ICE officials with nothing to go on. At the very least, María Fernanda said, the staff at the bus station was gracious and treated her well. There, a hopeful intercession happened, like the many others that had appeared randomly, at the most unusual moments and in the most unexpected circumstances in their long journey. María Fernanda met a woman who was having problems with her phone, and Pedro, adept at electronic devices, offered to help fix it. In return, the woman let María Fernanda call her brother. Happy and surprised, he wanted to buy her a ticket immediately; but tickets to the Texas town where he lived were sold out. Memorial Day was the next day, and the station would be closed. Furthermore, the scheduled buses to her destination were sold out until Wednesday, which meant 3 long days of waiting without shelter. Her brother could not drive to them; it was too risky for an undocumented person. He arranged for his boss to get María Fernanda and the kids. The boss agreed to meet them in San Antonio; buses there were still operating, although the one they needed to board would arrive at midnight on the same day. They took the bus, arrived around midnight, and were met by her brother's boss. After knowing true, deep pain, this was "all the suffering we had to go through" after release, María Fernanda said. She was grateful to her brother and his boss.

At the time of the interview, the family lived in their own place in Austin, near the Little Walnut Creek Library, María Fernanda and Valeria said the early days had been hard, especially because Javier was not released until 2 months later. They settled in with Javier's brother and his wife, but there was tension between the wife and María Fernanda. They were grateful that the uncle had taken them in while they waited for her dad to be released. He was the person who gave them shelter and food until they were able to find their footing as a family. Once Javier was released and found a job, they moved out. It was a tough call since they would be paying twice what they were giving Javier's brother. María Fernanda did not want any problems; they had helped them in their time of most need. Rent at the new place would be due soon at the time of our meeting in the library, but they still did not have enough money to pay. Javier would work hard to make that month's rent, María Fernanda said as she ran her fingers through her hair continuously, scratching her scalp in worry.

Valeria felt that she grew closer to her family after what they had been through. They spent most of their time together, enjoying a more carefree family life in their adopted hometown. Like any other family, she said they get stressed about money or other things, but she said that her parents make sure not to involve or blame her. Her parents resolve the issues by themselves. Javier and María Fernanda were working at regaining their footing as parents again. They were proud to have overcome all they had been through and were pushing forward through more trials. Valeria wanted to move forward and focus on the positive. She had parents she could rely on. They had devoted everything to her and Pedro during the hell they had faced down. While it was still hard to communicate, Valeria felt she could talk to her parents about anything. "Nothing has ever happened to me that I can't tell my parents. I can tell them everything," Valeria told Tatiana. This was especially true with her mom. "I can talk to my mom when I'm sad, angry, happy. My brother talks to my dad. Men get each other more. Just like women get each other. It's just how it is."

Adjusting to life in the United States was still hard for Valeria. She felt fear every time she went to school, not with the regular new-school jitters but real fears that she would be kidnapped. The loneliness of being the new kid in school, barely speaking English, made Valeria feel unsafe walking home alone from school. A recurring fear was of arriving home after school and not finding her father there. "I still think about the moment my father was taken from us in detention. I have nightmares about it. Even when I'm awake, I still think they're going to take him away from me again."

Like thousands of immigrants, María Fernanda had not wanted to leave her home country and wished things had not happened as they did. She often advised people not to take the risk of migrating. Whenever people told her "I want to leave for the United States as well," María Fernanda would say, "It's difficult. It's the hardest thing there can be," to attempt to dissuade them. But people in Central America are living under conditions that they want to escape, and the terrible things they hear about the journey north—pain, suffering, deprivation, rejection, hunger, abduction, thirst, humiliation, exhaustion, assault, and even death—are risks worth taking. When María Fernando said "Don't do it" to those thinking about migrating, they would commonly reply, "We'll take a different route than the one you took." María Fernanda was convinced that she would not have made the journey north if she knew about the suffering, of putting her children through the risks and painful days.

Valeria was steadfast that they were better off and did not want to return to Honduras. As the interviews ended, she showed Tatiana the picture in the coloring book on which she was so intently focused. It wasn't the Disney princess she had just colored. It was Warrior Woman, the Marvel Comics superhero who transforms from a petite, short woman into a tall, statuesque superhero with enormous strength and lightning speed. Valeria looked up with a grin and said, "That's me!"

Notes

1. See Smith-Acuña, 2011, and Wolynn, 2016, for more information.
2. As recently as March 2022, conditions at one detention center in Torrance County, New Mexico, operated by CoreCivic, were deemed unsafe. Critically understaffed, the center held detainees in unsanitary conditions of clogged toilets, moldy sinks, and water leaks throughout the facility. See US Department of Homeland Security, 2022c, and Sacchetti, 2022.

13

Sufrir, *Sufrimiento*, and Hallucinating the Invisible Killer Girl[*]

The psychological effects of migration, detention, separation, threats, and physical suffering are as varied as the children and parents with whom we spoke. We met children, adolescents, and parents who reported nightmares, night terrors, depression, anxiety, panic attacks, insomnia, overeating or undereating, and in a few cases psychotic episodes. We also encountered children with intellectual and cognitive limitations and other disabilities that predated the migration but which were no less affected. The accumulation of stress and trauma can be damaging, but solid coping skills, grit, and resilience can offer a balance.

"Sufrir en la calle, hambre, frío, sol, y todo . . . mucho sufrimiento" ("To suffer on the street, hungry, cold, sun, and everything . . . a lot of suffering"). That is how Antonia summarized the mid-migration journey through Mexico. Antonia was using the word *sufrir* to express a physically felt harm, pain, even punishment. *Sufrimiento* holds a different connotation than suffering. *Sufrimiento*, in Antonia's usage, means deep sorrow, a moral or spiritual pain that one has to endure with patience and conformity, even with martyr-like resignation. Both are words that migrants often use to describe their journey, expressions that sum up the totality of their experience. This resignation helps blur out parts of their journeys, the times too hard or too painful to recall in the sharp relief of memories. Antonia's words are given dimensionality by the words of Mark Lusk and Georgina Sanchez Garcia of the University of Texas at El Paso who write of what they learned from the ordeals of migrants:

> Suffering cannot be defined solely in psychological frameworks. It is also existential, having to do with fundamental questions about life, existence, pain and one's place in the world. Migrants spoke frankly and directly about

[*] Case profile contributed by Hilda Torres with Jamie Turcios-Villalta and Tatiana Londoño.

Through Iceboxes and Kennels. Luis H. Zayas, Oxford University Press. © Oxford University Press 2023.
DOI: 10.1093/oso/9780197668160.003.0014

their hardships, but would quickly move on to topics that gave meaning to their hardship, such as family, faith, strength and hope.[1]

Hilda Torres met Antonia at the Migrant Resource Center during a visit with Jamie Turcios-Villalta and Tatiana Londoño. Outside the center on that day were small groups of Haitian immigrants, waiting or just passing the time until they boarded buses or airplanes to head out to other parts of the country. Some spoke Spanish, but most chatted in Haitian Creole. The migrants looked at Tatiana, Jamie, and Hilda briefly as they approached the welcome center, before returning to their conversations.

Migrants seemed to be able to size people up quickly—friend or foe—a survival skill honed during their risky crossings. Yet, they remained friendly and approachable. It was easy to chat with a group of women from Honduras who had been at the center for a few days, their nights spent sleeping on the pews of a local church that converted its sanctuary at night into a dormitory for the weary. Despite the women's tired faces, they said they were doing well. Age is a hard thing to assess from the faces of people who have undergone extreme physical and mental hardship, who have labored to feed their families and have now taken one of the most dangerous passages imaginable. Some of the women were about Hilda's age, but their struggles in lives of elusion, danger, and exhaustion were etched on their brows and visible in their eyes. The women Hilda approached, who seemed older, didn't understand our study but seemed to pick up on Hilda's nervousness and comforted her naturally with their warmth and friendliness. Women who had undergone adversity that might never be known to anyone but them, who themselves had needed help, were now helping Hilda do her job. Hilda reflected later that these weary migrant women taught her something about authenticity: It was okay to be nervous.

Without time to process what she had just encountered, Hilda walked around to other tables. She made eye contact with an older woman who sat at a table with a younger woman. She greeted the older woman, who seemed eager to talk, having observed Hilda's conversation with the other women. She said they were doing all right and were just bored and tired. As she had done with the group before her, Hilda relayed her purpose, to interview people with children. The woman, who turned out to be Antonia, pointed to her son, Gabriel, 12, who was riveted by the television along with a group of black, brown, and Indigenous kids who typified the countenances of Africa, the Caribbean, and Central and South America. Hilda was surprised by how quickly this migrant woman agreed to talk to a stranger.

Antonia sat at a table with Gabriel. The team moved some chairs around so that Hilda could face Antonia while Tatiana spoke with Gabriel a few feet away. Antonia was 43 and had left Honduras in June. Like so many women escaping domestic violence, Antonia's husband wanted her back insistently and threatened her when she refused. With the combined threats of Gabriel's father and 18th Street Gang and with the help of friends, Antonia took off toward Guatemala with Gabriel. Most days they walked—so many miles that she lost a sense of how much distance they covered on foot—and rode in the occasional taxi or a *combi*, a passenger van modified to accommodate more people and luggage, when they could afford it. Antonia said she financed her escape by selling Avon products. She left owing the company and her clients about 4,000 lempiras (about $200). Guilt was in her voice as she relayed this story, but desperation fueled her reason.

They met other migrants on the same journey north. Bands of migrants connected quickly over their shared experiences and were ready to help one another. Trust was titrated: Among the new connections were people from the town they had just fled, catapulting Antonia and Gabriel into pit-of-the-stomach discomfort and wariness. Those people knew the gangs back home and could send back news of where they were, even get a reward for snitching. Antonia and Gabriel picked up the pace, away from their home-town, through parts of Honduras they had never seen and finally into Guatemala. Antonia explained that between Guatemala and Mexico there is a boundary, a safe place known as *La Linea* (The Line) where the Mexican police are not allowed to apprehend anyone. Antonia, Gabriel, and other voyagers laid low for hours at *La Linea* before they crossed into Mexico. Once they set foot inside Mexico, the police gave chase, but the group ran faster and managed to elude them.

Mexico proved even more difficult to traverse. There were three checkpoints they needed to pass through. The Mexican *federales* manned each checkpoint, and at each spot, the *federales* shook them down for money, threatening them not with deportation but with "getting them lost." Without a choice, Antonia gave them the little money she had. This happened at every checkpoint, whittling down what little money she had; but it was the only way they could keep going. Many forget, Antonia instructed Hilda, that Mexico is a tough country to cross, especially for Central Americans. She felt the slings of discrimination in Chiapas. "Hondurans only do bad things and all that" was one smear she endured.

"We Hondurans have an easy-to-spot accent, and Mexicans know who we are and don't trust us," she said. However, there were also kind Mexicans who offered her food and shelter, not distrust or disdain. In Palenque, Chiapas, deep southern Mexico, Antonia and Gabriel boarded a train that took them to Coatzacoalcos, Veracruz. Antonia said that Gabriel started to feel less fearful and thought that nothing bad would happen to him anymore—the farther from home they traveled, the greater the sense of safety. Once the train left them in Veracruz, they needed to find ways to make the next 650 or more miles to the US border. Walk. Pay for a bus or *combi*. Hitch rides. At one point, Antonia asked a passing car for a ride. The driver said he would take them. After some miles and pleasant conversation, the driver abruptly asked Antonia to have sex with him. If she agreed, he would take them farther north.

"It's true that a mother will do what she can, sacrifice for her son. But I let the man know that I would not do it." Stopping the car, the man said only, "Bájate" ("Get off"). Antonia shook her head as if to cast off the memory. A migrant woman had to tolerate those moments and worse, perhaps as part of *sufrimiento*. What fueled her and Gabriel was knowing they were that much closer to safety, or so they expected.

But to get to the safety of the United States, they had to cross the Rio Grande. Arriving around 3:00 in the morning near Piedras Negras, across from Eagle Pass, Texas, Antonia and Gabriel took cautious steps to make their way down to the banks of the Rio Grande with other migrants—some she knew from her group, others she did not know. As they got to the riverbank, the Mexican *migra*, or maybe it was the *federales*, began chasing them. Knowing there was no turning back and not knowing the river's depth or strength, desperation left only one choice: jump into the river or be deported to Honduras. "Pensé que íbamos a morir" ("I thought we were going to die"), Gabriel said, knowing that leaving Honduras behind called for a plunge into the strong river current.

Entering the water, Antonia and Gabriel saw four people ahead of them almost drown but still manage to make it to the other side. Now Antonia and Gabriel were more determined: "We can make it, too." A young mother with a 7-month-old baby, part of Antonia's group, became afraid to cross; Antonia and Gabriel stayed by her side and coaxed the frightened mother clutching her infant. Growing concerned, with *migras* behind them and the United

States ahead, the small group decided to wade toward the middle of the river. The Mexican officers shined bright lights on them and yelled at them to come back because Customs and Border Protection (CBP) would return them the following day anyway. Antonia and Gabriel grew more afraid of going deeper into the river. As the water rose to their chests, the group linked hands and stood strong—10 adults and children, an infant in its mother's arms, braving the river for life's sake. No way would they go back. They would not. *¡Jamas!* ("Never!").

The tired and hungry group fought the water for 4 hours, bracing themselves against the current and defying the Mexican forces. From Mexico, Antonia heard a man shout, "¡Desgraciados, van a matar a sus hijos! ¡No se arriesguen así!" ("Wretches, you're going to kill your children! Don't take chances like that!"). How ignorant, Antonia thought, we were risking our kids and ourselves to get away from the dangers of corrupt authorities, like them. From the United States, a CBP officer called out to the courageous migrants that a boat was coming for them, words that gave them hope and resolve to hold on for life.

By 7:00 in the morning, as the sun rose, Gabriel began to lose hope, feeling his fingers wrinkling: "Pensé que no iba llegar nadie a salvarme" ("I thought no one would come to save me"). Everyone was tired and cold, their feet and legs cramping. But they kept encouraging each other. Additional encouragement came from a CBP officer, who shouted again, "Hold on. The boat is coming." Hold on. Hold on. Sure, the battered group thought as the river washed away every bit of their energy, the cold, strong current dragging them downstream. When they sighted the CBP boat approaching them, the group was overcome with joy, weeping, and thanking God for the help he had sent. The sound of the boat restored their strength to hold on. Gabriel thought about his future in the United States as he saw the boat. His fear faded.

They were rescued and arrested. In a *perrera*, they were inspected by the officers, who took away all of their belongings and put them inside white bags. After about half a day, the migrants recovered some of the items—missing were things ruined by the long stay in the river, like their water-logged shoes. Given rubber sandals, the group was relocated to a *hielera* in a punishing cold. "Tratan como de que uno aguante frío ahí . . . tratan como de que sufra," Antonia concluded ("They try to keep you cold there . . . they try to make you suffer"). To Gabriel, the *hielera* was like being arrested, criminalized for seeking safety. They sat in the brutal cold with only a crinkly foil blanket, no sweaters, hats, or dry clothes. Antonia described *hielera* bathrooms as others had before and since: half walls, with no door or covering, exposed to other detainees and officials, dirty. Lone women and mothers with children stayed together, men were held apart from them, and men with children were also separated. Gabriel saw CBP officers taking pictures and fingerprinting his mom. Officials looked through Antonia's bag of blood pressure medication. The doctor sent to her said that she needed to relax because she could not leave the facility with her pressure so high. Easy for him to say—how easy could it be to relax after their ordeal and imprisonment in a *hielera*? She took a pill and worried that if her blood pressure did not drop, she would be made to stay longer. The timeline in the *hielera* was blurry to Antonia, but eventually officers told her to form a line along with other detainees and their children and walk to waiting buses. They were taken to a shelter, where Gabriel felt he was finally going to be where he wanted to be. In the shelter, they were better treated and given a place to shower and sleep, a couple of sets of clothes, a Bible, and food. The staff was kind to them, so generous that Gabriel looked like he was ready to open a mini-mart with all the things they gave him. It was the only humor Antonia could find to share with Hilda about their journey. They chuckled.

Nightmares and psychotic episodes, like the break with reality that Valentina suffered in detention during our meeting as told in Chapter 3, were rarer events but still part of the display of effects on people under extreme, prolonged, and intense stress that mounts day in and day out. Lucas was a case in point.[2] He described a disturbing psychological reaction, apparently a psychotic one, which shows how stress and deprivation can emerge and haunt a person for years. Lucas, his older brother Benjamin, and his mother Michelle told their stories to Rocio Morín, Tatiana Londoño, and Jamie Turcios-Villalta, respectively, late one afternoon in January 2020, a year after arriving in Texas. They met in a corner of the Spicewood Springs Branch Library in Austin, an angular red-brick building dating to 1985.

Benjamin was only 12 years old when he left Honduras. The *pandillas* had taken the lives of his uncles. His father, Pedro, would be next. It had become increasingly dangerous for Benjamin and his family because they knew the gruesome reality: The *pandillas* would not stop with his father; they would kill them all and continue to cousins, aunts, and grandparents. That's how they operated, Michelle concluded. The *pandillas* destroyed families, one by one. His parents knew they had no choice but to leave, not just because of the impending threat of murder—Benjamin was nearing his 13th year and would reach the age to be forced into gang membership. The plan they decided upon was to have Pedro leave Honduras immediately, alone, and Michelle and the boys would follow a few weeks later, not drawing attention to Pedro's absence.

It was a short-lived getaway. Michelle and the two boys made it to Mexico, arriving on Christmas Day. Whatever holiday hopes they had were dashed when they were picked up by the police. It was a Christmas experience they would never forget. Many Central American migrants told our researchers of the trying experiences they endured, and Michelle's was no different. They had been so close to crossing the Rio Grande when Mexican authorities chased them and their traveling companions. One by one they were stopped and apprehended. Michelle and Lucas could not elude the police who held pistols in their hands. Benjamin and the older boys got a jump on the police and outran them. They ran as fast as they could until Benjamin stumbled and fell to the ground. He heard his mother's screams and looked back as the police took hold of Michelle and Lucas. The boys stopped running, too, looking back at their families, now in the hands of Mexican police. "No la podía dejar sola. No tenía valor," Benjamin said ("I couldn't leave her alone. I didn't have the courage"). Benjamin and the other boys turned themselves into the Mexican police. Once in custody, the travelers were split up, and Michelle and her sons were locked in a windowless room for a week. The boys cried every day; Michelle blamed herself for bringing them to this traumatic moment, one she had no control over. All they could do was wait. Their hopes were kept alive by the thought of being released and continuing on to reunite with Pedro. But release came with disappointment when they were deported back to Honduras.

There was no homecoming. Word spread quickly that Michelle and her boys had tried to escape Honduras. They now became targets, well aware that they could not stay very long in their *colonia*. (A *colonia* in Latin America is a neighborhood that has no jurisdictional autonomy or representation but may have a postal code.) The second escape attempt came a month later on a bus to the outskirts of their town. There, they met up with a *coyote* Pedro had hired for them. The *coyote* then took them from one bus to another, three buses in total, Benjamin recalled, and then to a truck heading toward Guatemala. The possibility of an accident or kidnapping was undeniable and worried Michelle and Benjamin. Lucas did not speak about it, perhaps because he was too young to conceive of the possibilities. But on this second effort, Pedro had arranged for a *coyote* they trusted. He took good care of them and managed to get them to Guatemala safely. Traveling to Guatemala was relatively tranquil, nothing like Mexico the first time. They once had a scare when the Guatemalan police stopped them. The travelers were taken off the bus and interrogated briefly without any trouble. However, it was only a few minutes, and they soon continued on their journey to Mexico. But once deeper into Mexico, their travels became scary and complicated again. Mexican locals looked at and treated the family of three with contempt and suspicion. It was especially frightening when they had to ride in an enclosed semi-trailer filled with other migrants. There were no windows, and there was no room to breathe. It was filled with too many people and was traveling at a high speed, or so it seemed in the confinement of the trailer. The fear was in their minds, as it was in the minds of other migrants, that the truck would roll over. Benjamin and Lucas did their best to stay calm as they looked around the truck filled with other people, trying to reach loved ones on the other side as well. They struggled to breathe; the ride seemed endless; fear consumed them. Telling it now, in the safety of a public library in Austin, hindsight smoothed out the fear. Nothing tragic happened to anyone on board, although a woman fainted in the truck. She was given water and revived. Benjamin recalls how the group they traveled with helped each other throughout the journey. They all wanted to make it to the United States.

After entering Mexico, they slept in hotels while they waited for their *coyote* to take them to their next destination, the home of a Mexican family, where they stayed for a few days. The hosts had nothing to do with them, no interaction save bringing them the evening meal. The days were long while at the house, being watched and ignored at the same time. Benjamin and his little brother stayed close to their mother, quiet and vigilant. From there, the family was taken to Reynosa, where they were once again placed in a safe house. This time it was only for a short period, while the *coyote* prepared for the journey to cross the Rio Grande. Benjamin was ready to cross the river, although scared and worried. They had been on the road 17 days.

Seeing the Rio Grande reminded Benjamin of the first time they attempted to cross before. On this second attempt, there was thankfully no drama. Now they just boarded a small boat that would take them across the river. It was a risk they were willing to take to reunite with Pedro and leave Honduras behind. Michelle had heard the horror stories of children drowning. She prayed. Benjamin worried that the boat would capsize. The river current was furious and deep, but the boat ride went well.

Finding the Border Patrol in the barren land of south Texas to turn themselves in took time. Along the way, they ran into a mother and her young daughter who needed help, and Benjamin and the group of migrants aided her. Benjamin was scared at how much time they were spending in the desert, and they had no water. Out of desperation, they drank from the river and continued their search for Border Patrol. They walked for hours it seemed until they came upon utility poles. Their eyes followed the cables to the faint lights of a distant ranch, guided by the electric cables. It wasn't long after that they were found by CBP agents before they reached the ranch. Michelle breathed a sigh of relief that it was US Border Patrol and not Mexican police. They were now one step closer to being reunited with Pedro.

The CBP officers had the migrants sit on the ground to question them. The questions intimidated Michelle. They were told to remove hair ties, earrings, shoelaces, and anything else Border Patrol officers deemed potentially lethal or nonessential. They were fingerprinted as they waited to be taken to an immigration facility. They were given water and cookies. Eventually, a truck arrived to take the group to a *hielera* where other parents and children in wet clothing were all cramped into one cold room. Michelle and her sons spent 1 day in that *hielera* before being moved to a *perrera*, where the conditions were not much better. It was a bigger space compared to the *hielera*, but it was nothing more than an indoor cage. They were given food, warm milk, and thin mattresses to sleep on.

They slept in the *perrera* for 1 night before being taken to another *hielera* the next day. "It was always so cold, we were forced to sleep on the floor, and were only given aluminum blankets," Benjamin recounted. They stood in line to pick up their food, a choice between an unappetizing sandwich and an undercooked burrito with a juice box, both usually cold. Then it was back to waiting for the numbers to be called. It was for this reason that the officers wouldn't let anyone sleep, or so they said because detainees needed to be awake to hear their number called. They would even yell at the child if they attempted to rest. The officers were cold and glared menacingly at the immigrants. Benjamin and his family kept to themselves to avoid drawing any trouble.

As Benjamin told his story to Jamie and Michelle told hers to Tatiana at the library on that winter afternoon, Lucas was revealing to Rocio a powerful incident that occurred in the *hielera* and continued to haunt him a year later. At the time of his interview, Lucas was 7 and appeared small for his age. Initially shy, he soon warmed up to Rocio, fiddling with a toy he had picked out from among those the researchers had laid out on the library table. Lucas described detention differently, more naively than Benjamin or Michelle. He described the detention facilities as "apartments." In detention with them was the "invisible girl who kills." Lucas could not see her, but he felt her presence. He would often hear the girl "make a lot of noise." She may have been invisible, but he knew she was there; and Lucas "knew that she ended up in detention because she killed someone." She had followed him to his new home in the United States, and her presence made it difficult for Lucas to sleep alone at night. He often joined Benjamin in his bed for protection from the scary girl. Still, she made noises, and Lucas felt her in the room or the house somewhere. He knew she was there. Fear rattled in Lucas's voice as he talked about her presence in his home. As he described her, his voice filled with fear, and it was apparent that the thought of the invisible girl was still putting a strain on Lucas's mental health and his ability to sleep.

Rocio decided wisely to move away from the topic. There was no point in asking questions that might inflict further strain on Lucas's mental state. We didn't know how much he could tolerate, and the library was no place to pursue this kind of terrifying psychological material. The boy needed professional mental health services. The lingering fear of the invisible killer girl and the pain of the topic may have been too much for Lucas, who, after saying he missed his father, asked to end the interview.[3] Jorge's nightmares about the *chupacabra* in Chapter 10 were disturbing but not persistent memories, and Jorge understood that the *chupacabra* was imaginary. Lucas seemed more convinced of the reality of the invisible girl. It was challenging to make clinical sense of Lucas's invisible killer girl based on what he had told Rocio and on how far she could safely probe. Was it a hallucination that he experienced and may still be experiencing? Could it have been a frightening nightmare so powerful that it felt real to Lucas? Was it a nightmare so real that it was filed in his memory as an actual event? But how would we explain its persistence in his emotional life? Was it a persistent delusion, that is, a fixed but false belief triggered by stress? Research shows that refugees suffer psychotic features mostly in the form of auditory hallucinations and persecutory delusions.[4] Lucas's invisible killer girl had similar features.

While Lucas hallucinated the invisible killer girl, his brother and mother provided him a good deal of support. Less known to him was that his mother and brother had their own set of worries and sorrows. For Michelle, it was the credible fear interview that made her extremely nervous. Would the interviewer believe the reasons she was seeking asylum? Put simply, this was the interview that would determine if they stayed in the United States or not. Michelle had watched as others left their interviews with anger and tears and still others with different expressions that she could make out as joyful or hopeful. Some people would receive a slip of paper that indicated that they had not passed the credible fear standard and would be returned to their country. Other expressions were more inscrutable. Michelle was relieved that her interviewer was kind to her. He asked her a series of questions, took her fingerprints, and called her husband Pedro to let him know that Michelle and the boys were fine. More importantly, the interviewer told Pedro to purchase three bus tickets for his family to take them to him. Michelle and Lucas returned to Benjamin and shared the good news.

Benjamin's set of worries began when he was separated from his mother and brother, just before being released. The officers told them it would only be for a little while, but it was hard for the family to believe. They had heard the stories of families being separated for long periods of time and worried that this would happen to Benjamin. Michelle was horrified and thought repeatedly, "What if I never see him again? I will not leave without him." She did not rest or sleep for the day and a half that they were separated. What makes family separation so stressful and possibly traumatic is the uncertainty of when and if the children will be reunited with their parents. Ambiguity can be worse than cold *hieleras* or hunger. Telling Jamie of the separation, Benjamin's voice softened. Separated from his mother, Benjamin was alone with no one who knew him or cared. Soon, though, two familiar faces entered the room of other boys separated from their families. They were two boys he had befriended from the migrant group. They had not seen each other since they'd crossed the river and been taken away by immigration officers. Each of their families had been taken in separate directions by officers. Seeing his friends brought Benjamin a bit of hope. He was not completely alone anymore. The three of them spent the time talking, playing, and sleeping. They watched *Toy Story*. During meals, Benjamin and his friends would gather in a circle and place their food at the center to share; their portions felt larger this way. The three of them took care of each other, while they waited to be reunited with their parents. Hopefully.

Having friends in detention did not inoculate Benjamin from the scorn and threats by guards. In one incident, Benjamin went to use the bathroom but did not know it was closed for cleaning. A guard yelled at him, threatening to place him in a room alone with no bathroom, no food, while his mother was released. Using the bathroom became frightening, and avoiding the guard was a method of survival. Benjamin avoided the facilities as much as he could. He stayed with his three friends until one by one they were called to leave.

In another area, Michelle and Lucas waited. Michelle was worried that she would be forced to leave without Benjamin, something she would refuse to do. After a day and a half, her family's number was called, and they were released from detention. As Michelle walked out holding Lucas's hand, she saw a boy who might be Benjamin. As he came closer, her eyes confirmed that it was her son. They had a tearful but joyous reunion, embracing as though they had not seen each other in years, relieved to be reunited and released. They had spent a total of 5 days in detention.

From the *perrera*, they were taken by bus to another place, a church. It was much better compared to the places they had been in previously. The church looked like a house with many rooms to house migrant children and families. It was a center for refugees before they were released to their sponsors in the United States. Benjamin and his family were given hot meals, clothes, bedding, and everything else they needed. At the church, they were finally able to shower, change their clothes, and brush their teeth. Benjamin remembers that the day they arrived at the church, staff had made chicken and rice soup. He enjoyed his time there because "we were free to go outside and get some fresh air." There were toys and telephones to call Pedro. The staff said they would be going soon. After just 1 day, their number was called, and they were one step closer to seeing their father. The church staff gave Benjamin blankets and lots of food and even made food for the bus ride, this time en route to be reunited with Pedro. They were exhausted but knew that this was the final leg of their journey. As the bus came to a slow stop, they saw Pedro standing on the platform waiting for them. Lucas in the lead, they shuffled hurriedly to get off the bus. Lucas sprinted to his father's arms. Then Benjamin and Michelle joined the hug.

Pedro had found a job and a place for his family to live. He did his best to make sure his family had their needs met by the time they joined him. He made enough money that he was able to help his sister and niece flee Honduras and migrate to the United States as well. When Jamie asked Benjamin about the reunification with his father, he lowered his head as if to tighten his body into a cocoon, as if trying to hide from the question. His voice turned to a whisper, "He's in detention." Tears were in his eyes. The father's arrest happened not too long after the family reunited, just as they were settling into their new life together. Pulled over for a traffic violation while on his way to work, Pedro was taken to an immigration detention center, where he had now been for nearly 3 months.

"It should not have turned out like this," Michelle said. The family was heartbroken. Her husband had worked so hard to make sure his family would be safe from the harm of the *pandillas*. He didn't deserve this fate, and Michelle felt helpless. They didn't have money to pay for a lawyer and didn't know how to raise that kind of money. Her husband was the breadwinner, and Michelle cared for the children at home. "All he wanted was for us to be together again and now they've separated us, and they might deport him," said Michelle. Michelle said that Pedro would entertain the boys while she cooked and cleaned. He took the family to explore new places in the city and buy them things when he could. They visited local parks and stores and drove around in the city. These experiences helped Benjamin and Lucas to adjust to this new life and familiarize themselves with what was out there. Before his sons began school, Pedro insisted that they rest and regain their strength after everything that they had gone through. This was a very thoughtful decision by Pedro and unusual in our research since most families did not speak of the residual exhaustion that their children might feel after being held in detention. After a period of rest, Benjamin entered middle school and Lucas second grade. While the young boys found school difficult, they liked it and were always learning something new. Benjamin was learning English and would often talk with his classmates in the newfound language, a way of making his mark in a new life.

At the time of the interview, they had no idea what was going to happen to their father. He had a court date scheduled for a few weeks later. Michelle said that Benjamin cried every day, while Lucas tried to hold it in during the day but let it all out at night, perhaps as the invisible girl appeared in his room. Lucas worried that he would never see his father again. Despite the hardships, Michelle remained hopeful for the future saying, "as time goes by, you begin to adapt and to learn." Making ends meet was difficult, but she knew that she was doing her very best to make everything work. All she cared about was ensuring that none of them were deported back to Honduras; they had made it this far.

The sun was setting, and the waning rays of light coming through the window were striking the books on the shelves of the library. Independently, Benjamin and Michelle concurred that they no longer lived in constant fear of the gangs or other bad people who had threatened them in the past. Michelle no longer worried that the gangs would reach her children while they rode the bus to school. Her children now have more freedom; they are safe at school and can walk around the neighborhood without having to look over their shoulders.

Notes

1. Lusk & Sanchez Garcia, 2021, p. 6.
2. Case profile contributed by Jamie Turcios-Villalta with Tatiana Londoño and Rocio Morín.
3. As we did in all such cases, our team spoke to his mother about their concerns for Lucas's psychological state and made a referral to a free clinic near their home.
4. See Nygaard et al., 2017.

14

Four Generations of Mothers
and Daughters

The many families that you have met in this book have had, in general, a pre-migration stage of a few years. The families told of a migration stage of 1, 2, maybe 3 years before things got so bad that they had to leave. Conditions in their countries, we know, existed longer than that. It was when the danger of the streets arrived at their doorstep that parents decided to act and move from the first stage of the model to the second stage. Usually, a specific moment or series of events, threats, or tragedies occurred in the previous month or two that triggered their emigration. That was what we were accustomed to hearing.

Then, a family appeared in our research whose exceptional history went back more than 50 years and covered four generations of women in one Salvadoran family.[1] We heard the story from two of the four generations of mothers, daughters, and granddaughters. Their parents, the first generation, were alive and present but did not speak with us, although they were profoundly affected by the decades of pain inflicted on their offspring. Our first interviews were with two sisters, 54 and 62 years old, the second generation of the family. Missing entirely from the story was the third generation, the daughter of one of the sisters who had been killed by the *maras* of El Salvador when her child was 2. That child, representing the fourth generation, was now 14 years old and participated in conversations with our team. This family's story is worth telling for its reach to the political exigencies that began well before the 1960s and came to a tipping point in the early 1980s. In 2008 and 2018, tragic events and threats returned to remind everyone in the family of the fragility of life in El Salvador. Stresses and traumas were plentiful in all four generations of this family.

Our first contact was with Daniela, 62, who had eluded the crushing dictatorship of El Salvador about 38 years before. It was not just a moment of government corruption and repression that she fled in 1982 but an entire history of colonization, oppression, and inequality. El Salvador, like much of

Through Iceboxes and Kennels. Luis H. Zayas, Oxford University Press. © Oxford University Press 2023.
DOI: 10.1093/oso/9780197668160.003.0015

the Central American isthmus, was colonized by Spain in 1524 and then underwent a series of changes in its sovereignty in the centuries that followed. It became a sovereign state in 1841, but instability was part of its history from the late 1800s to the mid-20th century: chronic political and economic variability that included coups, authoritarian rulers, revolts, and civil unrest. The social and economic disparity was widespread, sparing almost no one.

The modern era of El Salvador could be said to have started in October 1979 when a military–civilian junta toppled the president, General Carlos Humberto Romero. After decades of brutal repression that went as far back as 1932, the 1979 coup ended a government that had ruled El Salvador through massive election fraud, corruption, and brutality. But it also marked the start of the Salvadoran Civil War that lasted until 1992, a conflict pitting the US-backed military government supported by the country's economic elite against a coalition of left-wing groups under the banner of the Farabundo Martí National Liberation Front. When the junta overthrew the previous government, a military government took its place and found support from Presidents Jimmy Carter and Ronald Reagan. The chokehold of the previous, corrupt government was replaced by the strangulation of a military junta, exercising its will over the Salvadoran people. In January 1980, the killing of 50 people by Salvadoran national guard troops during a peaceful march became the first of many more massacres in the weeks, months, and years that followed. In February, 234 people were killed and, in March, twice that number. Death squads made sure that if a citizen helped anyone opposed to the government, they too would be killed. The killing on March 24, 1980, of Archbishop Óscar Romero, a prominent critic of the death squads, as he celebrated mass stunned and outraged the world. But not the Salvadoran government: At Romero's funeral about a week later, government-sponsored snipers killed 42 mourners. In May, the national guard and other paramilitary groups aligned with the government carried out the massacre of 600 civilians, mostly women and children. Closing out the bloody year, the national guard raped and murdered four churchwomen from the United States who were part of a relief mission. At least 50 church-affiliated individuals were murdered by the government. By the end of 1980, the Salvadoran army and security forces had killed an estimated 11,895 people in less than 2 years following the coup, mostly peasants, trade unionists, teachers, students, journalists, human rights advocates, and priests. Before the conflict ended with a peace accord in 1992, more than 75,000 lives had been lost, and tens of thousands had emigrated to the United States. By 2008 Salvadorians were one of the largest immigrant groups in the United States. A negotiated settlement reached in Mexico City in 1992 established a multiparty constitutional republic, which remains in place to this day and is as ineffective as other governments in El Salvador's long history.

In 1982, Daniela and her new husband abandoned the middle-class life their parents had built in a small town outside of the capital, San Salvador. Daniela's politics and those of her husband were not stridently anti-government but certainly were critical of it. No matter how tempered the opinions that most Salvadorans held about the government were, they could never be expressed openly. To do so would make them the targets of government ire and likely death as it had for so many young people, rich and poor, White and Indigenous. Silence and emigration meant survival. Daniela left behind two sisters, a nephew, and both of her parents in the country of her birth.

Daniela and her husband settled in Texas. As time went by, they raised two children, worked, earned US citizenship, and established a stable, successful life. She kept up with her family across the decades. A daughter was born to her younger sister during that time. The civil war raged on in her homeland and affected her family as it did every family in the country. Fortunately for Daniela's family, they were spared the government's bloodshed. The civilian–military dictatorship that ended about 10 years after her departure was replaced, in time, by the dictatorship of the Mara Salvatrucha 13, a gang with origins in the Los Angeles area. In the 1990s, the United States began deporting many of its members, violent young men whose motto was quite literally *mata, roba, viola, controla* (kill, steal, rape, control). Deporting gang members meant exporting their violence to El Salvador, which then metastasized to other Central American countries. The government dictatorships of Central America, with their corruption and violence, were replaced by the lethal tyranny of the gangs.

The new dictatorship of the *maras* reached Daniela's family in 2008 when her niece, Beatriz, the mother of a 2-year-old named Alexa, disappeared and was presumed to have been killed; however, this was never confirmed officially. Beatriz's mother, Carla, took in the toddler and went on a relentless pursuit of her daughter's killers. Carla's mission was fueled by a mother's love. With small-denomination bills in her purse, Carla visited stores and spoke to clerks and owners who might have seen her daughter last. They took her money and gave her tips about where she might go next and who she might speak to next. Carla followed every tip and every trace of her daughter's whereabouts, where she was last seen and with whom, to little avail. There were frightening moments when she went into dangerous neighborhoods and entered small, seedy taverns, asking anyone who would listen about her daughter. But every tip and every lead went cold. Dead ends abounded everywhere. Everyone in town had heard of the maniacal mother searching for weeks and handing out bounties to anyone with information about her daughter. One collateral casualty was her son, Beatriz's brother and Daniela's nephew, who received death threats and was forced to take refuge in the United States, near Daniela in Texas. There came a terrifying moment when Carla came face to face with a *mara* and his buddies, the probable abductors and killers of her daughter. The tattooed, surly *pandillero* knew who she was and what she was doing. "You will not find your daughter. Not even a strand of hair," he said. The gang leader, a known killer, was serious: "You had better stop, or you and your little granddaughter will disappear in the same way your daughter did." Exhausted and now cautioned, Carla's search ended in this encounter, but her hope that someday her daughter or her remains would be found carried on. No news about Beatriz surfaced, and the suffering went on.

Ten years later, in 2018, the *maras* came back into the family's lives. This time they were after Alexa, who was now a budding 12-year-old woman. Carla told Hilda Torres in a series of telephone conversations what she faced and what she had to do.

> I took her out of the country because of the threats. One day when we were leaving school—I always picked her up from school—I was approached by some gang members. I noticed that one of them had a gun. He lifted his shirt just enough for me to see it, to be threatened. That's when I made my decision. I had already lost one child to the *maras*. I wasn't going to wait to let it happen again. I wanted Alexa to have a future, for her to prepare herself. Well, I knew that here it was no longer possible. That's why I decided to get her out of El Salvador. But I kept her in school because we couldn't just take her out, just like that. I started taking taxis to take her home. I let her finish the school year.

As part of her plan, and even without telling Alexa that they would leave the country soon, Carla started selling some of her possessions, quietly, trying to avoid drawing attention, to scrape up the money they would need to escape. No one knew. Not her elderly parents, her only surviving child, the son in Houston, or her sister who lived near her in El Salvador. Daniela did not know either. No one got a hint of what Carla was planning. She kept her secrets closely guarded.

No one in the family had told Daniela that her sister and niece were trying to get to her from El Salvador. No one knew that Carla had left El Salvador with Alexa. Even Daniela's parents who were visiting with her in Houston from El Salvador did not know of Carla and Alexa's escape. It had been a well-kept secret, even with the family.

That was exactly how Carla, Daniela's younger sister, wanted it.

"I knew that my sisters and others would not support the idea of fleeing, risking my granddaughter and myself. I planned. I invented excuses and schemes. I had no choice but to do what I did, and that's it," she said. Carla's tone and words were resolute. Her personality in the telephone interviews came across as that of someone who was steadfast, unwavering, and determined. She was clear about her decisions and stuck to them.

Carla, 54, and Alexa, 12, at the time of their escape from El Salvador, started their trek on April 28, 2018. With the money she had saved, Carla could afford a bus through Guatemala to Mexico and another from Mexico to the US border. Carla and Alexa made it through Guatemala with minimal interaction with others and the police. Mexico, she said, was risky "because they even know where you are from when you speak." They were afraid since they had heard of girls being raped and people assaulted. That was their fear. In Mexico, "you know that the federal government is on top of everyone, right?" The two women were scared. Along the way, they met other migrants, some of whom were making their second attempt to escape after having been returned to their home countries in their prior attempt. Being part of a collective from other countries who had experience in migrating helped relieve her fears, albeit only a little. Nothing major happened to them, thankfully, Carla added. Alexa didn't remember many details of the travel through Guatemala and Mexico, which matched Carla's description that it was an uneventful set of bus rides. Despite a general atmosphere of fear, Alexa seemed fine, not nervous, according to Carla. It was a great relief to Carla because she knew that "I was freeing my child from something awful in El Salvador." That sense of mission buoyed her.

Experienced migrants, the people they met along the way, helped them cross the Rio Grande. Between their expertise in crossing and her undeterred wish to bring Alexa to safety, Carla got the courage to board a raft with others. Bravery, she added, came fast because at that moment "the only emotion you have comes from knowing that you are crossing. You don't take danger into account." Crossing the river was frightening, Alexa remembered. She trembled uncontrollably—her lips, her legs, her feet, her knees—she recalled. She did not know what would happen when they got to the other side. "I was so nervous I didn't think about anything. I was just trying to calm myself down." She noticed that her grandmother was scared too, but she tried to act as if nothing was happening, trying to be calm. They held hands tightly and said nothing. For Carla, the journey she had planned stealthily had now reached its objective.

Alexa's recollection was sharpest in talking about the moment when they were arrested by Customs and Border Protection (CBP) after crossing the river and given blankets to keep warm. They were put in a cell with others who had come into the country the same way. The food was limited. When she spoke to the immigration officers, she was scared, mostly because she didn't understand much English. She tried to understand as best she could with her limited English. The cell in which they were first kept was in a one-story building, one of three similar structures set side by side. Alexa recalled that cars were parked in front, like any office building where people go to work, day in and day out. The serenity of the scene stood in stark contrast to what she was feeling. Alexa and Carla were kept together on the first day, but on the second day they were separated. It was 2018, and the Trump administration was furiously separating families.

Carla's well-laid plans had gotten them to the United States, but her optimism was derailed when immigration officers at the facility took her granddaughter from her side. Immigration officers told Carla that the separation was due to "a lack of documentation to prove that she was Alexa's legal guardian." That may have been the explanation they gave Carla, but the American public knew it was a presidential policy, not missing papers. "I was really scared," Alexa said, "when they separated me from my grandma. I turned around to look at her and she told me to stay calm, that everything was going to be all right. They took me to another place that was also cold, and we got a physical exam." (From the way she told her story, it does not appear that she was placed in a *hielera*, although she describes the place as cold.)

Alexa was taken to one of the other buildings in the small complex she had seen on arrival. There she was placed among other children, all under 18, where they slept on mats on the floor and were kept warm with Mylar blankets. The child detainees were awakened early in the morning, and their names were called out "to make sure we were all there." They were allowed to watch movies, talk, go to the bathroom, and eat. "We got apples, juices, burritos—but I didn't eat those. I just ate the fruits and the juices they had."

On the second day of confinement, Alexa and the other children were divided into groups and put in SUVs that took them to an airport from which they would be flown to cities closer to their US-based families or sponsors. That was her first time on an airplane. Alexa was placed with the Cayuga Centers, a non-profit social service organization that, among other programs, provides temporary foster homes for unaccompanied migrant children while working to unite them with their families. She was in one of their facilities for 2 months, the first time she had been separated from family for more than a day or two. She had not heard from her grandmother.

According to Cayuga Centers' self-description,

> Children are matched to bilingual foster parents who are familiar with the language and culture of their foster children. These children are placed in homes rather than a congregate facility, and those from the same family can stay together in a supportive and safe home. Foster parents are trained to work with these children and to support the treatment team in meeting the child's needs. What they offer immediately is a safe haven after a very long journey.[2]

This description matches what Alexa said of her experience there which was "a bit better because we were sent to homes after spending the day in, like, classes. At night, we would go to their homes and sleep." Homes sheltered groups of children, and Alexa felt that the family she was with was friendly and treated her and the group well. Alexa told Rocio that if she could say something to the house mother, it would be that she "misses her because she was a good person to me."

With separation and confinement, Carla's desperation grew. No one spoke to the *perrera* inmates, and even if they asked, no one was told anything. The officials were not going to bring her granddaughter back, no matter how much she tried. She was told that Alexa would be released, just not to her. It was at that point that Carla decided to speak to her sister in El Salvador. Taken to a room in handcuffs to make the call, the guard dialed the call for her.

"Where are you?" her sister asked, alarmed at receiving an international call from the United States. That's when Carla had to spill it; she had to reveal the long-held secret. In the short call, the sister learned the story of the emigration and the secrecy surrounding it and their separation by US immigration. Like the sister in El Salvador who received the first call, Daniela, her parents who were visiting from El Salvador, and Carla's son in Houston learned of their escape. Carla was unrepentant about her decision to save Alexa, even if it meant facing the dangers. But she was calmed knowing that someone else was also on the case—her sister in Houston would not rest until Alexa was safely in her home.

When we met Daniela in 2020, she was caring for Alexa, who was now 14 years old. Daniela said that one morning in 2018 a telephone call came that would upend her peaceful life in Houston. It was an American immigration official calling to ask Daniela if she knew Alexa. Telling the story, Daniela explained her confusion: "At that moment I did not understand the question, but then I understood when the person explained to me who they were, and I said 'yes.'" The official told Daniela that her grand-niece, Alexa, and her sister, Carla, were in detention in the United States. Daniela was alarmed and puzzled, then nearly fainted when she heard the news. Daniela identified herself as Carla's sister and Alexa's grand-aunt and offered to go pick them up and bring them to her home. The immigration officer left a number that Daniela dialed only a short while later. That's when she learned that the teenager was being transferred to a facility closer to her own home. They would let her know when Alexa would be at the local immigration detention. Two days passed, and Daniela did not get a call back from immigration. She called the number again and was told that her grand-niece had not yet arrived near Houston. Three more days passed, and Daniela tried the number again, this time getting a gruff reaction from the immigration employee: "Who told you that she would be near Houston? And who said it would be soon?" Daniela tried to explain the calls but to no avail. She was not going to get more information than what she had already been given. "We'll call you when we are ready to call you" were the last words she received.

Days later the fateful call came in: Alexa was near Houston. Based on the situation and what Daniela told us, it is fair to assume that the callers were from the Office of Refugee Resettlement (ORR), which is responsible for unaccompanied and separated minors. Daniela was told that another call would come to her soon, and they scheduled this incoming call. When it came, the voice at the other end was that of a young girl. It was Alexa.

"Are you okay?" Daniela asked. "Don't worry, I'm going to fight to get you out of there." That is when a 3-month struggle began, a paper chase in an intricate bureaucratic maze. Documents were sent, completed, and returned; and then a new set of papers came back to be filled out and signed. She had to show proof of residency and that she was a US citizen. Daniela and her husband were fingerprinted. They were asked about their health and if they had been sick or hospitalized. Did they have weapons in the house? Drugs? Pets? How many rooms in the house? Was there a separate bedroom for Alexa? "Everything," Daniela said. It wasn't easy, but she managed to get her grandniece out of the shelter.

> Oh my God! I turned everything upside down. I went everywhere. I did what they asked. What can I tell you? I lost 30 pounds in that time that I was struggling to get her out of there. Pure agony because my sister was imprisoned and my niece, too, but not together. I hired a lawyer. Luckily, I have my husband's support. I don't work and have lots of time and strength, but it was hard. There is no explanation for what one feels in those moments of wanting to help and not being able to help. It was horrible. To be thinking that the child was taken from my sister, knowing that my sister had raised her. It is her daughter, directly it is her daughter; she raised her from the age of 2.

A call came, and Daniela was told to send funds for the airfare. She refused to do so until she was given an exact date that Alexa would be released. She was told to expect Alexa on June 8, but no call ever came about the arrival on that date. The girl would not be with Daniela for another 3 weeks. Meantime, Daniela had to produce additional documentation. Through a friend of a friend in El Salvador, Daniela contacted the Salvadoran embassy. It was then that the news of Alexa came. ORR would place Alexa on a flight. Daniela paid the cost.

Alexa was freed, but Carla remained in detention, where her ordeal continued. From the *perrera* she was moved several times, and in the last location, she was given prison clothes. That location was a detention center near the Mexican border, a 6-hour drive from Houston. As soon as the family was able, Daniela set out to visit Carla, taking along her parents and Alexa. It was a hard trip and an equally difficult encounter. Carla's mother suffered from a heart ailment and her father from cancer. He would die about 5 or 6 months after seeing his daughter in detention. Daniela was moved at the moment when Alexa and Carla saw each other again after 2 months apart. It would be the only time they saw each other in person again. Alexa's attorney was concerned that passing CBP checkpoints on the highway and then having Alexa enter the detention facility might bring unnecessary attention to Alexa. All it would take was an unfair agent to raise questions and jeopardize Alexa's case even if there were no reason for an agent to do so. He said it was best not to have her enter the detention center. Daniela continued visiting Carla, saying "There wasn't a weekend that I didn't go." Alexa stayed at home.

Carla tried ingratiating herself with the guards, by being polite and friendly, referring to them always as "officer." The rest of the time, she kept her mouth shut. With that approach, she felt that she was treated far better than others. Maintaining this demeanor, Carla reasoned, might serve her well when she asked to remain in the United States with her granddaughter. She implored the officers to be kept with her child in the United States but was told that Alexa was not her daughter. Therein was the problem: The lack of documentation hindered her case. Keeping her polite but firm demeanor, following orders, and not challenging the authorities did not work. Three times Carla boarded a plane to be deported, and each time she was removed and returned to detention. Carla told our team,

> The lawyers filed papers to try to block my deportation. Three times they took me off the plane. "You're not leaving yet," they would say. The lawyers kept trying but the government did things to undercut their efforts. Finally, the government snuck me out. They took me out secretly because the lawyer was fighting for me to stay. The officers wanted me to sign a document. Some parents I saw signed the papers. They brought me the paper about three times, but I didn't sign because it meant renouncing my granddaughter and she would be turned over to the state. My lawyer told me not to sign it, too. "No," I told the officer. If I had signed, who knows where my child would be.

Carla's quiet deportation took place unexpectedly one night, without notification to her attorney. Carla connects the decision by the authorities to her refusal to sign deportation papers that relinquished her responsibilities for Alexa. In one instance, the government official handling her case said, "If you don't sign tomorrow, I'll put you and your child on the plane and the two of you will go," according to Carla. That night, Carla called her lawyer and described what she was facing with the Immigration and Customs Enforcement officers. It was not a long conversation, "But the officers must have been listening—they listen in on the calls—because after that night I could no longer make phone calls, even to my sister. That same night they took me out, put me on a plane, and deported me." Communication ceased, and Daniela waited and worried when her sister didn't call from detention. Making matters worse was that Daniela was blocked from calling the detention center. They did not speak until Carla was back in El Salvador. Thinking that it would be best for Alexa, the sisters decided not to tell the girl that her grandmother had been deported.

Back in her country, things were exceptionally difficult for Carla. She had to go into hiding since the *maras* knew that she had escaped and taken her granddaughter. Now she was their target. The only way to survive was to move to the capital city, keep her head down, and meld into the large urban crowd. She found work, but it wasn't easy and meant long hours alone, without her Alexa. Another sister of Carla's and Daniela's was forced to go into hiding as well and was helped by loyal co-workers and friends. They made it possible for her to continue working remotely.

According to Daniela, Alexa was traumatized when she took her in. When Alexa arrived, Daniela said, she had problems with frustration tolerance and would "throw herself on the floor, like a tantrum to get attention. She would sit at my feet." Alexa's sadness and anxiety were shown through overeating. Alexa cried alone in her room and would emerge with red eyes, refusing to speak to Daniela or her husband. All Daniela could do for Alexa was convey hope that one day her grandmother would come out of detention. Daniela recounted that Alexa would "grab a plate full of food. She did not even realize that she ate in large quantities. I didn't say anything." Alexa's teacher and the school nurse contacted Daniela with their concerns about Alexa's weight gain. With incidents like these happening more often, Daniela and Carla decided that Alexa needed to know that Carla had been deported; the truth was best. They were correct because Alexa accepted the fact that she would not see her grandmother and seemed comforted to know she was free in El Salvador. They agreed to have Alexa speak to her grandmother every day by telephone or Skype. This may have improved the relationship with Daniela.

Alexa had done well in her new school in spite of the emotional toll. It had been decided that Alexa would start a year behind her grade level—from sixth grade to fifth—to give her time to adapt and learn English. She watched movies in English and listened to English-language music on a computer tablet Daniela had bought for Alexa. While she would initially stay in her room and watch TV alone, Alexa gradually started coming out and sitting with her grand-aunt and grand-uncle to enjoy TV shows with them in the family room. Alexa says that she has a good relationship with her aunt and uncle. "I help them with chores. I cook with my aunt. Sometimes we'll watch a movie while we cook. We watch Spanish-language telenovelas and reruns of Chespirito."[3] Alexa didn't talk about her time in the shelter. In time she began to confide in Daniela that in the shelter she would help take care of the younger children, which filled her day with satisfaction.

Daniela says that Alexa has changed, "She's gone from a girl to a *señorita*. She seems more confident." Carla agrees, "She is adapting. I tell her that it is not easy, but it is what is best for her, to be in Houston. If I could have her with me, I would. Truly. Alexa doesn't have asylum yet. I hope she gets it. And thank God, the girl knows that I have left her in good hands, but I know that one day I will have the opportunity to be there with her." After the loss of a daughter, the daughter she was unable to protect from the *maras*, Carla was able to save her daughter's child.

Having her grand-niece living safely in Houston and knowing Carla can rest assured of Alexa's safety gives Daniela great satisfaction. Through her pride in her family and Alexa's growth, she clarifies that "Of course, what I can give is nothing like her grandmother's love. That's impossible." Daniela's voice and joy dim when she concludes that the blessing comes with a cost: "Still, Alexa is hurting." Alexa was the fourth generation of strong women in a Salvadoran family whose story spans 40 years and made it out alive through the determination and courage of her loved ones. Her family's patterns and desperation are seen in many Central and South American families who are not yet so lucky, who are still haunted by painful memories of dictatorships, murder, threats, migration, and detention.

Notes

1. The interviews were conducted by Hilda Torres, Rocio Morin, and me in 2020 and 2021.
2. As described by Cayuga Centers, retrieved from https://cayugacenters.org/services/#migrant. See also Yee & Jordan, 2018.
3. Chespirito, or "Little Shakespeare," was the plucky and uproarious superhero of *El Chapulín Colorado*, created by Roberto Gómez Bolaños, a Mexican actor, comedian, screenwriter, humorist, director, producer, and author. Gomez Bolaños played the role of Chespirito.

15

All That Comes After

It isn't surprising that efforts at deterring the arrival of people from the Northern Triangle countries have failed. Human history shows that migration is inevitable, inexorable, and inexhaustible. There will never be an era without migration. In the decade between 2000 and 2010, world migration grew by 48 million people and jumped again by 60 million between 2010 and 2020—possibly the largest flow of people in recorded history and a reflection of the humanitarian crises occurring everywhere around the globe.[1] In 2020, the number of *forcibly displaced* people stood at 34 million, double what it had been in 2000. Add to these numbers the refugees from Afghanistan in 2021 and Ukraine in 2022, and it is no wonder that streams of people continue to seek shelter in other places. To be forcibly displaced leaves people's material and practical matters unsettled and, worse still, leaves unresolved emotional and psychological issues, memories, ties, and identities. It is a powerful concept.

Most immigrant parents I met, whether from Guatemala, Honduras, or El Salvador, said they had never wanted to come to the United States. Leaving wasn't on their minds. They did not want to give up the lives they knew. And this is very understandable. We know that humans, in general, like to stay close to home. Most of the world's people live and die within a few miles of their birthplace. In underdeveloped countries, a person's entire life journey can span a 5-mile radius. In the United States and some other developed countries, the radius may be larger. Estimates for the United States indicate that between 60% and 70% of Americans live and die within an 18- to 44-mile radius of where they were born.[2] We can ask why some people move from place to place while others stay put. Those we might think of as "stuck" usually don't have the resources to leave even when they want to; they just can't leave. The "rooted" are those who can leave if they so choose but don't because they are content with the place, people, and pursuits right where they are. The "mobile" have the resources to get up and go. And they do, usually for new opportunities.[3] But, for the families described in this book, it is desperation and hopelessness that make the rooted and stuck become the

Through Iceboxes and Kennels. Luis H. Zayas, Oxford University Press. © Oxford University Press 2023.
DOI: 10.1093/oso/9780197668160.003.0016

mobile, the emigrants. They can be neither rooted nor stuck because to stay means that sooner or later they will suffer assaults, extortion, rape, death, or a child lost to gangs. Even for those whose hearts bend toward being rooted—content with life in their countries despite some economic and political hardships—the reality of violence forces them to leave. They have to abandon ancestral homes, businesses, friends, family, cultures, the ties of belonging to a place and a people, and their ways of life. They have no choice.

In *The Undocumented Americans*, Karla Cornejo Villavicencio encounters Octavio, a Guatemalan day laborer trying to make a living. Like a sagacious, laboring-class philosopher, Octavio captures the essence of why migrants do what they do.

> "I don't feel at home in this country," Octavio says. "Even immigrants in extreme poverty find a way to send their deceased loved ones back home to be buried. They won't be alive to feel happiness again, but they will feel at peace, finally a place to rest. All the dead want is a place to rest." He says this may be his last year before going back to Guatemala. He came here to make enough money to send his kids to school back home, and he did it. One is a mechanic, another is studying law, and the third is an aesthetician—Octavio financed her salon. "Everyone who kills themselves through their work is doing this for their children," he says. "If you don't have kids, why would you kill yourself like this?"[4]

Octavio's words ring true and speak for all of history. People do it for their children. But history is forgotten by the living. We seem to believe that history is in the past: old, quaint, irrelevant, and not instructive to the present. It all happened to people long ago who aren't like us and in places far away. Society as a whole has a short memory. Lost with a forgotten history is empathy.

More than once in just the last 100 years we have seen parents make the most agonizing decisions anyone should ever have to make. Jewish parents in Nazi Europe put their children on trains or handed them to underground operatives, out of harm's way but never to see them again.[5] Cuban parents between 1960 and 1962 placed more than 14,000 of their children aboard "Peter Pan" flights to Miami to escape Castro's takeover.[6] Many were never reunited with their children. Vietnamese parents herded their children onto American helicopters, planes, and boats as Saigon fell to North Vietnamese forces in 1975.[7] How many lived to see their children again? Sudanese parents in 1987 urged their sons to escape death as a civil war tore through their country. Half of the 20,000 "Lost Boys of Sudan" died on their trek to Ethiopia and then to the Kakuma refugee camp in Kenya.[8] Many Sudanese parents and sons never saw or heard from each other again. Long-running conflicts continue to drive refugees from Libya, South Sudan, the Central African Republic, northern Mozambique, Ethiopia, Cameroon, and other African hotspots, to other countries. Except for an occasional feature in a Sunday newspaper or television segment that reminds us of the innocent people caught and dying in the middle of these conflicts, we generally forget.

And in time, we will forget the things that we saw in August 2021 when Afghan parents tried to save their children, even at the risk of permanent separation, as the Taliban marched toward Kabul. One unforgettable image was of a mother passing her infant child toward border officials at the airport gates as thousands of Afghan women, men, and children pushed against a barbed wire fence that "separates hope from an uncertain future under the Taliban regime."[9] These families may never again see the children they saved. We will forget them, too.

In a smaller but no less poignant example, millions of viewers watching the evening news on television on March 30, 2021, saw how two unaccompanied children arrived in the United States. On that night, a Border Patrol agent operating a remote night-vision camera spotted an adult, presumably a man, straddling the border wall that rose about 20 feet in the desert near Santa Teresa, New Mexico. On the Mexican side, but out of view, was someone working with the man on the wall. The person in Mexico appears to have lifted a small child to the man on the fence. The straddling man is seen shifting as he lifts the child from the Mexican side over the wall to the US side. Stretching his arms, he drops the child, carefully, trying to break the child's fall from about 10 feet. It was a protective action by the *coyote*. The first child lays flat, face down on the ground not moving for about 20 seconds, probably stunned. She gets to her feet in the manner of a toddler. As she stands up, the man on the fence is lifting another child from the Mexican side and repeats the act of dropping the second child, also trying to soften her fall. She is larger than the first child. She lands on her feet and falls into a sitting position. The man on the wall drops a small package near the girls. As the *coyotes* run off into the Mexican night, the younger of the two sisters seems to be bending slightly to talk to or help her older sister. What must they have said? What fear and confusion must these two babies have felt from the moment they left their family's embrace to landing in the New Mexico desert?

The two sisters from Ecuador, ages 5 and 3 years, were rescued and taken to the Santa Teresa Border Patrol Station for medical evaluation and then to a hospital for further observation. Fortunately, neither girl was injured.[10] They were then turned over to the Department of Health and Human Services for placement.[11] The girls' parents had left their daughters in a remote, mountain town near the coast of Ecuador and had migrated to the United States. But the separation from their daughters was too painful. It was more than they could bear, and they made the desperate and risky decision to have their girls brought to the border. They contracted with *coyotes* to take the girls north. The girls were reunited with their parents.[12]

In 58 wordless seconds, we saw just two of the thousands of unaccompanied children arriving at our southern border. The parents risked their children's lives to bring them to where they could protect, succor, and nurture them, even with the chance that they might never see them. I may never know the girls' parents, but I don't blame them for their decision.[13] What conditions would drive parents to such desperation, entrusting their precious babies to strangers to carry them about 2,980 miles to New Mexico? What must their anguish have been not knowing their babies' fate?

As I write this concluding chapter in April 2022, Russia has invaded Ukraine, with the destruction, death, carnage, and flight of refugees broadcast on television news, social media, and newspapers. Fathers, mothers, daughters, and sons are taking up arms; and many are sending their children and parents to places of safety and security. The images coming from Ukraine show parents leading their children, aging parents, and the disabled out of the war zone to western Ukraine and nearby countries. More than 4 million Ukrainian refugees are now among the millions of forcibly displaced people. The worry on Ukrainian parents' and children's faces looks remarkably like that of families fleeing conflict in other parts of the world.

These examples didn't happen centuries ago. They happened in our lifetimes. Many of the people who made these life-and-death decisions in their children's interest, and the children who experienced these painful losses, are still alive today. They may feel the sorrow as keenly now as when it occurred. Will we forget them as time passes?

As we do with much of history, we forget the moments of crisis, the decisions parents have to make, their anguish and the confusion of children, and the loss, the deep, crippling loss that can never be fully mourned. As Elie Wiesel, the 1986 Nobel Peace Prize laureate, reminded everyone present in Oslo on the day of his award, "it is surely human to forget, even to want to forget." But remembering, holding the past in our memory, is essential to understanding the present as well as the past.

> Remembering is a noble and necessary act. The call of memory, the call *to* memory, reaches us from the very dawn of history. . . . It is incumbent upon us to remember the good we have received, and the evil we have suffered. . . . We must remember the suffering of my [Jewish] people, as we must remember that of the Ethiopians, the Cambodians, the boat people, Palestinians, the Mesquite Indians, the Argentinian *"desaparecidos"*—the list seems endless.[14]

The concerns that motivated me to write this book since that first drive to the Karnes County Family Residential Center remain today. There are questions as pressing now as they were then. Several are recurrent. What will become of the children and families who have gone through iceboxes and kennels and all the hardship that came before and after they immigrated? How will their lives turn out? How will they handle the stresses, small and large, that come with life? What will be the long-term outcomes after being scared, detained, and separated from loved ones? Now, just a few years since their detention and separation, what will their psychological adjustment look like? How about when they are young adults? In their 30s? If we were to trace their development, how will we plot the contours of their paths? What will their lives look like, and how will they and others characterize them?

Students ask me these questions in the classroom, and professionals ask them in small meetings and large conferences. The short answer to all of them is the same: "I don't know. It's simply too early to tell." Detention and separations by the thousands happened in just the past half-decade or so, far too early to make any predictions. The kids are still relatively young and are adapting to new lives in the United States or elsewhere. Years and decades from now, they will author memoirs, biographies, and histories of this period. Their works will provide answers to the questions we hear now and the questions that are yet to form. In the next decade, we should see studies that follow the children and parents over time, tracking their health and mental health, educational and occupational progress, and general well-being. Longitudinal studies of the children, parents, and siblings will illuminate the extent of the damage and if and how it is sustained. Research and literary products will yield examples of those who rose above impossible odds and those who succumbed in minor and major ways to the legacy of detention and separation.

Unquestionably the most daunting task for researchers will be finding the children and their parents, a colossal undertaking. The kids and families are dispersed throughout the United States and in their home countries or other parts of the world, not concentrated in a few places. The children who were never separated and those who were but were reunified will be forging lives in cities like Houston, Chicago, Los Angeles, and New York or smaller ones such as Tulsa, Asheville, and Kalamazoo. Others may be found on the dairy farms of Wisconsin and in central New York State, the orange groves of Florida, the fertile lands of Imperial Valley in California, ranches in New Mexico and Arizona, and the small towns of Louisiana, Missouri, Virginia, and Oregon. The children who were never reunited with their parents may be in state foster care systems, a labyrinth that can be impenetrable. Many formerly detained parents and children may just not want to talk with anyone or be counted in research. Federal government record-keeping was so sloppy that it will prove virtually impossible to obtain records, and they may simply not exist. In the event that a database does exist and can be obtained, it may be useless.[15] It may take dogged detectives to find the files and make sense of them.

What then can we do to change the future of immigration from Mesoamerica to the United States? How can US immigration enforcement policies be improved to be both effective and humane? There is no simple solution to the long-standing problems of Central America, where efforts that have been made by each country and with international support have met with very limited success. The United States and other countries have trained their police and armies, but little has changed. Fighting the drug cartels has been ineffective, for the most part. US foreign and economic policies have not had much success. We have heard for far too long that building democratic institutions and promoting the rule of law will be the way to change the conditions of Central America. But these systems too have not moved the needle. Yet, I hasten to add that they should not be abandoned; changing minds, institutions, and cultures takes multinational efforts and decades upon decades.

Dangling foreign aid is often at the center of US policy. The lion's share of aid is earmarked for military assistance, primarily to fight the drug business and tamp down the violence. The remainder of the aid goes for, in descending order, economic assistance, humanitarian aid, multilateral economic contributions, and bilateral development aid. The return on investment is minimal from what we can see, especially as corruption remains rampant. At every step of the way, crooked officials take their *mordida*, the Spanish word for "bite," an unambiguous expression of corruption, usually in the form of petty bribes.[16] Oftentimes, there is little that the US State Department can do about it. Removing corrupt officials through the ballot box is one approach, but they are often replaced by a new set of corrupt people. And just like dangling foreign aid has not stemmed the flow of migrants, building US border security has failed, primarily because it is often reduced to hiring more border agents and arming them with high-tech equipment. A wall will not stop the flow of immigrants. Instead, a border wall will only divide Americans further.

It is time for other approaches to be considered. Economic investment in Central America is one that has not been given the attention or support it deserves. Needed are government policies that encourage American companies to establish production and manufacturing facilities in the Northern Triangle countries and neighboring countries. The presence of large employers and manufacturing plants can help stabilize the countries' economies and provide employers with inexpensive labor. Production bases just a few hours by airplane from the United States would reduce the costs of overseeing the manufacturing activities from their US-based headquarters, permitting executives and managers to travel back and forth quickly and easily. Transporting the goods by airplane would be far less costly than airplanes or tankers coming from half a globe away. Bringing goods to American markets from Central America would cost a fraction of what it costs to ship goods from China, Vietnam, and Southeast Asia. Guatemalans, Hondurans, and Salvadorans don't want to leave their countries and families; and investing in Central America allows people to stay in place without the desperation that pushes them out. According to Steve Liston of the Council of the Americas, the United States can reduce the incentives to migrate by expanding economic opportunities. But it cannot happen through "development assistance or a few well-publicized investments by a group of multinationals. Instead, it requires broad trade and investment incentives that encourage the private sector throughout the Western Hemisphere to do more business in Central America."[17] The lower cost of production and transportation would benefit the United States and encourage manufacturers and investors to create engines of prosperity in Central America.

Another consideration is creating enterprise zones in which the manufacturers can cluster their plants, enhancing supply chain logistics and using a set of common carriers, thus reducing their individual costs. By clustering in enterprise zones, there would be greater security for businesses and safety for their workers. With investment in the region come economic opportunities and incentives for local people to start businesses. Education is improved, healthcare becomes accessible, and vital infrastructures are modernized.[18] Judicial and fiscal oversight will be needed to avoid a repetition of the past when powerful American and European companies acted imperiously and brutally to get their ways. Investing in building democratic governance, providing not aid but incentives tied to performance and outcomes, empowers people to build institutions that they can trust, especially the judiciary and executive branches of government of their countries. Proposals for sustainable development and investment exist, such as the Comprehensive Development Plan proposed by the United Nations (UN) Economic Commission for Latin America and the Caribbean. The plan's four pillars—economic development, social well-being, environmental sustainability, and comprehensive management of the migratory cycle—cover many areas of need.[19]

Any system put in place for greater economic investment in Central America must be one part of a "layered approach," if the purpose is to reduce emigration. Another layer is the establishment of in-country refugee resettlement zones, perhaps side by side or within proximity to the enterprise zones. Secure settlement zones within their countries can provide havens for people who do not want to leave their country and only wish to live with their loved ones near their jobs. "For many people," Ariel Soto-Ruiz and Andrew Selee of the Migration Policy Institute in Washington write, "in-country protection would be far preferable to having to seek refuge abroad."[20] In-country protection zones or safety areas might be overseen by multinational councils and protected by an international military presence, such as the UN's Blue Helmets. In-country settlement camps can provide layers of other life-affirming institutions that Central Americans need: schools, churches, recreation areas, and even incentives for starting small businesses. Applications for immigration to the United States or other countries could occur in an orderly fashion. Encouraging international investment in adjacent enterprise zones would provide a surcease from grinding poverty. A comprehensive investment plan would reduce the need to seek asylum and give young people hope, education, and jobs—the antidotes to the allure of gangs.

Until the far-ranging economic, political, and social circumstances that push Central Americans from their countries cease, the United States must enact policies and practices to handle asylum-worthy people more effectively. It will require, first, an uncompromising belief that border enforcement must abide by the principle of treating everyone humanely. There should never be justification for a government's deviation from the law or the principles of dignity and human worth. When asylum seekers pass the threshold labeled *The Crossing* in the stages of migration, as described in Chapter 8, immigration processing must observe commonly accepted principles of human rights. In theory, most US laws espouse this simple principle for citizens and non-citizens, but we don't always apply them. Government administrations have flouted the law even when federal court rulings have told them to follow it. A prime example is how detention and family separation violated the American Convention on Human Rights signed by the United States in San Jose, Costa Rica, on November 21, 1969. The family separation policy stomped on, first, the principle that "the family is the natural and fundamental group unit of society and is entitled to protection by society and the state" and, second, that "Every minor child has the right to the measures of protection required by his condition as a minor on the part of his family, society, and the state."[21] People have the right to seek asylum in another country to avoid persecution. This is not new; it is found in US law and international conventions. When it separated families, the government was not following the law and was not being transparent about the purpose of the policy. More maddening was that neither the judiciary nor the legislature could stop a president hell-bent on inflicting the most damaging harm possible. The protection against "cruel and unusual punishment," as enshrined in the US Constitution or as stated in the Universal Declaration of Human Rights that "No one shall be subjected to torture or to cruel, inhuman or degrading treatment or punishment" should be not an option but a requirement of any immigration enforcement system.[22] In a supreme example of irony, the Trump administration had to assume the care and cost of children it didn't want in the country in the first place. The government was strapped with costs that would not have been necessary if families had been kept intact.

Second, the US government must recognize that, in today's world, migration is inevitable, inescapable, and inexorable. We must recognize that south-to-north migration is not simply a matter of occasional surges but a permanent flow that will have its high tides and low tides. Despite the challenges of immigrating to the United States, about 78% of Hispanics who are not US citizens and do not have a green card say they would do it all over again.[23] From 2010 to 2020, when border protection was ratcheted up, the US Hispanic population increased by 23%, in contrast to the 7% growth of the overall population.[24] Many of these immigrants didn't want to come to the United States but have adapted to life here after their arrival. Coming to grips with the reality of the endless nature of immigration means that the United States must take steps to create permanent or long-lasting structures for an effective migration processing system. For far too long, the responses to immigration from Mexico and Central America have been makeshift and not permanent. Only when full recognition is given to the inexorable nature of migration can we shift from a deterrent and penal mindset to a reception and processing approach and convert it into an advantage for the country.

This recognition can help control costs, too. Detention is extremely costly, and the family separation policy brought to it unwanted attention.[25] Immigration and Customs Enforcement (ICE) tried to downplay the costs in fiscal year 2018 as a mere $133.99 a day on average to keep one adult detained, an expense officially considered a detention bed.[26] But others did the math with available data and arrived at about $200 per night.[27] A "family bed," in reality several beds for a mother and her children, cost about $320 per person per day. When children were separated, the cost per child per night in "tent cities" shot up to $775.[28] Thousands of children were held, and the figures grew astronomically, triggering the Government Accountability Office to uncover the glaring discrepancies between ICE's estimates and the true costs.[29] Even the libertarian Cato Institute, whose mission is to advance solutions on the principles of individual liberty, limited government, and free markets, proposed alternatives to detention that would cost far less.[30] Worse perhaps than the costs were the failures by ICE and private prisons to protect children and adults. In a span of 4 years—October 2014 to July 2018—more than 4,500 complaints of child sexual abuse in detention were filed.[31] Of the 1,303 cases considered the gravest, 178 accused staff members of rape, fondling, kissing, and watching children shower. Furthermore, the penal mentality and needless cruelty of guards led to deaths and suicides, mental health crises, hunger strikes, and other incidents among detained adults and children. Even when children were not directly affected, they were witnesses to the harsh actions that hurt others.

The monetary costs were immense and the human costs immeasurable. The uncaring policies and systems that came out of the collaboration among federal and state governments and private prison corporations—the prison–industrial complex—shouted to the world that America was no better than countries known for their gulags.

After decades and billions in monitoring the southern border, the United States has relied on a permanent border force that demonizes, jails, and deports migrants, without much regard for human worth. The United States must face the reality that migration will continue without an end in sight and design a permanent system to process migrants into the country or back to their homes in an orderly fashion. No doubt, the United States needs to remain in a state of readiness to process the huddled masses appealing for entry into the country. Therefore, another layer in reforming our immigration system is to build a permanent structure that reaches from the first point of contact with immigrants, at apprehension, to the subsequent steps of processing migrants and settling them in the United States or repatriating them, all done with humaneness and dignity. As conditions evolve, the systems and structures need to be adapted and refined with every new development. Dumping the punitive and carceral mentality of *hieleras*, *perreras*, and the use of prisons as family detention centers watched over by military-uniformed prison guards is a next step in establishing an immigration processing system that can be the envy of the world. Likewise, Mylar sheets, disgusting food, punitive treatment, overcrowding, and the insistent degrading of detainees by refusing them showers, clean clothes, and private commodes must give way to an accountable, humane system. Rather than using "detention" as deterrence or punishment, immigration processing will allow those with just claims to find safety and security and will repatriate those with criminal backgrounds or who cannot establish sufficiently their claims.

An improved and streamlined asylum administration system would give asylum officers discretion to decide initial claims in a fair and timely fashion and would provide legal counsel to migrants.[32] A case management system that expedites the review process for families with children and protects children throughout the adjudication process safeguards young asylees and their parents. Needed also would be permanent administrative processing centers and ample private offices for asylum applicants to meet with attorneys, which can be done through the construction of processing centers across the four border states—California, Arizona, New Mexico, and Texas—operated by non-profit social services with experience in the congregate care of children and family shelters under government contracts. It is far wiser to establish permanent campus-like environments where asylum seekers, namely parents with children and unaccompanied minors, can live for short or long stays. The iceboxes, kennels, and detention prisons would give way to housing that can come from new construction or from repurposing existing structures such as unused hotels and motels or army barracks redesigned as reasonable, home-like conditions with water, warmth, and nutrition. The separation of children from parents must never blemish our history again.

Contracting with non-profit organizations with sound backgrounds and experience in serving refugees, immigrants, the homeless, and the displaced could do the job far better at a fraction of the fees charged by profit-driven prison companies. Staff would include administrators and managers, licensed social workers, certified child care staff, chaplains, and, yes, security officers. Military veterans and former police officers can be part of the processing system but must understand that the border is neither a crime scene nor a war zone. Staff properly trained in immigration laws, policies, and practices, as well as the social and psychological conditions of immigrants, can protect migrants' rights to life, liberty, and security.

Alongside these permanent processing and resettlement centers would stand two essential services. First, schools operating year-round would ensure continuity in children's learning and preparation for American schools, emphasizing English language instruction and socialization for success in the US educational system. School psychologists and teachers would test children for grade level, aptitude, and academic performance and create an academic record that parents can take to the schools in their destinations, thus facilitating the integration of kids into schools and reducing the burden on local schools. Receiving schools would be informed about the child's needs and be prepared to arrange for the proper classroom settings. Second, health and behavioral health services would be staffed by pediatricians, internists, family physicians, nurses, dentists, social workers, physician assistants and nurse practitioners, optometrists and opticians, dental hygienists, pharmacists, laboratory technicians, and other allied health professions to provide the needed healthcare. Routine immunizations and physical, oral, and hearing exams would be joined with the psychosocial and developmental assessments performed by social workers. Like school records, health records for each family member would follow the families to their next physical and mental healthcare homes. The point of all of this is to respond compassionately, legally, ethically, morally, economically, and effectively to the ongoing arrival of desperate people knocking at our doors.

Finally, I turn to the behavioral health needs of the children and parents who experienced the *hieleras* and detention and the ones who suffered through government-sponsored separations. Dispersed throughout the United States, families will go through the settlement process in the post-detention stage of their journeys. They will make the physical, social, employment, housing, and educational accommodations that any transplanted family will have to make. They will find jobs, enroll their children in school, find a healthcare "home" in the community, access community services and organizations, and join first-generation communities and cultural resources that celebrate their cultures and remind them of home. They will worship in the ways they know to fill their spiritual needs. Schools, clinics, hospitals, and behavioral health centers in towns and cities across the United States have to be financed to prepare for the integration of these parents and children into their services. It will require federal funding from the Administration for Children and Families of the US Department of Health and Human Services to blanket the country, making services available in every hollow in the country. Training clinicians and educators to understand the experiences of these children during the stages of migration will make those professionals better qualified to treat the children and their parents.

It is in children's adjustment that we see the vestiges of their migration ordeals. The stresses and traumas that occurred in their home country, during their journeys, and after their arrival in the United States will be major sources of adjustment problems. Memories, nightmares, and sensations will remain and contribute to emotional problems. The bodies of these kids and parents went through extraordinarily stressful and traumatic moments that may have left them permanently damaged. Intervening early in their permanent communities will reduce the chances of long-term effects of the disruptions in children's physiology.[33] Events, memories, snippets, sights, sounds, and unique experiences endured during migration can each be tied to a specific place and time, giving them chronological or developmental order. But they are sensations and emotions that cascade into a plunge pool at the base of the mind, where time and place are indistinguishable. Only painful emotions and sensations are left after the ordeals of migration. It's not humanly possible to separate pre-migration, mid-migration, and detention stresses and traumas. Research shows that differential patterns of trauma exposure at each stage of the migration process and children's ages and developmental epochs may require targeted mental health interventions.[34] Skilled mental health therapists know that the work is slow and arduous, requiring sensitivity as they help children and parents peel away memories and emotions. Not unlike a surgeon working deftly with a scalpel while not causing any damage to the patient, therapists too must work cautiously, watching for signs of re-traumatization and the client's emotional limits. There are many well-tested psychotherapies that can be culturally adapted to the children's and the adults' needs, and these therapies should be in the therapist's toolkit.

Therapists can use psychoeducational approaches with mothers and fathers, and other caregivers, whether they migrated with children or just received them into their homes. The work is to help the adults understand their own emotional and psychological needs and to understand the meaning of their children's behaviors and what they are communicating. A child who goes from clingy to rejecting may be confused and show insecurity, ambivalence, and anger. Parents need to understand their children's behaviors and their emotional reactions. Sometimes a child will remain in the parent's arms but not cuddle, postured in a rigid, frozen state, not molding to the parent's body and caresses. The child may be confused and disorganized internally. Children may act out or not sleep well or fuss about eating, leaving parents at their wits' end. Older children will display their internal distress differently, maybe through defiance, lashing out, or risk-taking behaviors. They may turn the distress inward, shown by depression, self-injurious or suicidal behaviors, or drug use. When parents understand the sources and meanings of their children's behavior, they are more receptive to suggestions from therapists. There are a host of parenting and parent–child treatments that run the gamut from infancy through childhood and into adolescence. Whether the approaches are cognitive-behavioral or interpersonal, the evidentiary base is there showing their efficacy. It is a matter of making the proper adaptations of the treatments for the population at hand.

The approaches to giving help to the children and families of immigration and detention and separation are endless. What I have provided here are just some reflections on what social workers, psychologists, and mental health therapists from other disciplines can do. I am confident that, with sensitivity, therapists will develop creative means to help the healing process to take place and for children and families to do more than settle into their new lives. They will help them adjust in profound and important ways. They will help the children and parents learn to breathe free.

The journey that I began with a drive in August 2014 took me further than I ever could have dreamed, though I never left the United States. Much of the way migrants are treated in the United States is based on assumptions of their motivations for coming here. Listening to their stories, I learned of the productive and vibrant lives that families led in their hometowns in El Salvador, Guatemala, and Honduras before malignant and deadly forces drove them away. Through their stories of survival across challenging terrain and dangerous encounters, I witnessed a determination the likes of which I had never heard told. Through the iceboxes and kennels and long stints in detention, with insensitive prison guards and inadequate care, children, mothers, and fathers suffered together; yet each described it differently, from their unique vantage point. Some children survived by grit and exuberance. Some families were more resilient than others. What some parents perceived as traumatic, others saw merely as stressful. Children rode bravely through the most harrowing of experiences only to be beset by challenges once settled. I met heroic parents, and I met some who had made errors in judgment, some recovering their footing and others not. Regardless, all were deeply affected by their experiences. Even among the children and parents who are thriving, there will remain many scarred lives. As Americans, we have a duty to repair and heal them and to prevent damage to future generations of immigrants.

The situation in which we find ourselves may appear grim from all sides. But, as we have seen, there are concrete solutions for each stage of the migration journey, including healing the mind and body. It will take experts and professionals from all disciplines and walks of life, from every corner of our diverse and storied nation, to bring these weary, determined travelers to a place of safety, stability, and security. We must seek to add one final stage to the migration journey for these brave families—the stage that brings them to a place they can call home.

Notes

1. UN Department of Economic and Social Affairs, 2020.
2. Sixty percent of Americans, it's been reported, live within 18 to 44 miles from their birthplace, depending on where they live. In the United States, 60% to 74% of residents in places stretching from Iowa, Wisconsin, and Michigan to Ohio, Pennsylvania, and West Virginia and into Alabama, Mississippi, and Louisiana live in the state in which they were born. Between 71% and 75% of the populations of Louisiana, Michigan, and Ohio are native-born. In the deep South, the median distance between siblings and parents is only 6 miles, the shortest distance for all regions of the country. See Bui & Miller, 2015.

3. The categories of stuck, rooted, and mobile are adapted from Richard Florida, 2008.
4. Cornejo Villavicencio, 2020, p. 156.
5. Blakemore, 2018.
6. Hinckley, 2019.
7. Engelmann, 1990.
8. Bixler, 2006.
9. Bruno, 2021.
10. Hernandez, 2021.
11. Choi, 2021.
12. Fonrouge, 2021.
13. Zayas, 2021.
14. Wiesel, 1986, paragraphs 12, 14, and 26.
15. US Department of Homeland Security, 2021. The May 18, 2021, report by the Department of Homeland Security (DHS) inspector general opens with a summary of the problematic record-keeping. It reads,

> We confirmed that before July 12, 2018, migrant parents did not consistently have the opportunity to reunify with their children before removal. Although DHS and ICE have claimed that parents removed without their children chose to leave them behind, there was no policy or standard process requiring ICE officers to ascertain, document, or honor parents' decisions regarding their children. As a result, from the time the Government began increasing criminal prosecutions in July 2017, ICE removed at least 348 parents separated from their children without documenting that those parents wanted to leave their children in the United States. In fact, ICE removed some parents without their children despite having evidence the parents wanted to bring their children back to their home country. In addition, we found that some ICE records purportedly documenting migrant parents' decisions to leave their children in the United States were significantly flawed. For example, some records reflect that removed parents orally waived reunification prior to removal, but did not include the information ICE provided to the parent before the parent had to make the decision, or whether ICE gave the parent the option to reunify with his or her child. (p. 1)

16. Baez-Camargo, 2019.
17. Liston, 2022.
18. Ruiz Soto & Selee, 2022.
19. UN Economic Commission for Latin America and the Caribbean, 2021.
20. Ruiz Soto & Selee, 2022.
21. Organization of American States, 1969, Article 17, paragraph 1; Article 19.
22. United Nations, 1948.
23. Lopez & Arditi, 2021, p. 6.
24. Passel et al., 2022. The growth was higher proportionally in states like Georgia, North Carolina, Washington, and Pennsylvania, which are not known as historical settling places for Latinos. These places had a growth rate higher than in the usual Hispanic states, such as Arizona, California, Colorado, Florida, Illinois, New Jersey, New

Mexico, New York, and Texas, which experienced a smaller growth in the number of Hispanics arriving there.

25. Urbi, 2018.
26. US Department of Homeland Security, 2018.
27. Benenson, 2018.
28. Ainsley, 2018.
29. US Government Accountability Office, 2018.
30. Nowrasteh, 2018.
31. Hagg, 2019.
32. Meissner et al., 2018.
33. Dozier et al., 2006; Fisher et al., 2007.
34. Cleary et al., 2018.

Acknowledgments

There are many people who may never know the impact they had on this book or how deeply they touched, even changed me—like the two little girls dropped under the cover of night over a border wall in March of 2021 and my anguish for their safety; The Poet, who escaped the deprivation of detention through literature and the world of the mind; and Romeo, who was nearly blind but had extraordinary vision and courage. I learned about bravery and altruism from the girl with the broken leg and the unnamed angels who carried her. I wonder how the teenage boy who saved his mother from being swallowed by the raging Rio Grande is doing, as well as Danny, who drew such evocative pictures of the violent death of his uncle. How is the little boy in the video, now years removed from the moment in 2018 when he was reunited with his mother at the Houston airport but who rejected his mother's hugs? Thank you to the numerous families who gave of their time to tell us their stories. I am profoundly grateful to all the children, mothers, and fathers—known and unknown—who taught me about courage and sacrifice. They may never read this book, much less remember me. But I will forever remember them and the gifts they gave me. In my prayerful moments, I wish that they are all well and have found peace in their lives in the towns and cities of the United States or in the places that they now call home.

Collecting many of the stories told in this book was a remarkable group of researchers with a willingness to extend themselves to the children and families they met. The team was led by project manager Alice P. Villatoro and doctoral student Tatiana Londoño. With them were Hilda Torres, Jamie Turcios-Villalta, and Rocio Morín; and together they demonstrated intellect, authenticity, humility, vigor, passion, sensitivity, and dedication. As immigrants or the daughters of immigrants, this team understood far better than others the sacrifices that migrant families make to forge a future for their children. Thanks also to Joanne Sanchez and Gema Aleman for their help.

Many colleagues provided me with facts, documents, access to families, impressions, and conversations; and some read sections of this book for substance, fact, and style. They are many: Cheasty Anderson of the National Immigration Law Center and Esther Reyes of the Children's Defense

Fund–Texas; Allan Hugh Cole, Lauren Gulbas, Barbara Hines, and Yolanda Padilla of the University of Texas; Robert Hasson of Providence College; Laurie Cook Heffron of St. Edward's University in Austin; Olivia López, the heroic whistleblower; Carmen Zuvieta, Austin community activist; Claudia Muñoz of Grassroots Leadership, Inc.; journalist Bob Moore; Joe Van Kuiken of San Antonio's Migrant Resource Center; and attorneys Manoj Govindaiah and Alexandra Minnaar of the Refugee and Immigrant Center for Education and Services. Friends sustained me with good cheer, willing to hear passages from this book read to them late one night in Old San Juan: Carmen Andújar-Cantres, Miguel Cruz-Feliciano, Christine Miranda-Diaz, and Darice Orobitg.

Like any production, a book requires the help of people backstage. My sincerest thanks to Annalise Nakoneczny for her superb editorial assistance, Sharon Brennan who protected my schedule zealously, and Desiree Pacheco for typing and printing and reprinting countless drafts. I thank illustrator Danielle Jamison who took my crude pencil design and created Figure 8.1.

Finally, I give thanks to my family who joined me in Austin and formed a circle of love and companionship: Stephanie, who has been steadily by my side on this long road, and our growing family of Marissa, John, Charlotte, and Abigail Tesauro; Amanda Zayas and Rob Meyer; and Luis-Michael Zayas and Rebecca Fisher and all the family dogs. To them, my unconditional love.

References

Abram, K. M., Zwecker, N. A., Welty, L. J., Hershfeld, M. A., Dulcan, M. K., & Teplin, L. A. (2014). Comorbidity and continuity of psychiatric disorders in youth after detention: A prospective longitudinal study. *Journal of the American Medical Association, 72,* 84–93.

Abrego, L. J. (2014). *Sacrificing families: Navigating laws, labor, and love across borders.* Stanford University Press.

Acer, E., & Byrne, O. (2017). How the illegal immigration reform and immigrant responsibility of 1996 has undermined US refugee protection obligations and wasted government resources. *Journal on Migration and Human Security, 5,* 356–378.

Acevedo, N. (2019, May 29). *Why are migrant children dying in U.S. custody?* NBC News. https://www.nbcnews.com/news/latino/why-are-migrant-children-dying-u-s-cust ody-n1010316?fbclid=IwAR38n79Vu1jBLejqEPL8NCeCJ7qaGinN2TJOuTfEkVI1 BKJDyISX3Jee7Rs

Afifi, W. A., Afifi, T. D., Nimah, N., & Robbins, S. (2013). The relative impacts of uncertainty and mothers' communication on hopelessness among Palestinian refugee youth. *American Journal of Orthopsychiatry, 83,* 495–504.

Aguilar, J. (2019, March 28). What we know about undocumented migrants being housed underneath a bridge in El Paso. *Texas Tribune.* https://www.texastribune.org/2019/03/ 28/undocumented-immigrants-being-housed-underneath-bridge-el-paso/

Ainsley, J. (2017, March 3). *Exclusive: Trump administration considering separating women, children at Mexico border.* Reuters. https://www.reuters.com/article/us-usa-immigration-children-idUSKBN16A2ES

Ainsley, J. (2018, June 20). *Trump admin's "tent cities" cost more than keeping migrant kids with parents.* NBC News. https://www.nbcnews.com/storyline/immigration-border-crisis/trump-admin-s-tent-cities-cost-more-keeping-migrant-kids-n884871?utm_ source=newsletter&utm_medium=email&utm_campaign=newsletter_axio sam&stream=top

Ainsley, J., & Soboroff, J. (2018, July 3). *New Trump admin order for separated parents: Leave U.S. with kids or without them.* NBC News. https://www.nbcnews.com/politics/immi gration/new-trump-admin-order-separated-parents-leave-u-s-kids-n888631

Alexander, M. (2010). *The new Jim Crow: Mass incarceration in the age of colorblindness.* New Press.

Alfaro, M. (2018, December 27). Migrants detained at the border are kept in freezing cells nicknamed "iceboxes." *Business Insider.* https://www.businessinsider.com/migrants-detained-at-border-kept-in-freezing-cells-nicknamed-iceboxes-2018-12

Alvarez, P. (2019, March 4). *What happened to the migrant caravans?* CNN. https://www. cnn.com/2019/03/04/politics/migrant-caravans-trump-immigration/index.html

American Academy of Pediatrics. (2017, March 4). *AAP statement opposing separation of mothers and children at the border.* https://www.google.com/url?sa=i&rct=j&q= &esrc=s&source=web&cd=&cad=rja&uact=8&ved=0CAQQw7AJahcKEwjYtP3l2JT 7AhUAAAAAHQAAAAAQAg&url=https%3A%2F%2Fdocs.house.gov%2Fmeeti

ngs%2FIF%2FIF14%2F20180719%2F108572%2FHHRG-115-IF14-20180719-SD004.
pdf&psig=AOvVaw1biwwFlnD0rdPs3Klo05-E&ust=1667656736977790

American Psychiatric Association. (2013). *Diagnostic and statistical manual of mental disorders* (5th ed.).

Amnesty International. (2018, October 11). *Catastrophic immigration policies resulted in more family separations than previously disclosed.* https://www.amnestyusa.org/repo rts/usa-catastrophic-immigration-policies-resulted-in-more-family-separations-than-previously-disclosed/

Anwar, M. (2019, March 17). Who is Scott Lloyd? Trump's former ORR director is in some hot water. *The Elite Daily.* Retrieved from https://www.elitedaily.com/p/who-is-scott-lloyd-trumps-former-orr-director-is-in-some-hot-water-16962310

A.P.F. et al v. United States of America, 492 F. Supp. 3d 989 (D. Ariz. 2020). https://dockets. justia.com/docket/arizona/azdce/2:2020cv00065/1224648

Atlantic. (2018, September 7). *How Trump's family separation policy traumatized children* [Video]. https://www.theatlantic.com/video/index/569572/family-separation/

Attanasio, C., Burke, G., & Mendoza, M. (2019, June 20). *Lawyers: 250 children held in bad conditions at Texas border.* Associated Press. https://apnews.com/article/texas-immi gration-us-news-ap-top-news-border-patrols-a074f375e643408cb9b8d1a5fc5acf6a

Australian Human Rights Commission. (2014). *The forgotten children: National inquiry into children in immigration detention.*

Babineau, V., McCormack, C., Feng, T., Lee, S., Berry, O., Knight, B. Newport, J., Stowe, Z., & Monk, C. (2022). Pregnant women with bipolar disorder who have a history of childhood maltreatment: Intergenerational effects of trauma on fetal neurodevelopment and birth outcomes. *Bipolar Disorders.* Advance online publication. https://doi.org/ 10.1111/bdi.13207

Baez-Camargo, C. (2019). *Mordida (México).* Global Informality Project. https://www.in formality.com/wiki/index.php?title=Mordida_(Mexico)

Bakó, T., & Zano, K. (2020). *Transgenerational trauma and therapy: The transgenerational atmosphere.* London: Routledge.

Baldas, T. (2018, June 21). Torn from immigrant parents, 8-month-old baby lands in Michigan. *Detroit Free Press.* https://www.freep.com/story/news/local/michigan/ 2018/06/20/baby-boys-separated-immigrant-parents-michigan/714527002/

Bar-On, D. (1996). Attempting to overcome the intergenerational transmission of trauma: Dialogue between descendants of victims and perpetrators. In R. Apfel & B. Simon (Eds.), *Minefields in their hearts: The mental health of children in war and communal violence* (pp. 165–188). Yale University Press.

Beal, J. A. (2019). Toxic stress in children. *American Journal of Maternal/Child Nursing, 44,* 53.

Bean, T., Derluyn, I., Eurelings-Bontekoe, E., Broeckart, E., & Spinhoven, P. (2007). Comparing psychological distress, traumatic stress reactions, and experiences of unaccompanied refugee minors with experiences of adolescents accompanied by parents. *Journal of Nervous and Mental Disease, 195,* 288–297.

Beckett, C., McKeigue, B., & Taylor, H. (2007). Coming to conclusions: Social workers' perceptions of the decision-making process in care proceedings. *Child and Family Social Work, 12,* 54–63.

Benenson, L. (2018, May 9). *The math of immigration detention, 2018 update: Costs continue to multiply.* National Immigration Forum. https://immigrationforum.org/article/ math-immigration-detention-2018-update-costs-continue-mulitply/

Bixler, M. (2006). *The lost boys of Sudan: An American story of the refugee experience.* Athens, GA: University of Georgia Press.

Björkenstam, E., Burström, B., Brännström, L., Vinnerljung, B., Björkenstam, C., & Pebley, A. (2015). Cumulative exposure to childhood stressors and subsequent psychological distress. An analysis of US panel data. *Social Science and Medicine, 142*, 109–117.

Blakemore, E. (2018, December 18). The heartbreaking WWII rescue that saved 10,000 Jewish children From the Nazis: The desperate parents of Kindertransport refugees paid a terrible price for their lives. History.com. Retrieved from https://www.history.com/news/holocaust-child-refugees-kindertransport-britain

Boochani, B. (2018). *No friend but the mountain: Writing from Manus Prison.* Anasi International.

Bosquet Enlow, M., Devick, K., Brunst, K., Lipton, L., Coull, B., & Wright, R. (2017). Maternal lifetime trauma exposure, prenatal cortisol, and infant negative affectivity. *Infancy, 22*, 492–513.

Briere, J. (1996). *Traumatic symptom checklist for children.* PAR.

Bronstein, I., & Montgomery, P. (2011). Psychological distress in refugee children: A systematic review. *Clinical Child and Family Psychology Review, 14*, 44–56.

Brownfield, W. R. (2012, October 1). *Gangs, youth, and drugs—Breaking the cycle of violence.* [Transcript]. US Department of State Diplomacy in Action. https://2009-2017.state.gov/j/inl/rls/rm/199133.htm

Bruneau, T., Dammert, L., & Skinner, E. (Eds.). (2011). *Gang violence and security in Central America.* University of Texas Press.

Bruno, G. (2021, August 18). *Heart-wrenching video shows Afghan mothers "throwing babies over barbed wire" to escape Taliban at Kabul airport.* 7NEWS.com.au. https://7news.com.au/news/conflict/heart-wrenching-video-shows-afghan-mothers-throwing-babies-over-barbed-wire-to-escape-taliban-at-kabul-airport-c-3722658

Bucci, M., Marques, S. S., Oh, D., & Harris, N. B. (2016). Toxic stress in children and adolescents. *Advances in Pediatrics, 63*, 403–428.

Buch, J. (2016, November 18). Officials ban crayons for kids held at Karnes immigrant detention center. *San Antonio Express-News.* https://www.expressnews.com/news/local/article/Officials-ban-crayons-for-kids-held-at-Karnes-10623167.php

Bucheli, M. (2008). Multinational corporations, totalitarian regimes and economic nationalism: United Fruit Company in Central America, 1899–1975. *Business History, 50*, 433–454.

Bui, Q., & Miller, C. C. (2015, December 23). The typical American lives only 18 miles from mom. *The New York Times.* Retrieved from https://www.nytimes.com/interactive/2015/12/24/upshot/24up-family.html

Burnett, J., Carter, J., Evershed, J., Kohli, M. B., Powell, C., & de Wilde, G. (2010). *"State sponsored cruelty": Children in immigration detention* [Technical Report]. Medical Justice.

Bush, G. H. W. (1990). *Statement on signing the Immigration Act of 1990.* The American Presidency Project. http://www.presidency.ucsb.edu/ws/index.php?pid=19117

Byrne, M. W., Goshin, L., & Blanchard-Lewis, B. (2012). Maternal separation during the reentry years for 100 infants raised in a prison nursery. *Family Court Review, 50*, 77–90.

Byrne, O. (2015, December 18). *On the ground at Karnes: Children still harmed by family detention.* Human Rights First. https://www.humanrightsfirst.org/blog/ground-karnes-children-still-harmed-family-detention

Cantor, G. (2015). Hieleras *(iceboxes) in the Rio Grande Valley Sector: Lengthy detention, deplorable conditions, and abuse in CBP holding cells.* American Immigration Council.

Carpenter, Z. (2015, June 18). What it's like inside a Border Patrol facility where families are being separated. *The Nation.* https://www.thenation.com/article/archive/like-ins ide-mcallen-border-patrol-facility/

CBN News. (2018, June 21). *Sessions on immigration policy: "The optics haven't been good"* [Video]. YouTube. https://www.youtube.com/watch?v=hbJ3XkIAQMQ&t=19s

Chapman, D. P., Dube, S. R., & Anda, R. F. (2007). Adverse childhood events as risk factors for negative mental health outcomes. *Pediatric Annals, 37,* 359–364.

Children's Village. (2022, February 28). *Jeremy C. Kohomban, Ph.D.* Retrieved April 30, 2022, from https://childrensvillage.org/about-us/our-team/trustees/jeremy-kohomban/

Choi, J. (2021, March 31). Two toddlers dropped over a border barrier and left in New Mexico. *The Hill.* Retrieved from https://thehill.com/policy/defense/homeland-coast-guard/545870-two-toddlers-dropped-over-a-border-barrier-and-left-in/

Ching, E., & Tilley, V. (1998). Indians, the military and the rebellion of 1932 in El Salvador. *Journal of Latin American Studies, 30,* 121–156.

Clark, D. (2018, December 20). *"I am not a liar": DHS chief Nielsen defends immigration policies in heated hearing.* NBC News. https://www.nbcnews.com/politics/congress/i-am-not-liar-dhs-chief-nielsen-defends-immigration-policies-n950511

Clauss-Ehlers, C. S. (2019). Forced migration among Latinx children and their families: Introducing trilateral migration trauma as a concept to reflect a forced migratory experience. *Journal of Infant, Child, and Adolescent Psychotherapy, 18,* 330–342.

Cleary, S. D., Snead, R., Dietz-Chavez, D., Rivera, I., & Edberg, M. C. (2018). Immigrant trauma and mental health outcomes among Latino youth. *Journal of Immigrant and Minority Health, 20,* 1053–1059.

Cleveland, J., & Rousseau, C. (2013). Psychiatric symptoms associated with brief detention of adult asylum seekers in Canada. *Canadian Journal of Psychiatry, 58,* 409–416.

Clinton, W. J. (1996). *Statement on the executive order on illegal immigration.* The American Presidency Project. https://www.presidency.ucsb.edu/documents/remarks-the-immigration-policy-initiative-and-exchange-with-reporters

Cohen, E. F. (2020). *Illegal: How America's lawless immigration regime threatens us all.* Basic Books.

Committee on Oversight and Reform, House of Representatives. (2019). *The Trump administration's child separation policy: Substantiated allegations of mistreatment* (Serial No. 116–46). US Government Printing Office. https://docs.house.gov/meetings/GO/GO00/20190712/109772/HHRG-116-GO00-Transcript-20190712-U10.pdf

Congressional Research Service. (2019). *Immigration: Recent apprehension trends at the U.S. southwest border* (Report No. R46012). https://crsreports.congress.gov/product/details?prodcode=R46012

Cornejo Villavicencio, K. (2020). *The undocumented Americans.* One World.

Crawley, H., & Lester, T. (2005). *No place for a child: Children in UK immigration detention: Impacts, alternatives and safeguards.* Save the Children.

Crea, T. M., Lopez, A., Hasson, R. G., Evans, K., Palleschi, C., & Underwood, D. (2018). Unaccompanied immigrant children in long term foster care: Identifying needs and best practices from a child welfare perspective. *Children and Youth Services Review, 92,* 56–64.

Creamer, M., McFarlane, A. C., & Burgess, P. (2005). Psychopathology following trauma: The role of subjective experience. *Journal of Affective Disorders, 86*, 175–182.

Dallaire, D. H., Zeman, J. L., & Thrash, T. M. (2014). Children's experiences of maternal incarceration-specific risks: Predictions of psychological maladaptation. *Journal of Clinical Child and Adolescent Psychology, 44*, 109–122.

Dower, J. (1986). *War without mercy: Race and power in the Pacific war.* Pantheon Books.

Dozier, M., Peloso, E., Lindhiem, O., Gordon, M. K., Manni, M., Sepulveda, S., Ackerman, J., Bernier, A., & Levine, S. (2006). Developing evidence-based interventions for foster children: An example of a randomized clinical trial with infants and toddlers. *Journal of Social Issues, 62*, 767–785.

Dreier, H. (2020, February 15). Trust and consequences. *Washington Post.* https://www.washingtonpost.com/graphics/2020/national/immigration-therapy-reports-ice/?nid=top_pb_signin&tid=nav_sign_in

Dubowitz, H., Black, M., Kerr, M., Hussey, J., Morrel, T., Everson, M., & Starr, R., Jr. (2001). Type and timing of mothers' victimization: Effects on mothers and children. *Pediatrics, 107*, 728–735.

Dudley, S. (2020). *MS-13: The making of America's most notorious gang.* Hanover Square Press.

Eagly, I., & Shafer, S. (2016). *Access to counsel in immigration court.* American Immigration Council. https://www.americanimmigrationcouncil.org/sites/default/files/research/access_to_counsel_in_immigration_court.pdf

Earthjustice. (2022, February 8). *Private prison company poisoned immigrants at Adelanto for a decade.* https://earthjustice.org/news/press/2021/private-prison-company-poisoned-immigrants-at-adelanto-for-a-decade

Ebert, K., Liao, W., & Estrada, E. P. (2020). Apathy and color-blindness in privatized immigration control. *Sociology of Race and Ethnicity, 6*, 533–547.

Editorial: The government is still separating migrant families at the border. It needs to stop. [Editorial]. (2019, May 8). *Los Angeles Times.* https://www.latimes.com/opinion/editorials/la-ed-migrant-family-separations-continue-border-20190508-story.html

Encyclopaedia Britannica. (2021). Japanese American internment. *Encyclopaedia Britannica.* https://www.britannica.com/event/Japanese-American-internment [cited as Britannica]

Engelmann, L. (1990). *Tears before the rain: An oral history of the fall of South Vietnam.* New York: Oxford University Press.

Evans, G. W., & Kim, P. (2013). Childhood poverty, chronic stress, self-regulation, and coping. *Child Development Perspectives, 7*, 43–48.

Exec. Order No. 13841, 3 C.F.R., 83 FR 29435 (2018). https://www.federalregister.gov/documents/2018/06/25/2018-13696/affording-congress-an-opportunity-to-address-family-separation

Exec. Order No. 14011, 3 C.F.R., 86 FR 8273 (2021). https://www.govinfo.gov/content/pkg/FR-2021-02-05/pdf/2021-02562.pdf

Fazel, M., Karunakara, U., & Newnham, E. A. (2014). Detention, denial, and death: Migration hazards for refugee children. *The Lancet Global Health, 2*(6), 313–314.

Ferriss, S. (2019, December 16). The Trump administration knew migrant children would suffer from family separations. The government ramped up the practice anyway. *The Texas Tribune.* https://www.texastribune.org/2019/12/16/trump-administration-knew-family-separations-harm-migrant-children/

Finkelhor, D., Shattuck, A., Turner, H., & Hamby, S. (2013). Improving the Adverse Childhood Experiences Scale. *JAMA Pediatrics, 167,* 70–75.

Finnegan, M., & Barabak, M. (2018, January 11). "Shithole" and other racist things Trump has said—so far. *Los Angeles Times.* https://www.latimes.com/politics/la-na-trump-rac ism-remarks-20180111-htmlstory.html

Fisher, P. A., Stoolmiller, M., Gunnar, M. R., & Burraston, B. O. (2007). Effects of a therapeutic intervention for foster preschoolers on diurnal cortisol activity. *Psychoneuroendocrinology, 32,* 892–905.

Flores v. Johnson, 212 F. Supp. 3d 864 (C.D. Cal. 2015).

Florida, R. (2008). *Who's your city? How the creative economy is making where you live the most important decision of your life.* Basic Books.

Fonrouge, G. (2021, April 7). Family of little girls seen being dropped over border fence speaks out. *New York Post.* https://nypost.com/2021/04/07/family-of-little-girls-drop ped-over-border-fence-speaks-out/

Ford, G. (1976). *Statement on signing the Immigration and Nationality Act amendments of 1976.* The American Presidency Project. https://www.google.com/url?sa=t&rct= j&q=&esrc=s&source=web&cd=&ved=2ahUKEwj5vqb12pT7AhWwk4kEHeFDCN0 QFnoECAsQAQ&url=https%3A%2F%2Fwww.fordlibrarymuseum.gov%2Flibr ary%2Fdocument%2F0055%2F1669712.pdf&usg=AOvVaw0e3yBpvhXyoMAV3 LwW7ELz

Forkby, T., & Höjer, S. (2011). Navigations between regulations and gut instinct: The unveiling of collective memory in decision-making processes where teenagers are placed in residential care. *Child and Family Social Work, 16,* 159–168.

Foster, H., & Hagan, J. (2013). Maternal and paternal imprisonment in the stress process. *Social Science Research, 42,* 650–669.

Fuemmeler, B. F., Dedert, E., McClernon, F. J., & Beckham, J. C. (2009). Adverse child-hood events are associated with obesity and disordered eating: Results from a U.S. population-based survey of young adults. *Journal of Traumatic Stress, 22,* 329–333.

Gallegos, R. (2000). *Doña Bárbara.* Espasa Calpe. (Original work published 1929)

Galvan, A. (2014, December 9). *US Border Patrol: Female agents wanted.* Federal News Network. https://federalnewsnetwork.com/business-news/2014/12/us-border-patrol-female-agents-wanted/.

Garcia Hernandez, C. C. (2019). *Migrating to prison: America's obsession with locking up immigrants.* New Press.

Geneva Declaration on Armed Violence and Development. (2015). *Global burden of armed violence 2015: Every body counts.* http://www.genevadeclaration.org/measurabil ity/global-burden-of-armed-violence/global-burden-of-armed-violence-2015.html

GEO Group Inc. (2021, October 31). *The New York Times.* https://www.nytimes.com/ topic/company/geo-group-inc [cited as The New York Times]

Gerrig, R. J., & Zimbardo, P. G. (2002). *Psychology and life* (16th ed.). Allyn and Bacon.

Gerstein, J., & Hesson, T. (2018, June 26). Federal judge orders Trump administration to reunite migrant families. *Politico.* https://www.politico.com/story/2018/06/26/judge-orders-trump-reunite-migrant-families-678809

Ghosh, S., & Hoopes, M. (2021). Learning to detain asylum seekers and the growth of mass immigration detention in the United States. *Law & Social Inquiry, 46*(4), 993–1021.

Gogolak, E. (2016, December 26). Meet the Central American women the United States is detaining and deporting. *The Nation.* https://www.thenation.com/article/archive/meet-the-central-american-women-the-united-states-is-detaining-and-deporting/

Gomez Licon, A., & Coronado, A. (2021, June 2). *Texas push to close shelter for migrant kids alarms groups.* Associated Press. https://apnews.com/article/texas-immigration-coronavirus-pandemic-health-government-and-politics-462a36ca2ce66bda30e7abeb807a17a7

Gonzalez, C. (2015, April 9). *Karnes hunger strike organizer freed.* KSAT-TV 12. https://www.ksat.comnews/2015/04/10/karnes-hunger-strike-organizer-freed/

Government Accountability Office. (2020, February). *Southwest border: Actions needed to improve DHS processing of families and coordination between DHS and HHS* (GAO-20-245).

Grassroots Leadership, Inc., et al., v. Texas Department of Family and Protective Services 15-cv-04336 (Texas state trial court September 26, 2015).

Grillo, I. (2017). *Gangster warlords: Drug dollars, killing fields and the new politics of Latin America.* Bloomsbury Publishing.

Grinberg, E., Lynch, J., & Allen, K. (2018, July 4). *"They treated us as though we were animals": Letters from inside an immigration detention facility.* CNN. https://www.cnn.com/2018/07/03/us/detention-center-letters-grassroots-leadership/index.html

Haberman, C. (2018, October 1). For private prisons, detaining immigrants is big business. *The New York Times.* https://www.nytimes.com/2018/10/01/us/prisons-immigration-detention.html

Hagg, M. (2019, February 27). Thousands of immigrant children said they were sexually abused in U.S. detention centers, report says. *The New York Times.* https://www.nytimes.com/2019/02/27/us/immigrant-children-sexual-abuse.html

Hardcastle, K., Bellis, M. A., Ford, K., Hughes, K., Garner, J., & Ramos Rodriguez, J. (2018). Measuring the relationships between adverse childhood experiences and educational and employment success in England and Wales: Findings from a retrospective study. *Public Health, 165*, 106–116.

Hennessy-Fiske, M. (2015, July 27). Ex-worker at Karnes immigrant detention center says she saw unethical behavior. *The Los Angeles Times.* https://www.latimes.com/nation/la-na-olivia-lopez-karnes-detention-center-20150727-story.html

Hernandez, A. R. (2021, April 1). Video of Ecuadoran toddlers dropped over border barrier yet another reminder of the dangers migrants face. *Washington Post.* Retrieved from https://www.washingtonpost.com/immigration/toddlers-border-barrier-video/2021/04/01/a74eaace-9315-11eb-a74e-1f4cf89fd948_story.html

Hernandez Castillo, M. (2020). *Children of the land: A memoir.* Harper Perennial.

Hilton, W. S. (2015, April 10). A federal judge and a hunger strike take on the government's immigrant detention facilities. *The New York Times Magazine.* https://www.nytimes.com/2015/04/06/magazine/a-federal-judge-and-a-hunger-strike-take-on-the-governments-immigrant-detention-facilities.html

Hinckley, S. (2019, May 2). Separation and sacrifice: "Pedro Pans" who fled Cuba see echoes today. *Christian Science Monitor.* Retrieved from https://www.csmonitor.com/World/Americas/2019/0502/Separation-and-sacrifice-Pedro-Pans-who-fled-Cuba-see-echoes-today

Hirschfeld Davis, J., & Shear, M. D. (2019). *Border wars: Inside Trump's assault on immigration*. Simon & Schuster.

Hiskey, J. T., Córdova, A., Malone, M. F., & Orcés, D. M. (2018). Leaving the devil you know: Crime victimization, US deterrence policy, and the emigration decision in Central America. *Latin American Research Review, 53,* 429–447. https://doi.org/10.25222/larr.147

Holpuch, A., & Gambino, L. (2018, June 18) Why are families being separated at the US border? *The Guardian.* https://www.theguardian.com/us-news/2018/jun/18/why-are-families-being-separated-at-the-us-border-explainer

Human Rights First. (2021). *Delivered to danger: Trump administration sending asylum seekers and migrants to danger.* https://www.humanrightsfirst.org/campaign/remain-mexico

Huppke, R. (2018, March 6). Mother of Congolese girl being held in Chicago is released, reunification likely. *Chicago Tribune.* https://www.chicagotribune.com/columns/rex-huppke/ct-met-congo-mother-child-asylum-huppke-20180306-story.html

Huzard, D., Ghosal, S., Grosse, J., Carnevali, L., Sgoifo, A., & Sandi, C. (2019). Low vagal tone in two rat models of psychopathology involving high or low corticosterone stress responses. *Psychoneuroendocrinology, 101,* 101–110.

Hylton, W. S. (2015, February 4). The shame of America's family detention camps. *The New York Times Magazine.* https://www.nytimes.com/2015/02/08/magazine/the-shame-of-americas-family-detention-camps.html

Illegal Immigrant Reform and Immigrant Responsibility Act, P.L. 104-208 (1996). https://www.govinfo.gov/content/pkg/PLAW-104publ208/pdf/PLAW-104publ208.pdf

Immigrant Justice Corps. (2022). *Quality counsel changes everything.* https://justicecorps.org/about/#:~:text=Immigration%20judges%20ranked%20nearly%20half,time%20when%20they%20don't

International Organization for Migration. (2020). *World migration report 2020.* https://worldmigrationreport.iom.int/2020

Jacobs, J. (2019, April 6). U.S. says it could take 2 years to identify up to thousands of separated immigrant families. *The New York Times.* https://www.nytimes.com/2019/04/06/us/family-separation-trump-administration.html

Johnson, L. B. (1965). *Remarks at the signing of the Immigration Bill.* https://history.house.gov/Historical-Highlights/1951-2000/Immigration-and-Nationality-Act-of-1965/

Jonas, S. (2013). *Guatemalan migration in times of civil war and post-war challenges.* Migration Policy Institute.

Jordan, M. (2018a, July 27). "Why did you leave me?" The migrant children left behind as parents are Deported. *The New York Times.* https://www.nytimes.com/2018/07/27/us/migrant-families-deportations.html

Jordan, M. (2018b, July 31). A migrant boy rejoins his mother, but he's not the same. *The New York Times.* https://www.nytimes.com/2018/07/31/us/migrant-children-separation-anxiety.html

Jordan, M. (2019, November 6). U.S. must provide mental health services to families separated at border. *The New York Times.* https://www.nytimes.com/2019/11/06/us/migrants-mental-health-court.html

Jordan, M., & Dickerson, C. (2018, July 24). More than 450 migrant parents may have been deported without their children. *The New York Times.* https://www.nytimes.com/2018/07/24/us/migrant-parents-deported-children.html

Jordan, M., & Dickerson, C. (2019, March 9). U.S. continues to separate migrant families despite rollback of policy. *The New York Times.* https://www.nytimes.com/2019/03/09/us/migrant-family-separations-border.html

Jovanovic, T., Smith, A., Kamkwalala, A., Poole, J., Samples, T., Norrholm, S., Ressler, K., & Bradley, B. (2011). Physiological markers of anxiety are increased in children of abused mothers. *Journal of Child Psychology and Psychiatry, and Allied Disciplines, 52,* 844–852.

Kates, G. (2018, June 20). *Migrant children at the border—the facts.* CBS News. https://www.cbsnews.com/news/migrant-children-at-the-border-by-the-numbers/

Katz, A. (2021, December 1). Photographer who found Syrian toddler dead on Turkish beach: "I was petrified." *The Washington Post.* https://www.washingtonpost.com/news/worldviews/wp/2015/09/03/photographer-who-found-syrian-toddler-dead-on-turkish-beach-i-was-petrified/

Kopan, B. T. (2018, June 15). *DHS: 2,000 children separated from parents at border.* CNN. https://www.cnn.com/2018/06/15/politics/dhs-family-separation-numbers/index.html

Kovacs, M. (2011). *Children's Depression Inventory* (2nd ed.). Multi-Health System.

Kriel, L. (2017, November 25). Trump moves to end "catch and release," prosecuting parents and removing children who cross the border. *Houston Chronicle.* https://www.houstonchronicle.com/news/houston-texas/houston/article/Trump-moves-to-end-catch-and-release-12383666.php

Kronick, R., Rousseau, C., & Cleveland, J. (2015). Asylum-seeking children's experiences of detention in Canada: A qualitative study. *American Journal of Orthopsychiatry, 85,* 287–294.

La Sonrisa Productions. (2009). *The least of these* [Video]. https://vimeo.com/179342261

Laughland, O. (2016, November 17). US detention facility restricts use of crayons for migrant children. *The Guardian.* https://www.theguardian.com/us-news/2016/nov/17/migrant-children-crayons-banned-karnes-detention

Lavandera, E., Morris, J., & Simon, D. (2018, June 12). *She says federal officials took her daughter while she breastfed the child in detention center.* CNN. https://www.cnn.com/2018/06/12/us/immigration-separated-children-southern-border/index.html

Le Duc, J. (2019, June 25). "They wanted the American dream": Reporter reveals story behind tragic photo. *The Guardian.* https://www.theguardian.com/us-news/2019/jun/25/they-wanted-the-american-dream-reporter-reveals-story-behind-tragic-photo [cited as The Guardian]

Lee, E. (2003). *At America's gates: Chinese immigration during the exclusion era, 1882–1943.* University of North Carolina Press.

Leonard, T. M. (2011). *The history of Honduras.* Greenwood.

Levinson, R., & Cooke, K. (2018, July 18). *Migrants in U.S. custody describe life in "ice boxes" and "dog pounds."* Reuters. https://www.reuters.com/article/us-usa-immigration-conditions/migrants-in-u-s-custody-describe-life-in-ice-boxes-and-dog-pounds-idUSKBN1K82X1

Levintova, H. (2019, January/February). The Trump official who failed to reunify dozens of separated children is getting a new role. *Mother Jones.* https://www.motherjones.com/politics/2018/11/scott-lloyd-abortion-child-migrants-office-of-refugee-resettlement/

Linthicum, K. (2019, June 26). A photo from the Rio Grande captures the tragic end for a father and daughter. *Los Angeles Times.* https://www.latimes.com/world/la-fg-father-daughter-drowning-mexican-border-20190626-story.html

Linton, J., Griffin, M., & Shapiro, A. (2017). Detention of immigrant children. *Pediatrics, 139,* Article e20170483.

Liston, S. (2022, January 23). *To stabilize Central America, the US must craft better incentives for trade.* The Hill. https://thehill.com/opinion/finance/590727-to-stabilize-central-america-the-us-must-craft-better-incentives-for-trade

Loman, M., & Gunnar, M. R. (2010). Early experience and the development of stress reactivity and regulation in children. *Neuroscience & Biobehavioral Reviews, 34,* 867–876.

Long-Garcia, J. D. (2018, October 29). Humanitarian groups at U.S.–Mexico border prepare for the migrant caravan. *America: The Jesuit Review.* https://www.americamagazine.org/politics-society/2018/10/29/humanitarian-groups-us-mexico-border-prepare-migrant-caravan

Lopez, W. D. (2021). *Separated: Family and community in the aftermath of an immigration raid.* Johns Hopkins University Press.

Lorek, A., Ehntholt, K., Nesbitt, A., Wey, E., Githinji, C., Rossor, E., & Wickramasinghe, R. (2009). The mental and physical health difficulties of children held within a British immigration detention center: A pilot study. *Child Abuse & Neglect: The International Journal, 33,* 573–585.

Lovato, R. (2021). *Unforgetting: A memoir of family, migration, gangs, and revolution in the Americas.* Harper Collins.

L. V. M. v. Lloyd (1-18-cv-01453). Retrieved at https://images.law.com/contrib/content/uploads/documents/292/LVM-immigrant-children-complaint-.pdf

Lupien, S. J., McEwen, B. S., Gunnar, M. R., & Heim, C. (2009). Effects of stress throughout the lifespan on the brain, behaviour and cognition. *Nature Reviews Neuroscience, 10,* 434–445.

Lusk, M., & Sanchez Garcia, G. (2021). *Witness to forced migration: The paradox of resiliency.* Hope Border Institute.

Mares, S., & Jureidini, J. (2004). Psychiatric assessment of children and families in immigration detention—clinical, administrative and ethical issues. *Australian and New Zealand Journal of Public Health, 28,* 520–526.

Mares, S., Newman, L., Dudley, M., & Gale, F. (2002). Seeking refuge, losing hope: Parents and children in immigration detention. *Australasian Psychiatry, 10,* 91–96.

Martinez, O. (2016). *A history of violence: Living and dying in Central America.* Verso.

McCausland, P. (2018, July 13). *Government says around 2,551 migrant children still need reunification with parents.* NBC News. https://www.nbcnews.com/news/us-news/government-says-around-2-551-migrant-children-still-need-reunification-n891366

McLaughlin, K. A., Sheridan, M. A., & Lambert, H. K. (2014). Childhood adversity and neural development: Deprivation and threat as distinct dimensions of early experience. *Neuroscience and Biobehavioral Reviews, 47,* 578–591.

Meissner, D., Hipsman, F., & Aleinikoff, T. A. (2018). *The U.S. asylum system in crisis: Charting a way forward.* Migration Policy Institute.

Merchant, N. (2018, June 12). *Hundreds of children wait in Border Patrol facility in Texas.* Associated Press. https://apnews.com/article/north-america-tx-state-wire-us-news-ap-top-news-border-patrols-9794de32d39d4c6f89fbefaea3780769

Meyer, P., & Taft-Morales, M. (2019, March 27). *In focus: Central American migration: Root causes and U.S. policy.* Congressional Research Service.

Miller, K., & Rasco, L. (2004). An ecological framework for addressing the mental health needs of refugee communities. In K. E. Miller & L. M. Rasco (Eds.), *The mental health of refugees: Ecological approaches to healing and adaptation* (pp. 1–63). Lawrence Erlbaum Associates.

Miroff, N. (2018, June 9). A family was separated at the border, and this distraught father took his own life. *Washington Post.* https://www.washingtonpost.com/world/national-security/a-family-was-separated-at-the-border-and-this-distraught-father-took-his-own-life/2018/06/08/24e40b70-6b5d-11e8-9e38-24e693b38637_story.html

Montoya-Galvez, C. (2019, September 2). *11 migrant parents who were separated from their children can return to U.S., judge rules.* CBS News. https://www.cbsnews.com/news/family-separation-policy-some-migrant-parents-who-were-separated-from-their-children-can-return-to-u-s-judge-rules/

Montoya-Galvez, C. (2020, January 13). *Court refuses to further restrict administration's power to separate migrant families.* CBS News. https://www.cbsnews.com/news/family-separation-court-refuses-to-further-restrict-administrations-power-to-separate-migrant-families-2020-01-13/

Moore, R. (2019a, June 11). In El Paso, Border Patrol is detaining migrants in "a human dog pound." *Texas Monthly.* https://www.texasmonthly.com/news-politics/border-patrol-outdoor-detention-migrants-el-paso/

Moore, R. (2019b, July 15). *3-year-old asked to pick parent in attempted family separation, her parents say.* NPR. https://www.npr.org/2019/07/15/741721660/follow-up-what-happened-after-a-border-agent-asked-toddler-to-pick-a-parent

Ms. J. P. v. William P. Barr fka Jefferson B. Sessions, No. 18-06081. (C.D. Cal. July 12, 2018).

Ms. L v. ICE, No. 18-428 (S.D. Cal. Sept. 4, 2019).

Murray, J., & Farrington, D. P. (2005). Parental imprisonment: Effects on boys' antisocial behaviour and delinquency through the life-course. *Child Psychology and Psychiatry, 46,* 1269–1278.

National Immigration Forum. (2019, July 23). *Push or pull factors: What Drives Central American migrants to the U.S.?* National Migration Forum. https://immigrationforum.org/article/push-or-pull-factors-what-drives-central-american-migrants-to-the-u-s/

National Immigration Justice Center. (2021). A timeline of the Trump administration's efforts to end asylum. https://immigrantjustice.org/sites/default/files/content-type/issue/documents/2021-01/01-11-2021-asylumtimeline.pdf

National Scientific Council on the Developing Child. (2014). *Excessive stress disrupts the architecture of the developing brain* (Working Paper 3, updated ed.). Center on the Developing Child. https://www.google.com/url?sa=t&rct=j&q=&esrc=s&source=web&cd=&ved=2ahUKEwji2tWB35T7AhW8MVkFHSK1CsQQFnoECAsQAQ&url=https%3A%2F%2Fdevelopingchild.harvard.edu%2Fwp-content%2Fuploads%2F2005%2F05%2FStress_Disrupts_Architecture_Developing_Brain-1.pdf&usg=AOvVaw0ytt6lDDWHWYgExRcgbuCH

NBC News. (2018, July 18). *Jose was reunited with his son, but the 3-year-old is learning to trust him again* [Video]. YouTube. https://www.youtube.com/watch?v=zCCjznVFBI4

Nesmith, A., & Ruhland, E. (2008). Children of incarcerated parents: Challenges and resiliency, in their own words. *Children and Youth Services Review, 30,* 1119–1130.

Newman, L., & Steel, Z. (2008). The child asylum seeker: Psychological and developmental impact of immigration detention. *Child and Adolescent Psychiatric Clinics of North America, 17,* 665–683.

Nielsen, K. M. [@SecNielsen]. (2018, June 17). *We do not have a policy of separating families at the border. Period* [Twitter]. https://twitter.com/SecNielsen/status/10084674 14235992069

Nowrasteh, A. (2018, June 20). *Alternatives to detention are cheaper than universal detention.* Cato Institute. https://www.cato.org/blog/alternatives-detention-are-cheaper-ind efinite-detention?gclid=Cj0KCQiAzMGNBhCyARIsANpUkzPnEq8fj4Be4tltcdvsDQ Q7hXJDRD4yKX_zSMXGZfgLBRmP_Y1NalMaAhqBEALw_wcB

Nygaard, M., Sonne, C., & Carlsson, J. (2017). Secondary psychotic features in refugees diagnosed with post-traumatic stress disorder: A retrospective cohort study. *BMC Psychiatry, 17*, Article 5. Online Open Access. https://doi.org/10.1186/s12 888-016-1166-1

Office of Refugee Resettlement. (2015). *Children entering the United States unaccompanied: Section 1: Placement in ORR care provider facilities.* https://www.acf.hhs.gov/orr/ policy-guidance/unaccompanied-children-program-policy-guide

O'Neill, L., Fraser, T., Kitchenham, A., & McDonald, V. (2018). Hidden burdens: A review of intergenerational, historical and complex trauma, implications for Indigenous families. *Journal of Child and Adolescent Trauma, 11*, 173–186.

Onion, R. (2015). *The papers late-19th-century Chinese immigrants had to carry to prove their legal status.* Slate. https://slate.com/human-interest/2015/01/history-of-chinese-exclusion-certificates-required-by-the-geary-act.html

Opaas, M., & Varvin, S. (2015). Relationships of childhood adverse experiences with mental health and quality of life at treatment start for adult refugees traumatized by pre-flight experiences of war and human rights violations. *The Journal of Nervous and Mental Disease, 203*(9), 684–695.

Ordoñez, F. (2015a, March 31). Detained mothers launch hunger strike. *McClatchy, DC Bureau.* https://www.mcclatchydc.com/news/politics-government/article24782 515.html

Ordoñez, F. (2015b, July 29). Ex-family detention social worker speaks at congressional forum. *McClatchy.* https://www.mcclatchydc.com/news/nation-world/national/arti cle29147518.html

Organization of American States (OAS). (1969, November 22). *American Convention on Human Rights, "Pact of San Jose."* Costa Rica. https://www.google.com/url?sa=t&rct= j&q=&esrc=s&source=web&cd=&ved=2ahUKEwiKk5DR1pT7AhWqkokEHTD JAhMQFnoECAwQAQ&url=https%3A%2F%2Fwww.oas.org%2Fdil%2Ftreaties_b-32_american_convention_on_human_rights.pdf&usg=AOvVaw0Ioc5me5r5cjs1H jS46SoQ

Passel, J. S., Lopez, M. H., & Cohn, D. (2022, February 3). *U.S. Hispanic population continued its geographic spread in the 2010s.* Pew Research Center. https://www.pewresea rch.org/fact-tank/2022/02/03/u-s-hispanic-population-continued-its-geographic-spr ead-in-the-2010s/?utm_source=Pew+Research+Center&utm_campaign=c72108d 066-Weekly_2022_02_05&utm_medium=email&utm_term=0_3e953b9b70-c72108d 066-400734053

Pear, R. (1986, November 7). President signs landmark bill on immigration. *The New York Times.* https://www.nytimes.com/1986/11/07/us/president-signs-landmark-bill-on-immigration.html

Pechtel, P., Lyons-Ruth, K., Anderson, C., & Teicher, M. (2014). Sensitive periods of amygdala development: The role of maltreatment in preadolescence. *NeuroImage, 97*, 236–244.

Pelley, S. (2019, November 26). *The chaos behind Donald Trump's policy of family separation at the border*. CBS News. https://www.cbsnews.com/news/trump-family-separation-policy-mexican-border-60-minutes-investigation-greater-in-number-than-trump-administration-admits/

Phippen, J. W. (2016, May 6). Is it an immigration detention facility or a child-care center? *The Atlantic*. https://www.theatlantic.com/national/archive/2016/05/immigration-childcare/481509/

Pierce, S. (2015). *Unaccompanied child migrants in U.S. communities, immigration court, and schools*. Migration Policy Institute. https://www.migrationpolicy.org/sites/default/files/publications/UAC-Integration-FINALWEB.pdf

Plevin, R. (2020, January 3). 4 things we learned from GEO Group's lawsuit over immigration detention in California. *The Desert Sun*. https://www.desertsun.com/story/news/2020/01/02/4-things-we-learned-geo-groups-lawsuit-over-immigration-detention-california/2798568001/

Railton, B. (2013). *The Chinese Exclusion Act: What it can teach us about America*. Palgrave/Macmillan.

Ramel, B., Täljemark, J., Lindgren, A., & Johansson, B. A. (2015). Overrepresentation of unaccompanied refugee minors in inpatient psychiatric care. *SpringerPlus*, *4*, Article 131.

Rampell, C. (2015, August 28). Founding fathers, trashing immigrants. *The Washington Post*. https://www.washingtonpost.com/news/rampage/wp/2015/08/28/founding-fathers-trashing-immigrants/

Reeves, R. (2015). *Infamy: The shocking story of the Japanese American internment in World War II*. Henry Holt and Company.

Reilly, K., & Carlisle, M. (2019, September 30). The Trump administration's move to end rule limiting detention of migrant children rejected in court. *Time*. https://time.com/5657381/trump-administration-flores-agreement-migrant-children/

Richter-Levin, G., & Sandi, C. (2021). Labels matter: Is it stress or is it trauma? *Translational Psychiatry*, *11*, 385–394.

R.I.L-R v. Johnson, 80 F.Supp.3d 164 (D.D.C. February 20, 2015). https://scholar.google.com/scholar_case?case=17601999305528692568&q=R.I.L-R+v.+Johnson&hl=en&as_sdt=6,40&as_vis=1

Romero, S. (2019, March 31). Migrants moved out of holding pen under El Paso bridge. *The New York Times*. https://www.nytimes.com/2019/03/31/us/el-paso-bridge-migrants.html

Ruiz Soto, A. G., & Selee, A. (2022). *Beyond the border: Opportunities for managing regional migration between Central and North America*. Migration Policy Institute.

Ryo, E. (2019). Predicting danger in immigration courts. *Law & Social Inquiry*, *44*, 227–256.

Sacchetti, M. (2022, March 18). Inspector general, ICE clash over conditions at immigration detention facility in New Mexico. *The Washington Post*. https://www.washingtonpost.com/national-security/2022/03/18/ice-detention-unsanitary-new-mexico/

Salerno Valdez, E., Valdez, L. A., & Sabo, S. (2015). Structural vulnerability among migrating women and children fleeing Central America and Mexico: The public health impact of "humanitarian parole." *Frontiers in Public Health*, *3*, Article 163. https://www.frontiersin.org/articles/10.3389/fpubh.2015.00163/full

Schrag, P. G. (2020). *Baby jails: The fight to end the incarceration of refugee children in America*. University of California Press.

Seelke, C. R. (2016). *Gangs in Central America*. Congressional Research Service.

Select Commission on Immigration and Refugee Policy. (1981). *U.S. immigration policy and the national interest: The final report and recommendations of the Select Commission on Immigration and Refugee Policy with supplemental views by commissioners*. Congress of the United States.

Shalev, A. Y. (2009). Posttraumatic stress disorder and stress-related disorders. *Psychiatric Clinics of North America, 32,* 687–704.

Shear, M. (2021, January 1). Trump and aides drove family separation at border, documents say. *The New York Times*. https://www.nytimes.com/2021/01/14/us/polit ics/trump-family-separation.html

Shear, M. D., Benner, K., & Schmidt, M. S. (2020, October 6). "We need to take away children," no matter how young, Justice Dept. officials said. *The New York Times*. https:// www.nytimes.com/2020/10/06/us/politics/family-separation-border-immigration-jeff-sessions-rod-rosenstein.html?searchResultPosition=1

Shear, M. D., & Janno-Youngs, Z. (2019, August 21). Migrant families would face indefinite detention under new Trump rule. *The New York Times*. https://www.nytimes.com/2019/08/21/us/politics/flores-migrant-family-detention.html

Shonkoff, J. P., Boyce, W. T., & McEwen, B. S. (2009). Neuroscience, molecular biology, and the childhood roots of health disparities: Building a new framework for health promotion and disease prevention. *Journal of the American Medical Association, 301,* 2252–2259.

Siegel, R. (2017, October 26). The Trump official who tried to stop a detained immigrant from getting an abortion. *The Washington Post*. https://www.washingtonpost.com/news/post-nation/wp/2017/10/26/the-trump-official-who-tried-to-stop-a-detained-immigrant-from-getting-an-abortion/

Silove, D., Austin, P., & Steel, Z. (2007). No refuge from terror: The impact of detention on the mental health of trauma-affected refugees seeking asylum in Australia. *Transcultural Psychiatry, 44,* 359–393.

Smith-Acuña, S. (2011). *Systems theory in action: Applications to individual, couple, and family therapy*. John Wiley & Sons.

Soboroff, J. (2020). *Separated: Inside an American tragedy*. Custom House.

Soboroff, J., & Ainsley, J. (2019a, June 3). Botched family reunification left migrant children waiting in vans overnight. NBC News. https://www.nbcnews.com/politics/immi gration/botched-family-reunifications-left-migrant-children-waiting-vans-overni ght-n1013336

Soboroff, J., & Ainsley, J. (2019b, May 18). *Trump administration identifies at least 1,700 additional children it may have separated*. NBC News. https://www.nbcnews.com/news/us-news/1-700-additional-separated-migrant-children-identified-trump-adm inistration-n1007426

Steel, Z., Momartin, S., Bateman, C., Hafshejani, A., Silove, D. M., Everson, N., Roy, K., Dudley, M., Newman, L., Blick, B., & Mares, S. (2004). Psychiatric status of asylum seeker families held for a protracted period in a remote detention centre in Australia. *Australian and New Zealand Journal of Public Health, 28,* 527–536.

Stenson, A. F., van Rooij, S., Carter, S., Powers, A., & Jovanovic, T. (2021). A legacy of fear: Physiological evidence for intergenerational effects of trauma exposure on fear and safety signal learning among African Americans. *Behavioural Brain Research, 402,* Article 113017.

Stevens, J., van Rooij, S., & Jovanovic, T. (2018). Developmental contributors to trauma response: The importance of sensitive periods, early environment, and sex differences. *Current Topics in Behavioral Neurosciences, 38*, 1–22.

Stillman, S. (2018, October 11). The five-year-old who was detained at the border and persuaded to sign away her rights. *The New Yorker.* https://www.newyorker.com/news/news-desk/the-five-year-old-who-was-detained-at-the-border-and-convinced-to-sign-away-her-rights

Sullivan, E., & Qiu, L. (2018, December 11). Trump makes misleading border wall claims before and after meeting with Democrats. *The New York Times.* https://www.nytimes.com/2018/12/11/us/politics/fact-check-trump-border-wall.html

Sun, J., Patel, F., Rose-Jacobs, R., Frank, D. A., Black, M. M., & Chilton, M. (2017). Mothers' adverse childhood experiences and their young children's development. *American Journal of Preventive Medicine, 53*, 882–891.

Sweileh, W., Wickramage, K., Pottie, K., Hui, C., Roberts, B., Sawalha, A., & Zyoud, S. (2018). Bibliometric analysis of global migration health research in peer-reviewed literature (2000–2016). *BMC Public Health, 18*, 777–794.

Teicher, M. (2018). Childhood trauma and the enduring consequences of forcibly separating children from parents at the United States border. *BMC Medicine, 16*, Article 146.

Teicher, M., Samson, J., Anderson, C., & Ohashi, K. (2016). The effects of childhood maltreatment on brain structure, function and connectivity. *Nature Reviews Neuroscience, 17*, 652–666.

Thomas, D. S. (1952). *Japanese American evacuation and resettlement: The salvage.* University of California Press.

Thompson, G. (2018a, June 18). *Listen to children who've just been separated from their parents at the border.* ProPublica. https://www.propublica.org/article/children-separated-from-parents-border-patrol-cbp-trump-immigration-policy

Thompson, G. (2018b, November 27). *Families are still being separated at the border, months after "zero tolerance" was reversed.* ProPublica. https://www.propublica.org/article/border-patrol-families-still-being-separated-at-border-after-zero-tolerance-immigration-policy-reversed

Transactional Records Access Clearinghouse, Syracuse University. (2014). *Representation for unaccompanied children in immigration court.* https://trac.syr.edu/immigration/reports/371/

Transactional Records Access Clearinghouse, Syracuse University. (2017). *Asylum representation rates have fallen amid rising denial rates.* https://trac.syr.edu/immigration/reports/491/

Truman, H. (1962). *Public papers of the president of the United States.* Government Printing Office.

Trump administration's cruel treatment of migrant families was intentional and calculated [Editorial]. (2021, January 18). *The Washington Post.* https://www.washingtonpost.com/opinions/the-trump-administrations-cruel-treatment-of-migrant-families-was-intentional-and-calculated/2021/01/18/3c6b7d12-577f-11eb-a931-5b162d0d033d_story.html [cited as Washington Post]

United Nations. (1948). *Universal declaration of human rights.* https://www.un.org/en/about-us/universal-declaration-of-human-rights

United Nations High Commissioner for Refugees. (n.d.). *Children*. Retrieved April 27, 2022, from https://www.unhcr.org/en-us/children

United Nations High Commissioner for Refugees. (2015). *Women on the run: First-hand accounts of refugees fleeing El Salvador, Guatemala, Honduras, and Mexico.* https://www.unhcr.org/en-us/publications/operations/5630f24c6/women-run.html

UN Department of Economic and Social Affairs, Population Division. (2020). *International migration 2020 highlights* (ST/ESA/SER.A/452). https://www.un.org/development/desa/pd/news/international-migration-2020

UN Economic Commission for Latin America and the Caribbean. (2021). *ECLAC to officially present comprehensive development plan for El Salvador, Guatemala, Honduras and south–southeast Mexico.* https://www.cepal.org/en/news/eclac-officially-present-comprehensive-development-plan-salvador-guatemala-honduras-and-south

UN Office on Drugs and Crime. (2007). *Crime and development in Central America: Caught in the crossfire.* https://www.unodc.org/documents/data-and-analysis/Central-america-study-en.pdf

UN Office on Drugs and Crime. (2012). *Transnational organized crime in Central America and the Caribbean: A threat assessment.* https://www.unodc.org/documents/data-and-analysis/Studies/TOC_Central_America_and_the_Caribbean_english.pdf

Urbi, J. (2018). *This is how much it costs to detain an immigrant in the US: The economic cost of immigration detention.* CNBC. https://www.cnbc.com/2018/06/20/cost-us-immigrant-detention-trump-zero-tolerance-tents-cages.html

US Citizenship and Immigration Service. (2020). *Early American immigration policies.* https://www.uscis.gov/about-us/our-history/overview-of-ins-history/early-american-immigration-policies#:~:text=The%20general%20Immigration%20Act%20of,for%20new%20federal%20enforcement%20authorities

US Customs and Border Protection. (2018a). *Border wall replacement project starts near downtown Calexico.* https://www.cbp.gov/newsroom/local-media-release/border-wall-replacement-project-starts-near-downtown-calexico

US Customs and Border Protection. (2018b). *U.S. Border Patrol southwest border apprehensions by sector FY2018.* https://www.cbp.gov/newsroom/stats/usbp-sw-border-apprehensions

US Customs and Border Protection. (2020). *U.S. Border Patrol southwest border apprehensions by sector fiscal year 2020.* https://www.cbp.gov/newsroom/stats/sw-border-migration-fy2020

US Department of Health and Human Services, Office of Inspector General. (2019). *Care provider facilities described challenges addressing mental health needs of children in HHS Custody* (Report in Brief No. OEI-09-18-00431). https://perma.cc/2RPJ-WM5H

US Department of Health and Human Services, Office of Refugee Resettlement. (2012). *Who we serve—Unaccompanied children.* https://www.acf.hhs.gov/orr/policy-guidance/who-we-serve-unaccompanied-children

US Department of Homeland Security. (2015, November 24). *Southwest border unaccompanied alien children FY 2014.* Retrieved April 27, 2022, from https://www.cbp.gov/newsroom/stats/southwest-border-unaccompanied-children/fy-2014

US Department of Homeland Security. (2016). *Report of the Advisory Committee on Family Residential Centers.* https://www.ice.gov/sites/default/files/documents/Report/2016/ACFRC-sc-16093.pdf

US Department of Homeland Security. (2018). *Immigration and Customs Enforcement: Budget overview. Fiscal year 2018, congressional justification*. https://www.dhs.gov/sites/default/files/publications/ICE%20FY18%20Budget.pdf

US Department of Homeland Security. (2019). *DHS and HHS announce new rule to implement the Flores settlement agreement; final rule published to fulfill obligations under Flores settlement agreement*. News Archive. https://www.dhs.gov/news/2019/08/21/dhs-and-hhs-announce-new-rule-implement-flores-settlement-agreement

US Department of Homeland Security. (2020). *CBP separated more asylum-seeking families at ports of entry than reported and for reasons other than those outlined in public statements* (Report No. OIG-20-35). https://www.oig.dhs.gov/sites/default/files/assets/2020-06/OIG-20-35-May20.pdf

US Department of Homeland Security. (2021). *ICE did not consistently provide separated migrant parents the opportunity to bring their children upon removal* (Report No. OIG-21-36). https://www.oig.dhs.gov/sites/default/files/assets/2021-05/OIG-21-36-May21.pdf

US Department of Homeland Security. (2022a, February 18). *Detention facilities*. https://www.ice.gov/detention-facilities

US Department of Homeland Security. (2022b, March 17). *Refugees and asylees*. https://www.dhs.gov/immigration-statistics/refugees-asylees

US Department of Homeland Security. (2022c, March 16). *Management alert—Immediate removal of all detainees from the Torrance County detention facility* (Report No. OIG-22-31). https://www.oig.dhs.gov/sites/default/files/assets/Mga/2022/oig-22-31-mar22-mgmtalert.pdf

US Government Accountability Office. (2018). *Immigration detention: Opportunities exist to improve cost estimates* (GAO-18-343). https://www.gao.gov/products/gao-18-343

US Government Accountability Office. (2021, January). *Southwest border: DHS and DOJ have implemented expedited credible fear screening pilot programs, but should ensure timely data entry* (GAO-21-144.) https://www.gao.gov/assets/720/711974.pdf

US Immigration and Customs Enforcement. (2019a, February 15). *Karnes County residential center*. Retrieved April 27, 2022, from https://www.ice.gov/factsheets/karnes-county-residential-center

US Immigration and Customs Enforcement. (2019b). https://www.ice.gov/about-ice

Valdes, A., & Mejia, I. (2018, August 24). *"My son is traumatized": One separated family's reunion*. ACLU. https://www.aclu.org/blog/immigrants-rights/immigrants-rights-and-detention/my-son-traumatized-one-separated-familys

Vargas Alves Nunes, A., Odebrecht Vargas Nunes, S., Strano, T., Pascolat, G., Schier Doria, G., & Nasser Ehlke, M. (2016). Folie à deux and its interaction with early life stress: A case report. *Journal of Medical Case Reports, 10*, Article 339.

Vaughn, M., Salas-Wright, C., Huang, J., Qian, Z., Terzis, L., & Helton, J. (2017). Adverse childhood experiences among immigrants to the United States. *Journal of Interpersonal Violence, 32*, 1543–1564.

Villagran, L. (2021, June 8). Feds threaten to sue Texas over Gov. Greg Abbott's immigration "disaster" declaration. *El Paso Times*. https://www.elpasotimes.com/story/news/2021/06/08/feds-challenge-texas-governor-order-shut-unaccompanied-migrant-children-shelters/7601609002/

Vinograd, C., & Omar, A. C. (2015, September 3). *Aylan Kurdi is the Syrian toddler drowned on Bodrum Beach.* MSNBC. Retrieved April 27, 2022, from https://www.msnbc.com/msnbc/aylan-kurdi-the-syrian-toddler-drowned-bodrum-beach-msn a674781

Wakatsuki Houston, J., & Houston, J. (1973). *Farewell to Manzanar: A true story of Japanese American experience during and after the World War II internment.* Houghton Mifflin.

Washington, J. (2019, December 9). *The government has taken at least 1,100 children from their parents since family separations officially ended.* The Intercept. https://theinterc ept.com/2019/12/09/family-separation-policy-lawsuit/

Wheeler, W. (2020). *State of war: MS-13 and El Salvador's world of violence.* Columbia Global Report.

Wiesel, E. (1986). *Nobel lecture: Hope, despair and memory.* https://www.nobelprize.org/prizes/peace/1986/wiesel/acceptance-speech/

Wilson, W. (1915, January 28). *Veto message to the House of Representatives.* https://mille rcenter.org/the-presidency/presidential-speeches/january-28-1915-veto-immigrat ion-legislation

Wolynn, M. (2016). *It didn't start with you: How inherited family trauma shapes who we are and how to end the cycle.* Penguin Books.

World Bank. (2018a). *Groundswell: Preparing for internal climate migration.* https://www.worldbank.org/en/news/infographic/2018/03/19/groundswell---preparing-for-inter nal-climate-migration

World Bank. (2018b). *Intentional homicides (per 100,000 people).* https://data.worldbank.org/indicator/VC.IHR.PSRC.P5

World Food Programme. (2017). *Food security and emigration: Why people flee and the impact on family members left behind in El Salvador, Guatemala and Honduras, August 2017.* https://www.wfp.org/publications/2017-food-security-emigration-why-people-flee-salvador-guatemala-honduras

Yan, H. (2018, July 26). *The US must reunite separated families by today—But over 900 probably won't be reunited.* CNN. https://www.cnn.com/2018/07/25/politics/separa ted-families-by-the-numbers/index.html

Yee, V., & Jordan, M. (2018, October 8). Migrant children in search of justice: A 2-year-old's day in immigration court. *The New York Times.* https://www.nytimes.com/2018/10/08/us/migrant-children-family-separation-court.html

Yen, H., & Long, C. (2018, November 2). *AP fact check: President Trump's rhetoric and the truth about migrant caravans.* PBS Newshour. https://www.pbs.org/newshour/politics/ap-fact-check-president-trumps-rhetoric-and-the-truth-about-migrant-caravans

Young, E. (2021). *Forever prisoners: How the United States made the world's largest immigrant detention system.* Oxford University Press.

Zayas, L. H. (2011). *Latinas attempting suicide: When cultures, families, and daughters collide.* Oxford University Press.

Zayas, L. H. (2015). *Forgotten citizens: Deportation, children, and the making of American exiles and orphans.* Oxford University Press.

Zayas, L. H. (2021, April 28). Opinion: Helping kids arriving at border requires political will. *Houston Chronicle.* https://www.houstonchronicle.com/opinion/outlook/article/Opinion-Helping-kids-arriving-at-border-requires-16135771.php

Zayas, L. H., & Gulbas, L. E. (2017). Processes of belonging for citizen-children of undocumented Mexican immigrants. *Journal of Child and Family Studies, 26,* 2463–2474.

Zeanah, C., Berlin, L., & Boris, N. (2011). Practitioner review: Clinical applications of attachment theory and research for infants and young children. *Journal of Child Psychology & Psychiatry, 52*, 819–833.

Zechmeister, E., & Azpuru, D. (2017). *Topical brief: What does the public report on corruption, the CICIG, the Public Ministry, and the Constitutional Court in Guatemala?* Latin American Public Opinion Project, Vanderbilt University.

Zwi, K., Mares, S., Nathanson, D., Tay, A., & Silove, D. (2018). The impact of detention on the social–emotional wellbeing of children seeking asylum: A comparison with community-based children. *European Child and Adolescent Psychiatry, 27*, 411–422.

About the Contributors

Tatiana Londoño: Tatiana was born in Cali, Colombia, and immigrated to the United States with her parents who wanted to leave behind drug-related violence, kidnappings, and poverty. Growing up in Florida in a low-income household, Tatiana learned from her parents how to turn struggles into tools of empowerment. She volunteered in her immigrant community and found her passion in social justice work. Tatiana attended Vassar College, the first in her family to attend college, and graduated with a B.A. in neuroscience and behavior. While at Vassar, she worked part-time in a domestic violence shelter, where she learned about the unique struggles of other immigrants, especially Central Americans, who fled violence and abuse only to face the same along their journey and once settled in the United States. Tatiana continued her work in domestic violence services with immigrant communities and completed her master's degree in social work at the University of Texas at Austin, where she is now a doctoral student candidate. Tatiana studies how migration experiences and the context in the United States contribute to trauma and resilience among immigrant families from Latin America.

Rocio Morin: Rocio is a Houston native with parents who immigrated from Mexico. She grew up in a community where her close relatives and neighbors were also immigrants. This is where she saw the struggles of moving from one country to another and where she decided to be a support for her community. Rocio graduated from the University of Texas at Austin with a degree in sociology and Spanish.

Hilda Torres: Hilda is a first-generation college student who received her bachelor's degree in health and society from the University of Texas at Austin, where she is completing a master's degree in social work. The stories told to her by mothers and kids in the study resonated deeply with the experiences of her large extended Mexican family. Like the families she interviewed, her family migrated in search of a better life. Her mother immigrated to Baltimore with Hilda and a brother to reunite with her husband and four older sons. In Baltimore, Hilda attended a White school with an English learning program of just two students: Hilda and an immigrant student from Honduras. Hilda's parents expected her to excel in school, despite the challenges of a new educational system and language barrier. Her parents, "still working-class people," she says, worked tirelessly to break the many barriers they encountered.

Jamie Turcios-Villalta: Jamie received her bachelor's degree in health and society from the University of Texas at Austin and is currently a postbaccalaureate fellow with the Texas Behavioral Science and Policy Institute. Jamie was born in Canada to two courageous Salvadoran immigrants who then entered the United States to support an aunt who was ill, a move that left them undocumented. Jamie helped her mother clean houses as a child and spent after-school hours at a restaurant where her father was a cook. It was an arrangement filled with love and joy. Jamie's parents taught her to be kind, work hard, and *pelear la buena batalla* (fight the good fight). Eventually, her parents received temporary protected status, but Jamie did not qualify. As a teen, Jamie grappled with her own identity and became involved in the undocumented people's movement. She then received Deferred Action on Childhood Arrivals status. Jamie understands the uncertainty that families in this book feel navigating an immigration system that does not always work in their favor, yet "they had a lot of faith and planned to persist no matter what." Their stories were reminiscent of growing up hearing about the Salvadoran civil war and gang violence.

Index

For the benefit of digital users, indexed terms that span two pages (e.g., 52–53) may, on occasion, appear on only one of those pages.